Philosophical Issues
in Journalism

Philosophical Issues in Journalism

EDITED BY

ELLIOT D. COHEN

New York Oxford
OXFORD UNIVERSITY PRESS
1992

Oxford University Press

Oxford   New York   Toronto
Delhi   Bombay   Calcutta   Madras   Karachi
Petaling Jaya   Singapore   Hong Kong   Tokyo
Nairobi   Dar es Salaam   Cape Town
Melbourne   Auckland

and associated companies in
Berlin   Ibadan

Copyright © 1992 by Oxford University Press, Inc.

Published by Oxford University Press, Inc.
200 Madison Avenue, New York, NY 10016

Library of Congress Cataloging-in-Publication Data
Philosophical issues in journalism / edited by Elliot D. Cohen.
p. cm.   Includes bibliographical references.
ISBN 0-19-506898-X
1. Journalism—Philosophy.   I. Cohen, Elliot D.
PN4731.P48   1992   070.4'01—dc20
91-15437

1 3 5 7 9 8 6 4 2

Printed in the United States of America
on acid-free paper

To My Wife, Gale Spieler Cohen

ACKNOWLEDGMENTS

The editor would like to thank the following people for their supportive roles in the creation of this volume: Professor Richard P. Cunningham, Department of Journalism, New York University; Professor Albert Flores, Department of Philosophy, California State University, Fullerton; Dr. Rudolph Widman and Genevieve McMillen, Learning Resources Center, Indian River Community College; Professor Michael Davis, Center for the Study of Ethics in the Professions, Illinois Institute of Technology; Cynthia A. Read, Senior Editor, Oxford University Press.

"A Prolegomenon for a Theory of News" by Joshua Halberstam from *The International Journal of Applied Philosophy*, vol. 3, no. 3 (Spring 1987). Reprinted by permission of the publisher.

"The Significant Facts" by Berny Morson from *The International Journal of Applied Philosophy*, vol. 4, no. 2 (Fall 1988). Reprinted by permission of the publisher.

"The Virtuous Journalist: Morality in Journalism" by Stephen Klaidman and Tom L. Beauchamp from *The Virtuous Journalist* by Stephen Klaidman and Tom L. Beauchamp (Oxford University Press, 1987). Reprinted by permission of the publisher.

"Liberty of Thought and Discussion" by J. S. Mill from *On Liberty* by John Stuart Mill, edited by Alburey Castell (New York: Appleton-Century-Crofts, 1947).

" 'Censorship': Some Distinctions" by Judith Andre from *The International Journal of Applied Philosophy*, vol. 1, no. 4 (Fall 1983). Reprinted by permission of the publisher.

"Privacy, Morality, and the Law" by W. A. Parent from *Philosophy and Public Affairs*, vol. 12, no. 4 (Fall 1983), pp. 269–88. Copyright © 1983 by Princeton University Press. Reprinted by permission of the publisher.

"The Reporter's Refusal to Testify" by Philip Meyer from *Ethical Journalism* by Philip Meyer (New York: Longman Publishers, 1987). Reprinted by permission of the author.

"The Role of the Media in Shaping Public Policy" by Charles Green from *The Great Society and Its Legacy: Twenty Years of U.S. Social Policy*, edited by Marshall Kaplan and Peggy Cuciti (Durham: Duke University Press, 1986). Reprinted by permission of the publisher.

"Network News Coverage of the Presidency: Implications for Democracy" by Fred Smoller from *The International Journal of Appllied Philosophy*, vol. 3, no. 2 (Fall 1986). Reprinted by permission of the publisher.

"Stereotypes, Public Opinion and the Press" by Walter Lipmann from *Public Opinion* by Walter Lippmann (Macmillan, 1946). Reprinted by permission of Macmillan Publishing Co. Copyright © 1922 by Walter Lippmann, renewed 1949 by Walter Lippmann.

"Objectivity and News Bias" by Theodore L. Glasser from "Objectivity Precludes Responsibility" in *The Quill*, vol. 72, February 1984, pp. 13–16. Reprinted by permission of the publisher and the author.

"Multiperspectival News" by Herbert J. Gans from Deciding What's News: A Study of CBS Evening News, NBC Nightly News, Newsweek and Time by Herbert Gans. Copyright © 1979 by Herbert Gans. Reprinted by permission of Pantheon Books, a division of Random House, Inc.

"Some Reservations about Multiperspectival News" by Jay Newman from *The International Journal of Applied Philosophy*, vol. 1, no. 2 (Fall 1982). Reprinted by permission of the publisher.

"Understanding Errors and Biases That Can Affect Journalists" by S. Holly Stocking and Paget H. Gross from *The Journalism Educator*, vol. 44, no. 1 (Spring 1987), pp. 4–11. Reprinted by permission of the authors.

"Devices of News Slanting in the Print Media" by Howard Kahane from *Logic and Contemporary Rhetoric: The Use of Reason in Everyday Life,* third edition by Howard Kahane © 1980 by Wadsworth, Inc. Reprinted by permission of the publisher.

"Organizational Biases of Network News Reporting" by Edward Jay Epstein from *What's News*, edited by Elie Abel (Institute for Contemporary Studies, San Francisco, CA, 1981). Reprinted by permission Transaction Books, Rutgers—The State University of New Jersey, New Brunswick, NJ.

"Applying Philosophy to Journalism" by Anthony Serafini from *The International Journal of Applied Philosophy*, vol. 3, no. 4 (Fall 1987). Reprinted by permission of the publisher.

"What Can Philosophy Do for a Journalist?" by Franklin Donnell, from *The International Journal of Applied Philosophy*, vol. 4, no. 3 (Spring 1989). Reprinted by permission of the publisher.

CONTENTS

Philosophical Issues
in Journalism

General Introduction

The central task of this volume is to introduce students of journalism, mass communications, philosophy, and related fields to some persistent, hard questions relating to journalistic practice and training: What makes a story newsworthy? What is the relationship between good journalism and moral goodness? When, if ever, are attempts to suppress the free expression or free publication of ideas justified? How far should reporters go in protecting the privacy of their news sources? What political powers and responsibilities do the media bear? Is journalistic objectivity possible? Is a multiperspectival approach to the news a viable answer to the problem of news bias and news distortion? What logical standards are possible for the detection and/or elimination of cognitive errors and prejudices in news reporting? What value might the study of philosophy itself have for journalistic education?

These questions, and many related ones surrounding them, generate *philosophical* issues. At the same time they are also *practical* questions. They are practical because any attempt to address them can have significant impact upon journalists' behavior. For example, an answer to the question of what makes a story newsworthy can bear upon what stories editors actually select for publication.

These questions generate philosophical issues because they invite philosophical argument and analysis. For example, the question of the extent to which reporters are justified in protecting the privacy of their news sources invites conceptual analysis and argumentation about the nature and value of privacy itself. And the question of whether journalistic objectivity is possible presupposes an understanding of what is meant by "objectivity" in the first place.

Philosophical issues, including those addressed here, involve hard, persistent questions in the sense that they cannot be settled by empirical means alone. For instance, the question of whether and when a percentage of journalists would be prepared to resist subpoena in order to

3

protect the privacy of their sources is an empirical issue that can be answered, with some measure of probability, by conducting a survey. In contrast, the question of whether and when a journalist would be *justified* in resisting subpoena for this purpose is a philosophical issue that cannot be resolved *simply* by taking a survey or purely by any other empirical means. (This is not to say that answers to empirical questions are always easy or that they cannot have relevance to answers to philosophical questions. For instance, an answer to the rather difficult empirical question about the possible effects of journalists' compliance with the courts upon potential news sources is relevant to the philosophical question of whether and when journalists should resist subpoenas.)

The philosophical issues addressed herein are also *general* issues in the sense that answers to the questions they raise are assumed by, and have implications for, particular journalistic decisions. For example, journalists might favor "hard" journalism over "soft" journalism because they take the former to be more "objective"; and editors may print an editorial by a neo-Nazi in the midst of public outcry from the Jewish community because they believe that not even unpopular or objectionable viewpoints should be suppressed. These decisions presuppose answers to general questions about the nature of objectivity and free speech. Accordingly, careful philosophical analysis and argument addressing such issues could inform these decisions.

While each essay in this text is itself philosophical in the sense discussed earlier (they engage philosophical analysis and argument concerning hard, persistent questions of a general nature), a deliberate attempt has been made to avoid, as much as possible, technical philosophical vocabulary and reference to complex philosophical theories with which many students may not be familiar. In this way, a philosophical treatment of journalism is made available to a wider interdisciplinary audience.

Each chapter contains a carefully prepared introduction to the chapter readings that attempts to summarize, relate, and critique some key ideas falling within the purview of that chapter. The readings themselves (usually two per chapter) are written from contrasting perpectives, thereby attempting a "balanced" treatment of the subject at hand. Discussion questions at the end of each chapter are intended to direct and stimulate students' philosophical thinking about key issues and concepts related to the chapter. Finally, a selected bibliography, listing further suggested reading, completes the volume.

The issues raised here also accord with professional domains outside of journalism. For example, the privacy of news sources issue can be compared to issues of privacy and confidentiality raised in other professions, for example, ones arising in the practices of law and medicine. In addition to its use in courses within the schools of journalism and mass media communication (for instance, journalistic ethics and media and society courses), this volume may therefore be suitable for supplementary use in more general professional ethics courses as well as other "applied philosophy" courses.

The philosophical issues addressed in this volume are not intended to be all-inclusive. However, they do represent ones that have either been greatly neglected in the past (for instance, the question of how the study of philosophy itself may benefit students of journalism) or that underlie a number of difficult decisions practicing journalists inevitably confront (for instance, the question of morality and good journalism).

What is the value of the study of philosophical issues in journalism? Hopefully, those planning a career in journalism will, as a result of having carefully reflected upon the issues contained here, be better prepared to meet the philosophical challenges that underlie many problems of journalistic practice. Moreover, it is arguable whether such philosophical reflection can itself serve as a catalyst toward the cultivation of a general habit of critical thinking. A more complete discussion of the role(s) of philosophy in journalistic education will, however, be saved for the final chapter.

While there is no essential order in which chapters *must* be read, Chapters 6 through 8 are perhaps best read in the order in which they are presented. In Chapter 6 the general problem of journalistic objectivity is examined from contrasting perspectives. In Chapter 7, a particular solution to this problem, the "multiperspectival" approach, is examined. In Chapter 8, the logic of media errors, prejudices, and biases is examined as at least a partial response to the problem of objectivity— one that follows Walter Lippmann's plea for the construction of a "machinery of knowledge," presented in Chapter 7. Since these three chapters are related attempts at dealing with "journalistic epistemology"— that is, with the question of objective journalistic knowledge—it might be helpful if students were to read each in the order presented here.

It might also be useful for students to consider Chapter 9 after they have worked through the other chapters. Since this chapter deals with the question of the utility of philosophy itself for journalists, it might be helpful for students to actually have *done* some philosophy before turning to this "metaphilosophical" issue—a philosophical issue that is itself about philosophy.

It is noteworthy that many of the articles collected in this volume have been previously published in *The International Journal of Applied Philosophy*. In his capacity as editor-in-chief of the latter periodical, the editor of the present volume has in the past decade made a special effort to publish high quality philosophical literature in journalism. This special effort seemed justified by virtue of the paucity of existing published philosophical literature in this field. It is therefore no accident or mere fluke that many of the articles in this volume have been drawn from that periodical. It is, in fact, a product of a number of years of planning by this editor to make philosophical literature in journalism available to students of journalism, mass communications, philosophy, and related areas in a systematic and organized fashion.

One significant influence on the development of this volume is due to Professor Albert Flores, professor of philosophy at California State University, Fullerton, who, in the spring of 1986, organized and directed the California State University, Fullerton Philosophy Symposium entitled "Philosophical Issues in Journalism and the Media." Some of the proceedings of this symposium were, with the kind cooperation of Professor Flores, published in the Spring 1986 (Vol. 3.2) issue of *The International Journal of Applied Philosophy*. While only one of these published articles (Fred Smoller's article) is contained in this volume, this symposium gave credence to the idea that journalists and professionally trained philosophers could join forces. In this regard it is noteworthy that such interdisciplinary cooperation is presently common within such areas as business, law, medicine and engineering, but much less common within the field of journalism (which does, indeed, explain the current dearth of philosophical literature in journalism).

One further uncommon instance in which a philosopher has joined forces with a journalist to write philosophically on journalism is the recent book entitled *The Virtuous Journalist* (Oxford University Press, 1987), co-authored by journalist Stephen Klaidman and philosopher Tom L. Beauchamp. A selection from the latter book appears in Chapter 2 of this volume.

Some classical pieces have also been included. For example, carefully edited selections from John Stuart Mill's essay "On Liberty," and Walter Lippmann's book on *Public Opinion* are included. Since these classical selections set the framework for much contemporary discussion, including that occurring at several junctures in this volume, they are intended to serve an important integrative textual function as well as providing, in themselves, a rich source of philosophical insight.

The field of journalism is presently in a state of self-scrutiny. Those in the field are not united about its present or future identity. For example, there are some who would like to see journalism evolve into a full-blown profession (for instance, one on the style of law and medicine), defined by a common set of rules and regulations, entrance requirements, and binding code of ethics. Others would find such professionalization to be constraining. However, whatever direction journalism takes, individual journalists will inevitably confront philosophical problems in their practices, ones that cannot satisfactorily and finally be resolved through codes of ethics or legislation. (For example, the *Canons* of the American Society of Newspaper Editors, Canon 5 says that "News reports should be free from opinion or bias of any kind" but this greatly oversimplifies the problem of journalistic objectivity in news reporting as even a cursory reading of Lippmann's essay will suggest.) Philosophical issues are persistent, hard issues that cannot simply be codified away. The exploration of philosophical issues in journalism is, therefore, bound to be a timely pursuit, perhaps one that might even aid in journalism's search for its own identity.

1

What Makes a Story Newsworthy?

A key concept surrounding the development of a "news philosophy" is that of *newsworthiness*. Given the vast number of items that compete for limited news space, why are some items newsworthy while others are not; and, relatively speaking, why are some items *more* newsworthy than others? Indeed, these questions are broad philosophical ones which seem to underlie many specific criticisms of individual editorial decisions and policies concerning news selection.

In the first essay of this chapter, "A Prolegomenon for a Theory of News," Joshua Halberstam attempts to take some first steps toward a philosophical understanding of the concept of "newsworthiness." Beginning with a general characterization of "news" as the report of current events, he examines three theories of newsworthiness. According to the first, news may be analyzed on a "speech act" model, a relativistic conception of news according to which any report of a current event counts as news and is newsworthy by virtue of its being *published*. On this view the news and the newsworthy are created, not discovered, by the press through its act of publication—they are "whatever the news people say they are." Second, newsworthiness may be analyzed in terms of the degree of *importance*, or significance, of the news item in question. Third, it may be analyzed in terms of people's *interests*.

Halberstam, himself, provides a partial defense of a version of the third approach. In his view, the concept of newsworthiness is linked to the satisfaction of *actual* interests, especially those interests that we share with others, and which mark us out as members of specific communities. However, this view can be interpreted quantitatively to imply that the *amount* of interest in an event determines its newsworthiness. For example, on this understanding, a sports event could be more newsworthy than the discovery of a cure for diabetes, provided that more people shared an interest in the former than in the latter. As Halberstam acknowledges, such a purely quantitative approach might be amended by construing newsworthiness not in terms of actual interests but rather in terms of those interests that people *ought* to have. But a major difficulty he notes with the latter view is that of providing an adequate standard for identifying those interests.

According to one such standard, the interests that people ought to have are those that are *important* for them to have. While Halberstam dismisses the latter notion of importance, Berny Morson takes it seriously in the second essay of this chapter, "The Significant Facts." According to Morson, "facts become meaningful only to the extent that we recognize some significance in them"; and "facts are significant to the extent that they imply consequences for people's lives." For example, the facts surrounding the neglectful treatment of the patients at the Ridge Home for the mentally retarded were "meaningful" or newsworthy because they had serious consequences for the lives of residents at homes like Ridge as well as for their families.

According to Morson, the reporting of the significant facts, in a manner that conveys their significance, may be a "question of art" calling forth a literary presentation, especially in cases where the content of the purported facts are *human emotions*. In this regard, he discusses by example some literary techniques a reporter can use in promoting an empathetic understanding of different points of view. Quoting John Dewey, he contends that "artists have always been the real purveyors of news, for it is not the outward happening in itself which is new, but the kindling by it of emotion, perception and appreciation."

One major problem with Morson's view is that his concept of "significance" is ambiguous. As Halberstam queries, is this concept to be construed in terms of the *moral* significance of the facts? If so, then a murder in Brooklyn would appear to be more newsworthy than the destruction of the Mona Lisa. Second, is it the significance of the facts themselves or the significance of *reporting* the facts (or some combination of both) that constitutes the standard of newsworthiness? For example, a fact, say that of a covert government operation, may have significance as such but it may also have further social consequences by virtue of being promulgated by the media. Third, how many people must an event affect before it is newsworthy? Indeed, are events newsworthy *only* for those whose lives are significantly affected by them?

Finally, it is arguable that a relatively insignificant fact may still be newsworthy provided there is some degree of interest in it. For example, the fact that former President Nixon was hospitalized for a phlebitus attack may be newsworthy despite that it has little impact upon the lives of most people.

On the one hand, relativistic, subjective conceptions of newsworthiness (such as the "speech act" conception or those in terms of actual interests) may, upon reflection, suggest the need for a more "objective" ground of newsworthiness (such as one in terms of consequences for people's lives). On the other hand, the attempt to articulate a standard of the latter kind itself meets with further problems such as those noted above. Perhaps an adequate understanding of newsworthiness must incorporate all three theories discussed herein. In any event, a reflective study of the two essays contained in this chapter should shed light on central issues and problems raised by this concept.

A Prolegomenon for a Theory of News

JOSHUA HALBERSTAM

We often express bewilderment at what passes for news in the daily media. Supposedly, we recognize "real" news when we see it. Defining news, however, is far more complicated than one might initially suppose and the wide range of definitions offered by sociologists, communication theorists and the more speculative among journalists gives one additional pause.

Is there a philosophical problem here as well? The expanding philosophical interest in the methodology of journalism and the array of moral dilemmas generated by the news profession presumes an understanding of what constitutes news but comparably little direct attention is paid to the concept of news itself. A comprehensive theory of news must address two basic questions: a) What is news? and b) What makes some piece of news newsworthy? The present aim, then, is to offer some beginning steps in a theory of news and, *pari passu,* to indicate the philosophical interest in constructing such a theory.

1

Not everything in a newspaper is news: Advertisements are not news, nor are cultural reviews, obituaries, TV listings, recipes and letters to the editor. In fact, the greatest part of most newspapers or the "news" on TV and radio is not news. Genuine news is distinguished by a number of features but I focus here on three:

(a) News is about events, not states-of-affairs.
(b) News aims at current rather than past or future events.
(c) News is the report of an event, not the experience of an event.

These features not only help distinguish news from that which surrounds it, but also explain a number of other characteristics of news, *e.g.,* why news rapidly becomes obsolete, why single calamities are more newsworthy than a series of smaller calamities, why no news is good news.

(a) *News is about events.* A new development entails some change in the world and at least that much metaphysical similarity is captured in the etymological relationship between "new" and "news." News is about events and facts. The existence of an intact fifth century Mayan tomb is not news but its discovery is, as is the report that S died this morning but not the fact that she is dead.

This event orientation can be tuned finer still: News is nominalistic. Trends, statistics, patterns and classes of events may be sturdy entities in the inventory of the social scientist but the basic furniture of the news world is the single event. How to identify an event, establish its duration and extension, are troublesome issues in the determination of news as they are in describing all events. Nonetheless, it is this nominalistic orientation which guides the selection process by which some events become news items. The death of ten people in a single car crash is bigger news than the death of twenty people in five unrelated car crashes. It isn't the aggregate number of fatalities that counts, but the extraordinariness of a single event, and, as a rule, five unexceptional events do not add up to one exceptional event.

This emphasis on single events also illuminates that old adage "no news is good news." If we insist on being grimly pedantic about it, the maxim must be dismissed as plainly false—no news is not any news, good or bad. However, in a more expansive spirit, we'd note that if no news is good news then good news is no news and it is certainly the case that bad news rather than good news dominates our news media. The standard explanation for this is that the press trades in the sensational and tragic because people enjoy reading and hearing about other people's misfortunes (as to why they enjoy it, we are free to trot out our favorite explanatory psychological insight). This may be true but a more straightforward explanation for this tendency is that good events are infrequently reported because good events infrequently occur.

Consider how many distressing incidents can happen within the next five minutes: you can fall and break your toe, or your arm, or your skull. Your Aunt Bertha can fall and break her toe, arm or skull, any of these bad breaks can befall your friend Freddy. Good things, on the other hand, generally, don't just happen but develop; a deep romantic relationship doesn't suddenly arise though it can suddenly end, as when one of the partners dies. (This can be viewed as another manifestation of the (thermo-) dynamics of all systems, *i.e.* an operative system can more easily be impaired than improved). This is not to deny the existence of single fortunate events; the signing of a peace treaty, a righteous poverty-stricken individual winning the lottery, or, if you care for such things, the coronation of a king are felicitous happenings and genuine news items. Nevertheless, because it is in the nature of things for these agreeable events to occur far less frequently than unpleasant events, good news will be rarer than bad news.

(b) *News is aimed at current events.* News quickly becomes obsolete. Many would walk a mile for this morning's edition of a newspaper but not twenty feet for yesterday's. But why is a report of an earthquake in this morning's paper of interest but the same piece of "news" two days later no longer topical? It isn't that antiquated news is history. Clarifying the difference between news and history not only elucidates how news becomes superannuated, but also helps explain why we are attracted to the news in the first place.

A number of differences between history and news are readily apparent. History, for one thing, is only about people or events that directly impinge on the lives of people; the movements of the earliest ice floes belongs more to the study of geology than history. In addition, some insist that historical accounts include inferences to people's intentions and reasons in addition to their behavior. While news too is primarily concerned with the actions of people, motives are often immaterial to a news story. In fact, news need not concern people at all: it's news when a hen in Nebraska lays three purple eggs even if this occurrence has no significant consequences for anyone.

News, we noted, is nominalistic, but history ranges over series of events. In addition, historical recitals associate events in a narrative style which differs markedly from news reports.[1] In the 1830's, the German historian Ranke exhorted his colleagues to record only the facts of the past—"*wie es eigentlich gewissen.*" But historical facts never speak for themselves for they need to be embedded in some historical context. History is not mere chronicle, not simply a matter of accurately ordering events: 'Lincoln was shot,' 'WWI began,' 'Coolidge said, "I do not choose to run,"*t' 'Reagan was reelected' is the correct sequence of these events but not historical writing. Historical narrative requires *some* explanatory schema, be it a cover-law model, causal or other linking structure. News reports, on the other hand, need not be explanatory and those explanations which do appear in news accounts are often adscititious intrusions.

History is about the past while news aims at the present. The precise demarcation of the Peloponnesian Wars may be a matter of dispute and future discoveries may alter our understanding of that war, but the war, all of it, is decidedly over and an appropriate subject of historical investigation. Because the earlier and succeeding events of an historical subject have transpired, historians can evaluate the earlier events by reference to the later ones. Thus, Lincoln's decision to see a play at the Ford Theater has historical significance even though no such importance could have been attached to that decision at the time it occurred. News events, however, do not achieve their distinction by reference to their consequences for these effects may not yet be known. When, some time ago, a Russian satellite dropped to within twenty miles of the earth's atmosphere, it was the major news story of the day, though, in retrospect, the historical importance of the incident was negligible.

News aims at the present. We are attracted to news because we seek to satisfy our desire to be informed of what transpires beyond the limited range of our immediate experience. The history of news is, in part, the history of the attempt to shrink the temporal lag between the occurrence of an event and the report of its occurrence. The "latest news" is tantamount to the fastest means of delivery at our disposal. One remarkable consequence of the electronic news medium is that it has accelerated the speed of news transmission to its limiting case, to "live coverage" simultaneous with the event itself.

News becomes obsolete when it is superseded by more current developments. But like an old joke which retains the formal structure of a joke—it has a punch line though no punch—old news reports retain the former and formal characteristics of news; these reports become historical documents but not historical writings.

(c) *An event becomes news only when it is reported.* When I watch a fire in progress, attend the Superbowl or observe a robbery, I am not witnessing news but what will become news when I recount my experience to others. Anything that happens can become the subject of news but nothing that happens is itself news. The language employed in describing news contributes to this categorical confusion: we label news good or bad, shocking or uplifting, trivial or momentous, when these ascriptions apply only to the event and not the telling of the event. (This was a costly confusion to the royal messengers of old who paid with their lives bearing bad tidings.)

The essential purpose of the news is not to warn, instruct or amuse but to inform.[2] We may be entertained by a news feature, and the media, notoriously, is often more interested in entertaining than informing, but insofar as a report does provide information, it counts as news. Therefore, film clips of the day's sports events or space shots are news even though these events are dressed in graphic adornments which are not part of the news report *per se.*[3] . . .

II

I now want to consider three promising candidates for identifying newsworthiness: (1) news as speech acts, (2) news as a matter of importance, and (3) news as a matter of interest.

1. News as Speech Acts

The term "speech act" is borrowed from the philosophy of language—the pertinent idea is that "saying it's so, makes it so." The judge pronounces you married and you are; you utter the words "I promise" in an appropriate context and thereby place yourself under an obligation. Similarly, in this view, it is useless to posit a general, objective criterion for newsworthiness. None exists. While not everything published is news—on no account would we describe a crossword puzzle as news—any published item which meets the formal conditions stipulated above counts as news and is newsworthy: "news is whatever news people say it is."[4]

New reports certainly create news. No country can claim a psychological victory over its enemies without the media creating the impression that it has achieved such a victory. Studies indicate that voters believe that the important issues in an election are those that receive the most coverage on television."[5] When a crime wave is declared by the media, the public perceives itself as in the midst of one and its response generates additional news. The news media can unify a society and solidify that unity when it warns of foreign threats to the nation and its reference to "national spirit."[6] The broadcast of official announcements provides the publicity needed for rendering a decree authoritative and binding, and media gossip assures the renown without which celebrity status withers.

According to this speech act approach, there is no news "out there" waiting to be reported; rather, events are transformed into news only if they meet the specific demands and practices of the news-making process: "events become news by the news perspective and not because of its objective characterisitics . . . (the) news process decontextualizes an event in order to recontextualize it within the news format.[7] Moreover, it is argued, not only does news do more than merely report events, it does not mirror values either. In reporting, say, a deviant event— man bites dog—the news media actively defines what is deviant and what is normative. As one proponent of this "interpretative" school of journalism writes, "news is perpetually defining and redefining, constituting and reconstituting social phenomena.[8]

To be sure, the news media can create news and news coverage is certainly filtered through the special machinery of the news process. Nevertheless, these observations do not in themselves solve the question of newsworthiness. For one thing, the speech act analogy is not wholly apposite. News reports are, after all, reports: the information that Paris is burning does not cause the fire and while we might not hope for total objectivity, news reports are still basically true or false, more or less accurate.

More importantly, the descriptive insights of this speech act approach does not address the evaluative component inherent in the notion of newsworthiness. For even if we allow that news is whatever the media says it is, we must still ask for the grounds on which the media decide which events to report and which to ignore, which to emphasize and which to note in passing. We still need a criterion for newsworthiness.

2. News as a Matter of Importance

This is a more plausible proposal and most commonly offered as the central criterion of newsworthiness. Thus, the declaration of a red alert by the Joint Chiefs of Staff is more important than the result of last night's hockey game and therefore, more newsworthy. What is newsworthy is what makes a difference in our lives.

The notion of importance, however, is complicated. Should we think of importance in terms of consequences without regard to the actual public interest in those consequences? But what sort of ramifications are we to consider? Moral implications? But surely the murder of an individual anywhere in the world is morally worse than the ruination of any painting, yet no newspaper would give priority of coverage to a killing in Brooklyn over the destruction of the Mona Lisa. Should we stress the depth and extensiveness of an event's effects, deeming as more newsworthy events whose effects are long lasting rather than transient? Following this guideline we'd read a lot less about the machinations of local politicians and the goings-on of athletics and movie stars—a de-

velopment which can easily be applauded. But on these grounds information about wars and inflation would recede as well in favor of such
news as the report of a stellar explosion whose effects will include the
distruction of the earth seven billion years hence. In fact, if we appeal
to importance construed in terms of long-term effects on human life,
our newspapers would become a digest of articles from the *New England
Journal of Medicine, Physical Review,* and perhaps even philosophy
journals.

Suppose we interpret importance not as a function of an event's effects
but in terms of the consequences of *reporting* the event: what is newsworthy is what is important for people to know. In this amended for-
mulation, what is newsworthy is information which affects people's lives
and decisions. This view of newsworthiness underlies the traditional
emphasis on the role of a free press in a free society; only an enlightened
citizenry can make the informed decisions required in an effective
democracy.[9]

This revised interpretation of importance is inadequate as well. As
before, the adoption of this criterion of importance would result in a
radical alteration in the way news is presented. On the previous interpretation of importance, the discovery of an event pointing to the destruction of the planet in seven billion years was especially newsworthy,
while in the present approach in which importance is a function of the
consequences of the *revelation* of the event, this discovery would hardly
be newsworthy at all. Unnewsworthy, too, would be such curiosities as
the news that a lady in New Jersey had won the state lottery for the
fourth time or any other extraordinary but inconsequential event. And
while the appeal to the utility of publicity might further democratic aims,
it could also sanction censorship of any material deemed harmful to the
general good. An appeal to the demands of national security would not
only justify quashing provocative news reports but, according to this
criterion, provocative reports would be rendered unnewsworthy. For
example, the discovery of extraterrestrial life or any other wondrous
development would not be newsworthy if the public would be better
served by remaining ignorant of what occurred. But this is to confuse
what is newsworthy with the "worthiness" of reporting what is
newsworthy.

The second explication of importance improves on the first in directly
connecting the notion of newsworthiness to its consumer's needs. However, in focusing on the consequences of news and disregarding the
actual interests of those to whom it is directed, the essential feature of
newsworthiness is ignored.

3. News as Interest

Any event can be news and anything that happens can be of interest to someone for some reason or other. If we identify newsworthiness with interest then any news is potentially newsworthy. Fluctuations in the price of old nickels is newsworthy to numismatists, the results of Aunt Shirely's kidney operation is newsworthy to Uncle Harry, and the amount of salt the president poured on his eggs this morning is news-worthy to someone researching the effects of diet on presidential foreign policy. Accordingly, local or specialized news is not less newsworthy than global or national news but merely newsworthy to a smaller audience.

Can we define newsworthiness in purely quantitative terms without regard to the quality of the news? The fact that thirty percent of Americans read only the sport pages while far fewer follow developments in scientific research might seem insufficient grounds for deeming sports more newsworthy than science. To meet this objection, we might wish to base newsworthiness not on what satisfies those interests that people *do* have but on what satisfies interests that people *ought* to have.

This approach, albeit appealing, is misguided. The immediate difficulty is the absence of any procedure for determining which interests we are supposed to pursue. Presumably, we should be interested in what is important, but the difficulties attending the idea of importance have already been noted. Moreover, any attempt to ground newsworthiness in importance or any other value other than *actual* and immediate interest is questionable. Certainly, we do care about much that does not effect us directly, and certainly too, we can meaningfully distinguish between cultivated and prosaic interests, between serious and trivial concerns, but what do these distinctions have to do with newsworthiness? Being newsworthy is akin to being shipworthy; a shipworthy vessel gets you where you want to go but where you want to go is your decision; similarly, what is newsworthy is what satisfies your curiosity, but what you *should* be curious about is a different matter. The identification of newsworthiness with the satisfaction of interest becomes clearer when one considers why people follow the news in the first place.

Keeping up with the news serves to establish an ongoing sense of community and connection to the world around us. To think of the news only as a source of needed information is to miss the crucial role that news plays in our lives. Robert Nozick, for example, fails to appreciate the important social function of the news when he disparages reading the daily news as "shallow" and a "waste of time." Nozick writes:

... Newspaper readers devour the details of the previous day, but how many would similarly read through the daily papers of 1984? Yet we cannot affect most of today's details or their follow up; (nor will we be affected by them except as we read them)—they will sink rightfully into last year's ephemera. Why then should a person choose to be a prisoner of his time, selling such a large portion of his consciousness with its details? There are many other interesting things he can fill it with: history of whole other cultures, some of the great works of literature, music and art he has not encountered or exhausted (is this all of them?), deep scientific theories, and so forth. What rational being would choose instead to concentrate on the machinations and lies or honest but boring doings, speeches, and contests of today's mayors, senators, presidents, junta leaders, celebrities, and other assorted uninspiring seekers after power and attention?[10]

But this is a false dilemma. Is it similarly irrational to spend one's time cooking, at the movies, at sport events, or staring at sunsets? None of these activities—including following the news—is incompatible with the more serious pursuits favored by Nozick. Granted, what we learn from the news is of less consequence than what we learn from studying "deep theories of science" or great works of literature, but education is not the sole, nor even the main, purpose of news.

The news is the focus of much of our anger, hopes, curiosity and ruminations. It also provides a common set of topics about which individuals can exchange ideas and engage in social dialogue. On yet another level, following the news reflects and affirms our membership in a community of shared interests.

The network of our membership is composed of many intersecting strands. We belong to families, friendships, cities, countries, nations, political parties, unions, and professional associations. But more: those who follow baseball belong to the sports public, those who play chess seriously are part of the chess world, and those who frequent the theater are part of the theater communities—an undue emphasis on political developments and the pronouncements of politicians is perhaps what motivates Nozick's impatience with the current news media. We belong to various groupings with varying degrees of intensity; correspondingly, we seek out news concerning these different communities with varying degrees of interest. (Thus, the different allocation of space for international, national and local news will vary with the respective interests of a newspaper's readership.)

This linkage to community also underlies our greater attachment to news about present developments than to facts about past events. Suppose you have the choice of learning the details about one or two earthquakes. One earthquake occurred fifty years ago, the other this morning. Suppose, furthermore, that the two earthquakes are equal in scale and damage and, suppose too, that nothing you do will have more impact on this morning's earthquake than on the earthquake of fifty years ago. Other things being equal, we can assume that you would rather hear about today's tragedy. For while we do not know the victims of either earthquake, today's victims are our contemporaries with whom we share a history. However latent the feeling may be, these individuals are part of our immediate world and, in an important sense, our larger human community to a greater degree than inhabitants of either the future or the past. Only thoroughgoing hermits belong to no community whatsoever; and thoroughgoing hermits do not keep up with the news.

It is precisely in these quotidian pursuits that one's interests, values, and social reality are manifested. The commonplace attention paid to the news is, therefore, an important expression of our commitments and concerns.

NOTES

1. This may be something of an overstatement. Was Herodotus a journalist or an historian? Was Thucydides, an historian or correspondent?

2. Is the notice that an artist will appear at Carnegie Hall news or advertisement? According to one guideline, it is news the first time it is announced and advertisement thereafter.

3. Perhaps a news report that is only written but never disseminated should be considered news as well, provided that the report is written with the intention of dissemination. For a related discussion on the difference between news and gossip, see Sabini & Silver, *Moralities of Everyday Life* (NY: Oxford University Press, 1982).

4. See David L. Altheide, *Creating Reality: How T.V. News Distorts Events* Vol. 33 (Berkeley: Sage Publications, 1986) p. 17.

5. P. G. McCombs & D. L. Shaw, "The Agenda Setting Function of Mass Media", *Public Opinion Quarterly* 36 (1972):176–187.

6. Herbert J. Gans goes further: "The primary purpose of the news derives from the journalists' function as constructors of nation and society, and of managers of the symbolic arena. The most important purpose of news, therefore, is to provide the symbolic arena, and its citizenry with representative images (or constructs) of nation and society." *Deciding What's News: A Study of CBS Evening News, NBC Nightly News, Newsweek and Time* (N Y: Pantheon Books, 1979), p. 143.

7. Altheide, op. cit., p. 25.

8. Gaye Tuchman, *Making News: A Study in the Construction of Reality* (NY: The Free Press, 1978), p. 184.

9. See, for example, Robert A. Hutchins, *A Free and Responsible Press* (Chicago: University of Chicago Press, 1947), p. 29.

10. Robert Nozick, *Philosophical Explanations* (Cambridge: Harvard University Press, 1985), p. 525.

The Significant Facts

BERNY MORSON

One January morning, a powerful committee chairman, speaking from the floor of the Colorado House of Representatives, referred in passing to a discussion of problems at the Wheat Ridge Regional Center, one of the state's three homes for the severely retarded. The comment caught my attention as I sat at the press table at the front of the House chamber.

Problems at "Ridge Home" had cropped up with some frequency over the years. Each time, the story involved mistreatment or non-treatment of the multiply handicapped and hopelessly retarded residents of the home, who were of course unable to speak out on their own behalf.

So when the committee chairman came off the floor, I asked about the latest problems. He handed me a sheaf of correspondence from several federal agencies describing appalling conditions at Ridge Home. In addition to the usual problems of overcrowding, federal investigators had found care so lax that broken bones had gone untreated.

"One resident was found with a femur segment protruding through the skin," said a letter signed by William Bradford Reynolds, the assistant United States attorney general for Civil Rights. "Another resident was found with a left arm that was swollen and loose and floppy at the shoulder. Both these residents had broken bones, but staff were unaware of how the injuries occurred. Similarly, staff were unable to explain how a resident suffered second degree burns on his arm."

Reynolds' letter, which was addressed to Colorado Governor Richard D. Lamm, continued, "Our consultant found approximately 20 adult women being cared for by one person amid great disorder and confusion. Many of these women were partially undressed; one was urinating on the floor of the living area, and several were engaging in self-abusive behavior. Under such circumstances, appropriate supervision is impossible, and the physical safety of residents is threatened. . . ."

"A large number of Wheat Ridge residents suffer from severe contractures of their limbs and other body deformities due to the absence of necessary physical and occupational therapy," Reynolds continued.

22

"Residents who come to Wheat Ridge with some ambulatory ability or other mobility often lose these physical capabilities due to atrophy of muscles."

Such conditions violate the civil rights of the residents, Reynolds warned. Separately, the Department of Health and Human Services threatened to halt $10 million a year in Medicare payments to the facility unless the quality of care was improved.

The next morning, my story appeared on the front page of the *Rocky Mountain News* under enormous headlines. With more than 300,000 readers, the *News* has the largest circulation in the Rocky Mountain region. My story drew immediate, widespread attention to the problem at Ridge Home. Parents of Ridge residents demanded improvements, and state officials promised to comply. The Legislature moved quickly to allocate additional funds for the home, while department heads took steps to improve staff training. And one year later, a new federal investigation concluded that conditions had improved dramatically.

Sixty years ago, John Dewey wrote, "Opinions and beliefs concerning the public presuppose effective and organized inquiry."[1] The Ridge home story is an example of how much inquiry is conducted and the results published in the daily press. Of course, the federal government was capable of demanding improvements at Ridge without the help of the *Rocky Mountain News*. But absent the moral suasion of an outraged public, such change might have occurred only after years of litigation, or the problem might have been forgotten amid the multitude of other matters facing federal and state officials. Meanwhile, the state funds allocated to improve staff training and reduce overcrowding at Ridge would have gone instead to the pet projects of legislators.

More important, treatment of the handicapped is an on-going public policy issue, with advocacy groups urging new standards of care and an end to the "warehousing" of the retarded at large institutions such as Ridge. To form an intelligent opinion on the issue, citizens must know about conditions at institutions like Ridge and know the cost of alternatives. They also must know something about the people who live at Ridge. They must have "facts."

But which facts? As a legislative reporter, I hear debate each day on bills dealing with everything from public school graduation standards to a sales tax exemption for straw used as bedding for chickens. I can write about only a small fraction of these occurrences. The comment about Ridge leaped out at me because I knew the troubled history of the institution and of similar facilities in other states, and I was familiar with the debate swirling around the issue of care for the handicapped. Other reporters were in the House chamber that morning, but failed to catch the significance of the comment about Ridge Home, and so missed the story.

The point is that facts become meaningful only to the extent that we recognize some significance in them. In and of themselves, unsifted facts add up only to what William James called a "buzzing, blooming universe," a meaningless stream of occurrences. Facts are significant to the extent that they imply consequences for people's lives. Of itself, the average rainfall of a given country is trivial. Rainfall becomes significant if the amount is so low as to result in drought and famine or so great as to result in flood. What facts portend constitutes their significance. To cover the news takes a combination of formal education and past experience that permits the reporter to judge among available facts and to choose those that are of significance to the community. To make sense of events requires intelligent selection among the facts.

Once found out, the events at Ridge Home are of obvious significance in the context of American values. Americans abhor mistreatment of the handicapped and will always demand a halt to such practices. But all reporting is not so simple. Sometimes the significance of facts is not obvious, either because the subject matter is unfamiliar or because the context itself is at issue. The nascent environmental movement raised such problems beginning in the late 1960s. For years, suburban housing developments provided livelihoods for builders and homes for millions away from the core of older cities. The environmentalists, embracing a new set of values, saw such development as a blight upon the landscape and called for state and federal regulation. The dispute brought angry clashes in many communities. Developers argued that the right to own property includes the right to build on it, while the environmentalists countered that poorly planned development increases traffic and air pollution, degrading the quality of life for everyone.

Boulder, Colorado, has long been a leader nationwide in land-use planning. The city began buying open space in the late 1960s to preserve scenic areas and to "shape" development. Construction is subject to rigid aesthetic codes, with even stricter rules in historic zones. From the beginning, environmentalists pressed for restrictions on development outside the city limits, fearing that growth barred under municipal ordinances would take place in unincorporated parts of the county. Environmentalists and developers battled subdivision by subdivision for 10 years in zoning hearings before the Boulder County commissioners.

The Armageddon of zoning battles came in 1985, when the county commissioners proposed a ban on all development, except for a few isolated houses, on land outside incorporated cities. The proposal, which affected more than 5,000 tracts totalling 38,700 acres, drew sharp dissent from property owners outside the path of urban annexations. With the farm economy in perpetual shambles, many Boulder County farmers were hoping to cash in on their land and retire. Other land was owned by people who had invested their savings on the assumption that the property could be developed at a profit. Now they envisioned their property values deflating like a stuck balloon.

I tried to use direct quotes to make vivid the feelings of property owners faced with a sharp decline in land values. When a member of the county planning department tried to explain the proposal at a public meeting, one crusty old land owner stood up and said, "Somebody get a rope." In another instance, property owners, wielding signs and shouting crude epithets, disrupted a press conference called by environmental groups to voice support for the proposal. The land owners called the environmentalists "communists" and "bird-watchers."

"They're trying to take people's property rights without notice and without payment," said one developer. "I never thought it could happen in America."

Such emotional appeals are meaningful under the assumption shared by most Americans that development of property is a right, guaranteed by the Constitution. Legally, that assumption is incorrect; decisions by the United States Supreme Court grant broad authority to local governments to regulate development. But the assumption is understandable since governments rarely exercise that authority, and the issue rarely arises at public forums or in the popular press. I tried to report the concerns that led county officials to adopt a strategy that runs counter to the popular assumption about property rights. From the standpoint of the planners, development of rural land would provide a cozy retirement for a few farmers, but the other 185,000 Boulder County residents would be left to finance uneconomical urban services. Development of homes miles from existing cities would require the widening and paving of roads that now are little more than dirt lanes. Law enforcement officials, called to emergencies in outlying developments, would leave the rest of the county unprotected for long periods.

"If we're doing our planning correctly, we put our development where it can be most efficiently served," explained one county planning official. "It's cheaper for a police car to circle a [city] block with [many] homes than for the sheriff to circle a block with [only] four homes. That's obvious." Development prevented under the re-zoning was sufficient to generate 162,000 additional automobile trips per day, the official pointed out. And each trip would be longer—and would generate more air pollution—than if development were directed to sites close to shopping and places of work.

In the end, the County Commissioners adopted the zoning proposal. And a year later, a commissioner prominently identified with the plan was easily re-elected, partly, I believe, because a majority of citizens was sufficiently able to untangle their own interests from the emotional web spun by the landowners.

To report this sequence of events required an ability to recognize an emerging intellectual framework in which development is judged from the standpoint of the community as a whole, rather than of a relatively few property owners. Some reporters, unable to assimilate an unfamiliar point of view, got bogged down in the emotional appeals of the land-owners. They produced stories about good farmers pitted against bad bureaucrats. Ultimately, that "angle" on the news was not useful in understanding why the county commissioners voted as they did and why the public backed them at the polls. The significance of behavior—even of customary behavior that occurs every day, such as housing construc-tion—is not fixed once and for all, subject to a single, unvarying inter-pretation. The planning officials saw new implications in actions previously taken for granted. Even historical events, seemingly dead to new interpretation, take on altered meaning with each generation. To report current events without regard to the evolving significance of be-havior is to miss the point of the news. Because the way we view events guides future action, the changing significance of behavior is itself news. . . .

Often we talk about the need for reporting to be "objective." The term usually refers to the duty of the reporter to give the facts "as they are" and without distortion, as a camera might record a scene. Such a cascade of facts, unsifted with regard to relative significance, would be worthless. The job of the reporter is to make an intelligent selection among available facts. Reporting is objective to the extent that facts, once selected, are communicated as accurately as possible.

Of course, the facts of a case are not always obvious, and the very existence of facts is a matter of doubt in some instances. At this writing, for example, it is a matter of speculation whether South Africa has nuclear weapons. Because reporters live with daily deadlines, they must often write articles before all the facts of a situation are known. But not to know the facts or to perceive them indistinctly is different from the willful distortion of facts for gain or ideological advantage. Objective reporting is a matter of honesty and conscience in reporting the facts to the extent they are known.

Objectivity can take countless forms. Often articles about the same subject will differ, reflecting the diverse perspectives of the reporters. Many witnesses may testify in the course of a lengthy hearing. Reporters will differ as to which of the testimony is worth reporting and in what degree of prominence. The best report is the one that emphasizes those facts that prove most salient in understanding events. Because reporting occurs while events are in progress, that judgment can be made in many instances only in retrospect.

Reporting is called biased when facts are twisted or distorted to serve the ends of the writer, rather than the need of the reader to learn what transpired. I recall an editor of a small town paper many years ago who wrote atrociously inaccurate stories about land use planning. He always left out the reasons advanced by civic groups in support of better planning and emphasized facts that tended to bolster the case for development. One day while going through county records, a reporter for another newspaper discovered that this editor was a partner in a development firm with substantial real estate holdings in the area. This editor had a conflict of interest. He was pretending to be a disinterested observer of events, when in fact he had a financial stake in the outcome. He was incapable of selecting facts in terms of their significance for the community as a whole because his vision was bounded by his own narrow interests. And he was dishonest in failing to tell readers of his financial stake in events.

Bias also occurs when reporters are blind to all facts except those that accord with their own, long-held point of view. In the Boulder County case, some reporters were unable to recognize that the customary process of real estate development had taken on new significance for planning officials and a portion of the public. The resulting stories emphasized the wrong facts because the writers failed to see beyond their long held views about the right of property owners to develop their land. The stories were not willfully dishonest, but neither were they useful to readers in understanding events, particularly if they lived outside Boulder County and were trying to make sense of an unfamiliar attitude toward development.

Understanding is a process that takes many forms. In the case of Ridge Home, understanding meant realization that norms for treatment of the retarded were being violated. The story also added to the ongoing public discussion of how best to care for the retarded. In the case of the land use stories, understanding meant recognition that some development patterns are more economical than others. . . .

Understanding can also mean the ability to empathize with people in the news. By putting ourselves in their place, we grasp their anger and pain. As fellow human beings, we understand their responses at an intuitive level. A soldier is killed in war, and through vivid writing, we understand his suffering and the suffering of his family. Suddenly he is no longer a statistic, and war is more than an abstract problem. It is our problem, and events of the war become immediately significant for us.[2]

Some of the most important events of the 20th Century, such as the civil rights movement in the United States, are best understood in this latter way. In fact, *only* to the extent that we learned to respond to blacks as human beings did we understand their demand to be treated as human beings. As long as white people continued to relate to blacks as something other than human, we did not understand the humiliation they experienced under segregation, and their protest was baffling. In retrospect, the civil rights movement seems inevitable. But at the time, the sudden upheaval in an ancient caste system was not immediately apparent, particularly to white people who had little acquaintance with blacks. So the most important task for reporters was to convey the feelings of blacks.

I said earlier that good reporting requires an ability to recognize which facts are significant amid the stream of daily occurrences. The same principle is true of writing that conveys feelings, but different kinds of facts are important. The clothes people wear, the kinds of jobs they perform, their age or other distinguishing features—all these are significant for the writer who wishes to convey a sense of the men and women who are the subjects of news accounts. Descriptions of sounds and colors are used to create vivid images of the lives they lead. Direct quotation, as opposed to paraphrasing, helps us to "hear" the people as they describe their problems. Details of weather, landscape, or decor add a sense of place to the events being reported. The result is a word portrait, not unlike a novel or short story.

Here's how Jimmy Breslin of the now-defunct New York *Herald Tribune* described his plan of attack for a series during the civil rights era on life in Harlem, a large black community in New York:

"Take a woman at the supermarket. Get her order, can by can, and list it and what she paid for it. With almost no comment on it by me, this list will be meaningful to a housewife in Larchmont [a wealthy New

York suburb]. Maybe more meaningful than all the big words written of this thing.

"You follow this theory with everything. With the school-yards, which are crowded at 7:30 A.M. because parents have to leave early and the kids are locked out of the apartments and with nothing to do, they go to school. And with the furniture repossessions and water and gas and electric shutoffs and the gas-station habits—50 cents worth of gas for a Cadillac. You do this with facts from small people in the street and from merchants and bankers.

"But always you do it with people. You keep the facts alive with people."[3]

The kinds of facts Breslin selects are not dispositive of policy questions in terms of law, anthropology or other formal disciplines. His facts are ones that give a sense of what life is like for the people he describes— what they eat, how they make ends meet, how children get by without daycare. This approach later became enshrined as "the new journalism" in a volume of that name by Tom Wolfe. In fact, good journalists have written vividly about people for as long as there have been newspapers. New York newspapers at the turn of the century frequently wrote colorfully of the city's large immigrant population. Journalists have chronicled the life and death of soldiers in America's wars. As Dewey wrote: "Artists have always been the real purveyors of news, for it is not the outward happening in itself which is new, but the kindling by it of emotion, perception and appreciation."[4]

Sometimes, stories on the same or similar subjects present different perspectives depending on whether the writer takes a "hard news" or "feature" approach to the selection and organization of facts. The events at Ridge Home were presented in a hard news fashion. The significance of the facts—that public standards for treatment of the handicapped were being violated—was evident even when the facts were presented through quotation from dry legal documents. I dealt with similar issues in the case of a mother who did not want her severely retarded child, living at a state institution (not Ridge Home), to be educated in a public school. But in this case, events were presented almost entirely from the emotional perspective of participants.

As mentioned previously, advocacy groups have suggested that the retarded could live fuller lives outside large institutions. They propose that the retarded live in group homes, located in residential neighborhoods, and take advantage to whatever extent possible of such public amenities as schools, parks and public transit. Based on that view, Col-

orado officials proposed to bus a child identified in my account only as
"Tracy" from the state institution to a nearby public school each day.
Tracy's mother took the position that efforts to educate Tracy raised
false hopes that the child may someday recover—a point of view that
is understandable only to the extent that we grasp the suffering of a
parent with a profoundly retarded child.

I began with a description of the child:

"Tracy is curled up in a wooden box, her arms wrapped around her
misshapen head, her eyes alternately crossed or rolling aimlessly around
the room.

"Earlier in the day, a worker tried to establish contact by massaging
lotion into Tracy's wrists. But after 10 minutes, Tracy issued a series of
ill-tempered grunts that ended only when she was lifted back into the
box, which is lined with fuzzy carpet.

"All around Tracy, children sit in wheel chairs or lie on cushions.
Some are in braces; others are nourished by tubes that run directly into
their stomachs.

"The room is cheerful and filled with toys, but the children's eyes are
vacant. Over and over, a tinkly music box plays 'When You Wish Upon
a Star.'

"Nearly 13 years old and profoundly retarded, Tracy—her parents
asked that their last name not be used—is a resident at the Grand
Junction Regional Center, one of three state homes for the severely
disabled.

"She can't walk or feed herself or take care of her bodily needs. Snug
in her box, she smiles in response to some private vision. Her nominal
IQ of 1 may be an exaggeration—some tests indicate she is less developed than a new-born baby."

This description "sets the scene" by helping the reader to understand
the depth of this child's retardation. The fact of children being fed
through stomach tubes conveys the seriousness of their medical condition. The vacant eyes of these youngsters adds to the picture of retardation, as did Tracy's vacuous smile, unconnected to external events. I
used the detail of the music box, playing the same tinkling melody over
and over again, to symbolize the emptiness of these lives. The technique
of using visible or describable objects to symbolize unobservable mental
states is called "the objective correlative."

Then I described the feelings of Tracy's mother about proposals to
educate her child:

"In the past, officials at the center told her that Tracy was learning to stand. When the photographs arrived in the mail, she saw Tracy propped up in metal braces like a rag doll on a scaffold.

" 'You go through hope to depression again,' the mother says. 'You go through this constant yo-yo thing. It's not fair to parents.'

" 'She needs to be held and loved,' the mother says. 'But why subject her to the standing brace when she never can walk? To me that's just torturing the child'."

Using a flashback technique, I described the origins of Tracy's problem:

"A forceps delivery by a New York doctor left Tracy with severe brain damage. She suffers from a syndrome in which fluid builds up inside the skull, putting pressure on the brain.

"Tracy made some progress after neurosurgeons inserted a tube to drain the fluid to the stomach. The tube [called a shunt] is visible in her neck, just beneath the skin.

"By the time Tracy was 15 months old, she was behaving at a 12-month level. She could stand in a walker. She smiled and recognized people.

"But then the shunt failed. Doctors inserted a new shunt.

"Over the next five years, the shunt failed 19 times. Each time, doctors drew off the fluid by inserting a needle into Tracy's skull, then dug deep into the brain to replace the shunt.

"Each time, Tracy's development regressed. In the end, she recognized no one, not even her mother. She felt only pain. She was in severe seizures 20 hours a day.

" 'Essentially, it was like watching your child die before your eyes,' the mother says."

Officials at the institution cited federal law requiring that youngsters be educated in the most "normal" environment possible. Tracy was receiving some training at the home, but a public school would be a more "normal" environment, the officials said. They said Tracy might make progress in learning to drink from a cup or might one day learn to activate a toy by pushing a button.

Although Tracy was happy to drink from a bottle, curled up like a baby, workers at the home insisted she learn to use a cup instead. "When she reaches 30 years old, that won't look very normal to be drinking out of a bottle," one official explained. "The whole goal is to teach people to be as normal as possible."

"They can't accept [Tracy's] limitations," the mother said. "If I as a parent can accept it, why can't they?

"At Christmas, they send you a picture of Tracy in Santa's lap, and there she is, all contorted. That really does it at Christmas—you just sit there and cry."

Like the Ridge Home story, the events involving Tracy and her mother concern the public policy question of how to care for the retarded. But in the case of Tracy and her mother, the significance of available alternatives is measured entirely in feelings. The facts to be considered are not cost or legalities, but emotions. Direct quotes—"You just sit there and cry" and "To me, that's just torturing the child"—convey emotion. Comments also were included by parents who chose public school for their retarded youngsters. Those comments presented the other side of the issue in language every bit as emotional as the words of Tracy's mother.

Of course, the story about Tracy could have been structured around the cost of educating a profoundly retarded child. I would have gathered a different set of facts in preparation for such a story, concentrating on budget documents, for example. I probably would have interviewed Tracy's mother anyway, but in much less depth. Certainly we would not have discussed her depression at Christmas or her feelings about watching Tracy regress as a result of successive shunt failures. I would have scheduled interviews with state education officials to ask them whether the high cost of educating the retarded means less money for other programs. The result would have been a different, but perfectly acceptable story exploring an issue of public finance. Conversely, the story about Ridge Home could have been written from the standpoint of residents of that institution and their families. Discussion of legal and financial issues would have been given less attention in order to emphasize emotional impact. Both approaches present facts that are necessary to understand the issue, but from different perspectives. In fact, newspapers often run stories from both perspectives on major issues, sending two or more reporters, if necessary.

Facts that can be understood only through empathy are among the most difficult to recognize and the hardest for reporters to communicate. Both grief and joy are often silent, and even when revealed, the significance for others may not be apparent. But if the purpose of public policy is to further human good, it is just these facts that are often most significant.

An informed public requires facts in order to make policy decisions. But facts alone are not sufficient. Fires and murders are "facts," but only rarely are they more than of passing significance, except to those involved. Intelligent reporting is distinguished by the ability to recognize which facts are truly of significance to the community.

NOTES

1. *The Public and Its Problems,* Henry Holt and Company, New York, (1929, p. 177).
2. Of course, to empathize with people does not necessarily mean to agree with them. We can empathize with the land owners in Boulder County who stood to lose money through re-zoning, while at the same time recognizing that the plan was in the interest of the vast majority of people.
3. *The World of Jimmy Breslin* (New York: Viking Press, 1967), p. 66.
4. Ibid., p. 184.

DISCUSSION QUESTIONS

1. Halberstam argues that news is "nominalistic." What does he mean by this? Do you agree with him? Defend your answer.
2. Halberstam states that "bad news rather than good news dominate our news media." What is his explanation for the latter? Do you agree with him? Defend your answer.
3. What, according to Halberstam, are some major differences between news and history? Is his analysis correct? Defend your answer.
4. Halberstam states that "anything that happens can become the subject of news but nothing that happens is itself news." What does he mean by the latter remark? In your view, is he correct? Defend your answer.
5. What does the so-called "speech act" analysis of news and newsworthiness assert? What criticisms does Halberstam have of this view? Do you agree with these criticisms? Defend your answer.
6. Halberstam draws the following analogy: "Being newsworthy is akin to being shipworthy; a shipworthy vessel gets you where you want to go but where you want to go is your decision; similarly, what is newsworthy is what satisfies your curiosity, but what you *should* be curious about is a different matter." In your view, is the latter analogy a helpful one? (Is "getting one where one wants to go" a sufficient condition for calling a ship "shipworthy"? Is "satisfying one's curiosity" a sufficient condition for calling a story "newsworthy"?)
7. What, according to Halberstam, are some links between "community" and the newsworthy? Can a story fail to be newsworthy in spite of its being of interest to a nameable community of individuals? Defend your answer.
8. According to Morson, what makes a fact "significant"? In the light of Halberstam's discussion, what problems, if any, do you see in using "significance" (or "importance") as a standard of newsworthiness?

9. Halberstam points out that there is a difference between the significance of the facts and the significance of *reporting* the facts. In your estimation, does Morson adequately account for this distinction in his essay?

10. In what respects does Morson, like Halberstam, recognize links between community and the newsworthy? What differences in this regard exist between their views?

11. Morson maintains that "objective" news reporting involves the selection of facts on the basis of their significance. In your view, can the judgment of what facts are significant itself be "objective"? Defend your answer.

12. Morson quotes the famous contemporary American pragmatist philosopher, John Dewey, as saying the following: "Artists have always been the real purveyors of news, for it is not the outward happening in itself which is new but the kindling by it of emotion, perception and appreciation." Do you agree with Dewey's latter characterization of news? Must a good reporter be a good artist? Defend your answers.

13. How does Morson use "art" in his own work as a reporter to convey the significant facts? Discuss some of the specific techniques he employs in his article about "Tracy." What is the difference(s) between the approach he takes in the latter article and that which he takes in the article on Ridge Home?

14. Can an "eclectic" view of newsworthiness be constructed by incorporating ideas from some or all of the alternative theories discussed in this chapter? Discuss the nature and feasibility of such an approach.

15. In the light of your reflections, briefly present and defend some major aspects of your own view of the newsworthy.

2

Morality, Competence, and Journalistic Excellence

One general philosophical and practical concern in journalistic ethics is that of the place of morality in journalism. In particular, what is the relation between competence in journalism and morality? Must a good journalist be morally good as well? What is meant by "morality" in the first place? Is a journalist bound by the standards of ordinary morality? Is there a special "journalistic morality" that is separate and distinct from the standards of ordinary morality? Such questions are of philosophical interest; but, insofar as the answers individual journalists may provide to them can affect the manner in which they conduct their professional lives, such questions are also of significant *practical* concern. In this chapter, these matters are explored from contrasting perspectives.

In the first essay, "The Virtuous Journalist: Morality in Journalism," Stephen Klaidman and Tom L. Beauchamp discuss significant concepts of morality as they relate to journalism. According to the authors, the term "morality" itself denotes "culturally transmitted rules of right and wrong conduct that establish the basic terms of social life." Such rules, argue Klaidman and Beauchamp, are not merely matters of subjective preference but are, "absolutely essential to social stability and the preservation of human decency."

Klaidman and Beauchamp further distinguish between a morality of rights and duties and that of virtues. Whereas the former is expressed in terms of rules governing moral conduct, the latter is expressed in terms of character traits such as fairness, truthfulness, trustworthiness, and nonmalevolence. More precisely, they define a moral virtue as "a fixed disposition to do what is morally commendable, which entails a desire to act according to moral principles." While the authors favor the use of the latter terminology they acknowledge that being virtuous entails the execution of one's duties as well as respect for the rights of others.

What *practical* difference does it make whether morality is cast in terms of virtues or in terms of rules? According to Klaidman and Beauchamp, the meaning of rules may be unclear, and their interpretation and application uncertain, thereby prompting prolonged debate or reflection. Therefore, since journalists often work under time constraints and in crisis situations, the appeal to rules in order to make their moral decisions may be self-stultifying. On the other hand, the cultivation of moral virtue among journalists can make moral action in such contexts "a matter of course."

It is not clear, however, that the cultivation of moral virtue may circumvent the uncertainty surrounding the meaning and application of rules. This is so because even moral virtues entail "a desire to act according to moral principles"; that is, they involve the application of rules to contexts which may well be less than clear-cut.

Perhaps the cultivation of morally virtuous character among journalists has its most salient value in increasing the likelihood that a journalist will even *want* to be moral in the first place. Since the latter desire appears to constitute a prerequisite of moral action, a virtue-based concept of morality may, after all, provide a firmer and more reliable foundation of moral action than one that focuses primarily upon moral rules. However, the matter of *how* to cultivate such moral dispositions in prospective journalists then becomes a significant problem for those entrusted with the training and education of journalists.

According to Klaidman and Beauchamp, morality, whether in terms of moral virtues or in terms of rules, is not merely tangential to the professional activities of journalists. Rather, it is intrinsic to the idea of professional *competence.* That is, according to these authors, "moral criteria are embedded in our very conception of competent journalistic practice" since "standards such as fairness and accuracy are moral dimensions of competence." For example, while the ability to keep one's own personal biases and beliefs out of a news story may be part of the concept of general competence in journalism, it is also a moral consideration; or, for example, while the use of reliable sources may be a part of general journalistic competence, the question of *how many* reliable sources to use when reporting an item that has serious social implications is also a question about moral responsibility.

Klaidman and Beauchamp thus view morality (construed either from a virtue-based perspective or from a duty-based one) as a necessary condition of being a good journalist or of good journalistic practice.

What this implies is that a good journalist must harmonize the professional practice with the rules of morality, that there are internal moral constraints that set limits upon what he or she may do in the name of the profession.

In the second selection of this chapter, "Some Conflicting Assumptions of Journalistic Ethics," Stephen H. Daniel, in contrast to Klaidman and Beauchamp, argues that standards of ordinary morality are not intrinsic to journalistic standards but rather are often in conflict with them.

While Daniel agrees with Klaidman and Beauchamp that morality is not merely "subjective" or "personal," he also rejects the idea that morality is "culturally relative" (a form of relativism that appears to be implied by Klaidman and Beauchamp's definition of morality as "culturally transmitted rules"). However, Daniel admits that the meanings of moral terms are relative to particular groups or cultures. For example, the concept of a "good conscience" may be defined in a given way by a given group of language users; however, this does not mean that I ought to govern my life according to this particular definition. Indeed, I might (rightly) decide to behave in a way that would be regarded within this particular community of language users as indicating a "bad conscience." There is, therefore, according to Daniel, a difference between the *linguistic* use of moral discourse, in which I adopt a culturally relative definition of a term purely for purposes of communicating within that culture, and the *normative* use of such discourse in which I try to regulate my behavior, or that of others, by it.

According to Daniel, the standards of ordinary morality and those of "journalistic excellence" are, in effect, defined by two different communities or cultures of language users. For example, when seen from within the journalistic community, such activities as eavesdropping and other invasions of privacy for purposes of obtaining newsworthy items may be seen as being in compliance with high professional standards in journalism; whereas such activities, when seen from outside this community, from within the community of ordinary language users, may be regarded as morally reprehensible.

A major point Daniel is making is that journalists, *in their capacity as journalists,* are not bound by the *ordinary* rules of morality. Rather, in the latter capacity, "being moral" means fulfilling responsibilities to society, even at significant costs to self. For example, it is in this sense of "being moral" that a photographer who films his own assassin, in order to obtain photographs, is behaving morally. On the other hand, journalists are also, at the same time, members of the community of ordinary persons who (according to standards of everyday morality) ought to value their own survival. In *this* capacity, the definition of "being moral" may militate against such acts done in a professional capacity. Journalists, Daniel argues, are, thereby, torn between (in a state of conflict and tension between) these two different communities of language users.

Nevertheless, even if journalistic standards and those of ordinary morality do sometimes come into conflict, Daniel is clear that adopting the language of a given community does not mean that one must also accept that language in a *normative* way so as to govern one's conduct by it. What the latter means is that a journalist may still be free to choose whether to govern his or her life according to the one set of standards or the other in cases of conflict. It is only by assuming that the journalist who trangresses ordinary standards of morality in satisfying professional standards has no choice in the matter, that personal responsibility for those actions dissolves. The danger of making such an assumption, however, is that journalists may lose their personal identity, becoming, thereby, tools of society, mere cogs in a journalistic machine that grinds out the news.

In contrast to Daniel's view, Klaidman and Beauchamp see journalistic standards and those of ordinary morality as aspects of the same "ethics game" (to use Daniel's, not their, term). On this understanding, journalistic standards are circumscribed by, and entail, the same moral constraints that are recognized, in other contexts, by the general moral community.

To say that journalistic morality is governed by the rules of ordinary morality is not, however, to say that it does not ever tolerate actions that are ordinarily thought to be immoral. As Klaidman and Beauchamp make clear, "making moral judgments and handling moral dilemmas require the balancing of often ill-defined competing claims, usually in untidy circumstances." For example, even acts of eavesdropping and deceit may, at least in extraordinary circumstances, be tolerated, even by our ordinary understanding of morality—say when such acts are necessary means towards preventing a national disaster. Nevertheless, according to Daniel, "most journalists do not live and work in an environment of *ordinary* interaction and communication." If Daniel is right, then ordinary morality may, indeed, in the end, be too restrictive for the extraordinary demands of journalistic practice. But, as he suggests, an upshot of such a division between these two sets of standards may be the loss of development of an independent, autonomous, and personally responsible self amongst practicing journalists.

The Virtuous Journalist: Morality in Journalism

STEPHEN KLAIDMAN AND TOM L. BEAUCHAMP

MORALITY: ITS VIRTUES AND ITS RULES

. . . [W]hat do we mean by *morality?* This word denotes culturally transmitted rules of right and wrong conduct that establish the basic terms of social life. Because the rules are pervasively acknowledged and shared in a culture, morality is not merely a matter of what a person subjectively believes. That is, individuals do not create their morality by making their own rules, and "a morality" cannot be purely a personal policy or code. Sometimes morality is cynically or frivolously dismissed, as if it were no more significant than superstition, but this claim is untenable. Morality is absolutely essential to social stability and the preservation of human decency, and the fact that it is sometimes ignored serves only to emphasize its significance.

Morality in this sense is different from *ethical theory* and *moral philosophy,* which are synonymous terms referring to systematic reflection on morality. Moral philosophers reflect on social practices in order to bring them into a unified, clear, and consistent package of action guides.

Rules as Specifications of Duties and Rights

Moral philosophy also formulates principles to help develop and evaluate moral beliefs and arguments. All rights, duties, and obligations are based on these principles, most of which are already present in public discourse, but usually in an imprecise form. Fairness is an example. Any reader of editorials and op-ed articles will frequently encounter appeals to fairness—for example, in considering the fairness of the tax system. Editorial writers and columnists are not expected to analyze the concept of fairness and the rules of fairness with philosophical depth and precision. Their claims and conclusions are usually left at an intuitive or

39

common-sense level. The reason is that in the brief analyses typical of journalism, basic claims can only be presupposed rather than defended by lengthy, well-developed theories.

Consider as an example a comment by CBS Chairman Thomas Wyman about cable TV network owner and entrepreneur Ted Turner, who at the time was considering a hostile financial bid for ownership of CBS: "He [Turner] is not qualified because he doesn't have the conscience. When what you are broadcasting goes out to 70 million people, you better be thinking about something broader than the things I think occupy his thinking, and that includes money."[1] This comment typifies the moral criticism found in journalism. Wyman is, in effect, saying that Turner does not have either the character or the sense of responsibility required to run a network. Such comments are generally made without providing any supporting analysis or, as in this case, any idea of what conscience, character, or responsibility mean to Wyman.

This brevity or lack of analysis and supporting argument also typifies government in its dealings with the press. Wyman's comment about Turner derived from a context in which CBS sought to thwart Turner's hostile takeover bid by questioning whether Turner was fit to receive a transfer of CBS's broadcast license from the Federal Communications Commission. The FCC had routinely denied license applications in the past on grounds of deficiencies in moral character.[2] A criminal record, for example, generally was sufficient as a test of moral unfitness, but broader sets of criteria would be used as well. The underlying idea was that people who cheat, perjure themselves, and so on, are not likely to be responsible station owners and should therefore be disqualified. However, over the years it became clear that the FCC had no well-informed, systematic criteria or tests, and the role of these character judgments diminished. Now the agency is more narrowly concerned about whether a candidate would lie to the commission or otherwise violate its rules. But even under the narrower conception, the FCC still has no carefully drawn criteria or tests that inform its moral judgments.

The job of moral philosophy is to transcend moral intuition and purely contextual judgments by defining with precision such notions as conscience, responsibility, and fairness, without oversimplification or excessive abstraction. One objective of an ethics for journalism is proper interpretation of rules of conduct directed at the amelioration of specific professional problems. These rules are generally—although not necessarily—rules of duty, and they are often accompanied by correlative rights. Problems often arise over the demands made by rules about freedom, respect for privacy, fairness, avoidance of harm, and the like, and over how to handle situations in which the rules are vague. Because abstract rules cannot anticipate all possible situations, they must leave appropriate latitude for judgment and thus potentially for disagreement. Like many matters in life, sound judgment in applying rules is as vital as the rules themselves. (*Rules,* as we use the term, are statements either of duties or of rights that may or may not be formally recognized in a code of professional ethics; *responsibilities* are generally established by the rules of duty.)

Imagine, for example, a newspaper attempting to frame rules that specify when it will and will not publish confidential information obtained from sources. The bare fact that the information is confidential is not a sufficient reason to rule out publication. Publication is sometimes warranted by reasons that outweigh the standard reasons for protection. Conversely, there is no warrant for rules declaring that it is fair to publish all the confidential information a reporter can unearth. *The Washington Post* in 1971 briefly followed the so-called Bradlee rule (named for Benjamin C. Bradlee, the editor who devised it). This rule decreed that a maximal effort be made to identify all sources by name in one-on-one interviews and that press briefings be for direct attribution (or the *Post* reporter would leave). The rule was a stab at one aspect of source confidentiality. It was quickly dropped, however, because it was too confining and because other newspapers did not adopt it. The Bradlee rule tried to cover too much and demanded too much, although it was appropriate for many journalist–source relationships. A subtler, more selective rule of confidentiality was needed.

Newspapers should have a policy—neither too specific nor too vague—governing matters such as permissible use of confidential information, and they probably should also have procedural rules or guidelines that specify how editors and reporters should decide whether and how to use confidential information. We will [now] explore . . . the concept of virtue, which some moral philosophers see as substantially different from and more important than rules.

Virtues and Character

In the midst of the 1984 presidential campaign, columnist Richard Cohen wrote that Vice-President George Bush "has consistently shown a lack of character," something "reprehensible in a politician, frightening in a president."[3] Cohen wrote that Bush was arrogant and untruthful, confusing "truth and political expediency" and in various ways "stretching the truth." "To Bush," Cohen said, "truth is the sum of the votes on Election Day." We are not concerned with whether Cohen was right about the vice-president, but we are interested in character traits such as truthfulness and arrogance. Cohen is correct when he says we should expect good character in our national leaders, and the same expectations are justified for anyone in whom we regularly place trust.

One ironic example of a failure of character involved a writer who submitted a book manuscript to a publisher titled *Telling Right from Wrong*.[4] Along with the manuscript he also submitted a letter by the respected philosopher Robert Nozick endorsing the book. Although the publisher received rave reviews from those who read the manuscript, it turned out that the letter from Nozick was forged by the author in an attempt to get his book accepted. There is something more than faintly odd about a man who writes a book about how to tell right from wrong but lacks the character to act according to his own prescription. Even if we admire his intellect, he seems untrustworthy and dishonest. In this case knowledge has failed to enrich character.

The language of both *character* and *virtue* sometimes sounds ridiculously prim, as journalists occasionally delight in pointing out. Thus, Henry Allen writes that "'Character' is one of those horrible Victorian virtues that makes you think of cold baths, savings accounts, the Protestant work ethic, self-sacrifice, manhood, duty and so on in a list of everything we thought we'd ripped out of American culture like a weed."[5] However, despite their prissy connotations, *character* and *virtue* are accurate and appropriate terms for discussing moral behavior. Moreover, whether or not they recognize the nature of the appeal, editorial writers often use these concepts in stating their cases. For example, in an editorial on news credibility, *USA Today* said that the "so-called crisis of [news] credibility has been self-inflicted. With accuracy, balance, sensitivity, humility, and humor, those who bring the news to the nation can heal themselves."[6] Here we have an overt appeal to a list of virtues, and for sound reasons. Even journalists who are repelled by virtue language would probably agree that the public is better served when journalists perform well because of good character than because of sanctions, threats, rules, laws, regulations, and the like.

There is nothing novel about a virtue-based approach to professional responsibility, as the following example of virtue-based advice for physicians illustrates. In 1959 a Harvard anesthesiologist named Henry Beecher was deeply troubled by numerous experiments that physicians had performed on human subjects. Beecher was convinced that rules, regulations, and threats, if used to restrict experimentation in medicine, were "more likely to do harm than good." He argued that physicians needed to be more sensitive to sound training in scientific methodology and to the abiding importance of cultivating a virtuous character.[7] The most reliable safeguard against abuses in research involving human subjects, he proposed, is "the presence of an intelligent, informed, conscientious, compassionate, responsible researcher."[8] Accordingly, Beecher recommended educating physicians through a virtue-based rather than a rule- or duty-based ethic—an approach that may prove to be as sound for journalists as for doctors.

But what do we mean by virtue and character, and how do these concepts play an important role in our arguments about morality and virtue? A virtue, as we use the term, is a beneficial disposition, habit, sentiment, or trait, and a moral virtue is a fixed disposition to do what is morally commendable, which entails a desire to act according to moral principle. Almost all professions have virtues that are keys to success in the profession but are not moral virtues. Philip Dougherty, in his advertising column in *The New York Times,* quoted a member of Beber Silverstein and Partners to the effect that the key to their success in advertising is found in the virtues of "tenacity, talent, and perseverance."[9] These dispositions no doubt are virtues in business, but they are different from moral virtues such as respectfulness, kindness, gratitude, and benevolence. These latter virtues are fundamental to moral behavior, while the first set is fundamental to success in business.

Nora Boustany, who reports from Lebanon for *The Washington Post,* provided a striking account of how different people respond when moral and business virtues like those quoted by Dougherty come into conflict. She wrote as follows:

> Television cameras that had been set up outside the hotel to film [Anglican envoy Terry] Waite crossing the street from a news agency office caught the attention of a militiaman standing by an earth mound nearby. He fired a shot at nothing in particular. The driver of a yellow-and-black Austin happened to be driving down the street. He was killed instantly.
> Meanwhile, the fighting got worse—preventing rescue workers from getting near the car. Goskun Aral, a Turkish photographer working for the French Sipa agency, joined Visnews soundman Ali Moussa, a Lebanese, in a rescue effort. They dragged [an] injured man, Raja Fuleihan, an administrator at the American University Hospital, from the car under a hail of machinegun fire. *Other photographers displayed a different kind of courage. They braved the shooting and clicked away at their colleagues.*[10]

Aral and Moussa, whose good character provided their guide to action, did not need to stop and think. They acted to save a life at considerable risk to themselves. The other photographers displayed courage (which may be a moral virtue as well as a professional virtue) solely in the service of their professional goals. Saving a life meant less to them than getting the pictures.

Virtuous traits of all kinds are especially significant in crises and in environments such as journalism that are often too pressured to permit prolonged and careful reflection. By cultivating moral virtues, doing what is right in these situations can become a matter of course rather than a conflicted debate over how to interpret rules whose meaning and application may be less than clear. No one can be expected to possess all the moral virtues or to behave virtuously with complete consistency, but some virtues such as honesty and trustworthiness are fundamental to the notion of a morally virtuous character. If a single incident of moral failure were all we had to go on, we could not say that a person lacks character, because we need a pattern of action to justify such a judgment. At most we can say that a person made an error, which is an assessment of an action rather than character. Even several blameworthy errors do not necessarily indicate a failure of character.

Our arguments suggest that a person's character is good or bad, virtuous or vicious, praiseworthy or blameworthy, depending on the particular virtues or vices he or she possesses. But which virtues should journalists cultivate? To answer this question, contrast for a moment journalists with St. Francis, who was admired for the tenderness and compassion exhibited in his spontaneous displays of affection for others—such as embracing a leper or giving away his only blanket on a cold night. These virtues may be appropriate for a saint, but they are not the ones that leap to mind when deciding which virtues should be exhibited by reporters and editors. Rather, virtues like fairness, truthfulness, trustworthiness, and nonmalevolence (avoiding harm) come to mind. We should not look, however, for some finite list expressing the traits of virtuous journalists. . . .

As we hinted earlier, many writers in contemporary moral theory are undecided about whether their arguments are best expressed in terms of virtues or in terms of duties or rights. Although our book [from which this essay is taken] is titled *The Virtuous Journalist,* and the chapter titles are cast in virtue language, we do not mean to imply that virtues can or should replace rights and duties. The virtuous journalist acknowledges the execution of duties and respect for the rights of others as fundamental matters in moral conduct. These categories can all be used profitably in discussions of journalism ethics.

Whichever category is used, however, the standard of moral scrutiny must not be so high that the expectations for conduct are that the journalist be heroic or saintly. The rather heroic (even if flawed) character of *New York Times* reporter Sydney Schanberg and his even more extraordinary assistant, Dith Pran—as depicted in the film *The Killing Fields,* based on their wartime experiences in Cambodia—is certainly praiseworthy, but such character, while admirable, is not morally required. A virtue-based or duty-based ethics for journalism must be within reach of ordinary persons. It is not always easy to divide the moral life into the ordinary and the extraordinary, but if we were to forgo this distinction entirely, we would either set impossibly high standards or give up on the possibility of setting any standards at all.

A further word of caution is in order at this point. No system of ethics can provide full, ready-made solutions to all the perplexing moral problems that confront us, in life or in journalism. A reasoned and systematic approach to these issues is all that can be asked, while appreciating that practical wisdom and sound judgment are indispensable components of the moral life. The absence of neat solutions may seem to prop up the views of those who are skeptical or cynical about the possibility of journalism ethics, but such views are based on the false premise that the world is a tidy place of truth and falsity, right and wrong, without the ragged edges of uncertainty and risk. The converse is the case: Making moral judgments and handling moral dilemmas require the balancing of often ill-defined competing claims, usually in untidy circumstances. . . .

COMPETENCE IN THE CRAFT

Former CBS News President Richard Salant once said, "No two people, if they took 25 minutes [of videotape] and edited it down, would get the same two minutes."[11] Salant was probably right, but it does not follow that any two-minute segment is as fair, representative, or competently edited as any other two-minute segment. Tape can be edited accurately, fairly, and objectively, or it can fail to meet these criteria. The editing cannot justifiably be called competent unless they are satisfied, which suggests that moral criteria are embedded in our very conception of competent journalistic practice. That is, standards such as fairness and accuracy are moral dimensions of competence.

Many professional standards and codes of ethics make an open appeal to the concept of competence, even if the word *competence* is not specifically used in the code. "Be competent" may seem such an obvious rule that is scarcely deserves attention, but it is also among the more frequently violated norms of journalistic practice. Lying, conflict of interest, malevolence, unfairness, and lack of respect for persons are, quantitatively, minor moral problems compared to incompetence. For example, one criterion of competence that reporters often fail to satisfy is the ability to place a distance between personal beliefs and what is being reported.

A different but related problem of competence arises when reporters fail to keep their notes and writing or phrasing sufficiently distant from source materials. Roy Peter Clark reported the story of a *Miami News* reporter who wrote an article on stock car racing that was reprinted in an anthology Clark edited titled "Best Newspaper Writing 1982." The reporter, Tom Archdeacon, borrowed about a hundred words almost verbatim from a book written by Jerry Bledsoe of *The Greensboro Daily News and Record*. Bledsoe called the apparent plagiarism to Clark's attention. Clark responded that "Archdeacon told his editors that he admired Bledsoe's book, that he had used it for background on Linda Vaughn [a beauty queen], and that under deadline he had confused Bledsoe's words for his own in more than 100 pages of sloppily taken notes."[12]

The American Society of Newspaper Editors (ASNE) sponsored the competition in which Archdeacon's article was selected for publication. Its board, as quoted by Clark, issued a statement that said: "While what happened is a journalistic misdemeanor and not a felony—and appears to be a mistake rather than plagiarism—the board deplores that such gross carelessness and sloppiness could be part of the working procedure of such a talented writer."[13] Assuming that the ASNE board is right that there was no intentional plagiarism, when they accuse Archdeacon of gross carelessness and sloppiness they are describing incompetence with a moral dimension.

There is, of course, no single criterion of competence in journalism, moral or otherwise. If someone says, "Peter Jennings is incompetent," one might ask, "Incompetent to do what?" To make intelligent news judgments? To convince viewers? To write unbiased copy? Here we need to distinguish between general competence as a journalist and a specific competence in journalism. General competence refers to the ability to perform the myriad tasks that are basic to any journalist's responsibilities. Specific competence requires a specific context and a defined task. Although criteria of general competence are not well established in journalism, some criteria can be listed with assurance. Any generally competent journalist must be able to recognize a story (the intrinsic importance of an event, its inherent human interest, its novelty, its consequences, etc.), must be able to use language well enough to convey the story adequately to readers or television viewers, must be able to organize and edit copy so that a story can fit into a limited space in a newspaper or a limited time slot on television or radio, must be able to check facts quickly and accurately, and must be able to weigh the various elements of a story so that they are fairly represented in the final product.

Copy editors—who cut news stories to size; evaluate their coherence; check facts; correct grammar, syntax, errors of style, and organization; and write headlines—must have the same qualities to do their jobs competently. So must reporters, columnists, and editors with broader responsibility. But these criteria must be supplemented by others to describe competence in specific cases. Investigative reporters, for example, must be able to gain access to persons and information that are not easily available. Columnists must have insights and sources that make their analyses and opinions worthwhile. Editors with responsibility for planning coverage and making judgments about how stories are played in the paper or on the air must have a sure grasp of where stories fit in the broad sweep of events and what they are worth in the context of history and the day's news. This list is not meant to be a comprehensive set of criteria for competence. It merely suggests what is entailed by the notion of general and specific competence in journalism.

We indicated earlier that moral qualities are intrinsic to journalistic competence, an idea that apparently conflicts with the common assumption that simply possessing the required professional skills makes a professional competent. To emphasize that competence is not limited to these skills, consider how a reporter should answer the following questions: How many credible sources does a journalist need before reporting something as factual? Is one very reliable source sufficient? Must a reporter have at least two? Three? Must they be independent? Adversarial? During a televised symposium on national security and the press, Lyle Denniston of *The Baltimore Sun* took the position that one reliable source would be enough to publish secret government information on a CIA-sponsored covert operation.[14] Dan Rather of CBS, Jack Nelson of *The Los Angeles Times,* and others disagreed, arguing for at least two and generally three reliable sources for that kind of story. Despite the unavailability of a simple or definitive answer to these questions, any answer depends on taking a view about what constitutes a responsible use of sources. Moral criteria of responsibility are clearly linked in this example to general considerations of journalistic competence.

Incompetence in journalism therefore often results from moral failure, not merely a lack of professional rigor or experience. Here is an example involving an incompetent use of sources. When UPI reported on Israel's use of a "vacuum bomb" on August 7, 1982, it attributed its information to a U.S. congressional delegation. But *The New Republic* reported a few weeks later that "the official Congressional delegation turned out to be neither official, nor Congressional, nor a delegation."[15] The group was fraudulent, and so was the bomb; there was no such thing as a vacuum bomb. Nevertheless, UPI's hundreds of clients received a story on August 7 describing how such a weapon flattened an eight-story building in West Beirut.[16]

The New Republic offered this version of how the bomb story got on the wire: "[Brenda] Pillars [a member of the self-styled delegation] says the UPI dispatch stemmed from a conversation at Beirut's Commodore Hotel as a few members of the 'delegation' chatted with a few members of the press. Susan Hedges, who said she was doing research for [Sen. James] McClure (she was not), was discussing a bomb she claimed to have seen the previous day. Pillars says the report resulted from a misperception of a reporter."[17] A little checking into the nature of the "delegation," the credentials of Susan Hedges, or those of the leader of the group, Franklin Lamb, who had a record of fraud and deceit, would have saved UPI the considerable embarrassment of sending out corrections that never caught up with the original story. The failure to investigate Lamb and his group adequately is an unambiguous example of incompetence on the part of the reporter, and possibly the editors as well. It is no less an example of a moral than a professional failure.

A standard approach to this kind of problem is to say that a newspaper should have a policy to deal with such situations. However, the implication of this recommendation often seems to be that any among a wide range of possible policies will suffice, as long as there is some consistent policy to follow. We agree that policies may justifiably vary, but to adopt a policy just to have guidelines may provide more of an excuse than a morally satisfactory response. A policy can be a moral instrument, because it can be a means of expressing what counts as responsible conduct—in this instance, responsible use of sources and responsible corroboration of claims—and it is possible to argue in a morally principled way about the kinds of policies that are acceptable. . . .

NOTES

1. *USA Today,* March 14, 1985, Money section, p. 1.

2. See Elizabeth Tucker, "FCC Weighs 'Character' Issue," *Washington Post,* May 22, 1985, p. D3.

3. Richard Cohen, "A Question of Character," *Washington Post,* October 27, 1984, p. A19.

4. Timothy J. Cooney, *Telling Right from Wrong* (Buffalo: Prometheus, 1985), with an afterword by the author on the subject of the falsified letter.

5. Henry Allen, "Character Takes on Personality: A Victorian Virtue Is Trying to 'Find Itself' in the '80s," *Washington Post,* January 5, 1986, p. D5.

6. Editorial, "Media Can Improve, but Laws Won't Do It," *USA Today,* April 12, 1984, sec. A, p. 12.

7. Henry K. Beecher, *Experimentation in Man* (Springfield, Ill.: Charles C. Thomas, 1959), pp. 15–17; 43–44, 50.

8. Henry K. Beecher, "Ethics and Clinical Research," *New England Journal of Medicine* 274 (June 1966): 1354–60, esp. 1354–55.

9. Philip H. Dougherty, "Beber Silverstein on Move," *New York Times,* April 11, 1985, p. 45.

10. Nora Boustany, "A Lebanon Diary: Gathering News in the Heart of Darkness," *Washington Post,* March 30, 1986, p. D3. Emphasis added.

11. Eleanor Randolph, "Libel Jury Sees TV Outtakes," *Washington Post,* October 24, 1984, p. A12.

12. Roy Peter Clark, "The Unoriginal Sin—How Plagiarism Poisons the Press," *Washington Journalism Review,* March 1983, 42–47.

13. Ibid.

14. "National Security and Freedom of the Press," from "The Constitution—That Delicate Balance," PBS, November 6, 1984.

15. Laurence Graftstein, "The Implosion Plot," *The New Republic,* September 6, 1982, pp. 8, 9.

16. UPI wire story on vacuum bomb in Beirut, August 7, 1982.

17. Graftstein, "Implosion Plot," p. 8.

Some Conflicting Assumptions of Journalistic Ethics

STEPHEN H. DANIEL

Most ethical questions for the journalist arise out of the conflict between his business of gathering and disseminating the news and the professional vocation of informing the public. Admittedly, the journalistic profession is different from the medical or legal professions in that journalists do not have to master any specific body of knowledge and are not licensed or policed by recognized professional bodies. However, like doctors, lawyers, businessmen, and engineers, journalists do see (and historically, have seen) the need to regulate their behavior according to general professional standards. Just as we now find courses in medical and legal ethics being offered in the nation's medical and law schools, so also are we beginning to see courses developed in mass media and journalistic ethics.

My primary concern is to address the question of the role of the philosopher in evaluating and helping to formulate or highlight the presuppositions of journalistic ethics. More specifically, I would like to point out how some conflicting assumptions about the business of journalism generate ethical dilemmas for the individual journalist. I would also like to suggest two further points: first, that journalists can handle such dilemmas by recognizing how personal journalistic values and duties are different from social journalistic values and duties; and secondly, that a personal journalistic ethics is more fundamental than a social journalistic ethics, in that social ethics attempts to define moral good publicly, while personal ethics provides the individual with the justification for acting morally in the first place.

I. THE CONFLICT IMPLICIT IN THE CODES

From the outset, it should be noted that the topic of mass media ethics (seen from a philosophic perspective) cannot be understood as a gloss on what are referred to as the professional codes of ethics of newspaper editors, writers, and broadcast journalists. Such codes of professional conduct serve, for practicing journalists, as guidelines for behavior considered appropriate, desirable, and even commendable under ordinary conditions of human interaction and communication.[1]

Beginning in the 1920s, the recognition of the need for such codes and their adoption as statements of principle by groups like the American Society of Newspaper Editors and the National Association of Broadcasters paralleled the growing awareness of the extensive impact of the mass media. That is, as journalists became more aware of the extraordinary nature of their profession, they felt all the more the need to formulate explicit codes of conduct which embodied the ethical values of ordinary human interaction and communication. Thus, the conflict between the practical, daily, and often extraordinary demands of the profession, on the one hand, and the ethical values which journalists saw compromised within the profession, on the other, gave rise to codes of conduct which served (and continue to serve) as reminders of the strained attempt to include journalistic morality within general and ordinary morality.

Unfortunately, most journalists do not live and work in an environment of *ordinary* interaction and communication. They purposely attempt to minimize personal prejudices, to probe and challenge in ways which most people would otherwise find offensive, and even to continue coverage of material when their freedom or lives are at stake. The recent jailings of authors and deaths of photographers killed in the course of filming their murderers attest to the profound effect of the training which replaces even the ordinary interest in survival with the need to get the news and to prepare it for popular dissemination within often severe time and monetary limits.

Within such a context, it comes as little surprise that many journalists place little weight in philosophic arguments for respecting the privacy of individuals or for avoiding conflicts-of-interest, for such arguments are intended to apply to ordinary human interactions. Such a situation gives rise to comments such as those of the publisher of the *Louisville Courier-Journal,* who in 1974 argued that though eavesdropping activities of his reporters were "morally wrong," they exhibited "the vigorous enterprise and competitive spirit that is . . . a standard of excellence in journalism."[2] Such a statement highlights the fact that practicing journalists often are torn between a set of ethical values which is intended to be applied to all morally responsible beings, and a set of professional standards which assumes a special calling for journalists.

The values of truth-telling, honesty, and fairness which we apply to communicators in general fail to exercise a compelling force over many journalists other than in the codes to which they give lip-service. This is not to say that journalists have no ethical standards; rather, it says that the working ethical standards of the journalist are determined by what he sees as contributing to his own (and ultimately, the public) good through the survival of his paper, television station, or job. Though this might smack of an ends-justifies-the-means type of thinking, the point of remarking such a perspective is to indicate that the journalist asks a different question from that posed by the general ethicist: instead of asking "what is moral?" the journalist asks "why should I do this or avoid that, regardless of whether it is generally (i.e., ordinarily) considered to be moral or immoral?"

In short, the journalist asks the metaethical question of "why be moral?" primarily because he is so aware of the discrepancy between the extraordinary standards of excellence within his profession and the ordinary moral standards of his readership.

One way to get around such a contrast would be to point out how a consideration of the pressures from advertisers and owners can explain why journalists engage in what otherwise would be called immoral behavior. Editors and publishers often allocate space dealing with real estate, travel, and food news according to the amount of advertising space in such areas; and sponsors (or the lack of sponsors) often determine whether a program is aired.[3] In ways such as these, the monied interests in a community can indirectly determine what is presented for public consumption—again, based on circulation numbers or ratings (in brief, economic considerations).

There are numerous practical ways in which the integrity of the journalistic profession is compromised. Newspersons are often asked to appear chummy, to sell products, and to do other tasks in order to make their appeal to show-business–oriented consumers greater. Public relations material, provided by companies, groups, and individuals, is often used by the media without correcting the avowed promotional character of the material. The justification for the use of such material is based on the claim that the news which is provided by public relations departments is often significant and would not otherwise be made available to the public. This frees reporters to do stories on other matters for which there would not be public-relations coverage. In press releases, the polishing has been completed for the reporter or editor, thus saving valuable time and energy.[4] Of course—and this is the difficulty—P.R. people are paid to present only the self-complimentary side of a news event or personality; and this differs from the supposed task of the reporter to present a balanced view of his subject.

Overall, it might be argued that the larger and more financially solvent or independent a paper, station, or journalist might be, the more it or he is able to act in what might be recognized generally as morally responsible ways. In order to attain the status by which they might be able to refuse to engage in questionable journalistic practices, most journalists appear to have to bend according to the pressures applied to them in the business: before one can do the job of the journalist well, one has to be able to have the opportunity to do the journalist's job. Integrity (and the opportunity to act with integrity) thus seems to be a product of unethical behavior.

Perhaps nowhere is the conflict between general ethical values and the standards of journalistic excellence felt more strongly than in the publication of photographs. Most often, the problems arising out of such publication stem from the attempt to reconcile the sensitivities of persons involved in the news with the public's right to know. Where there is a major news break of momentous dimension (as, for example, the shooting of Lee Harvey Oswald or the killings at Kent State University), journalists and ethicists generally agree that the publication of pictures is acceptable. But those pictures which trade in the grief, tragedy, and violence of contemporary society—precisely those pictures which the journalistic community rewards as prizewinners in the business—are focal points of dispute for those concerned with ethical questions relating to privacy.[5]

The question of whether certain photographs should be published is an extension of the ethical dilemma faced by the photographer himself—viz., whether the task of the journalist is that of reporting the news (even when it involves a conflict with humanitarian inclinations) or, first, of taking the well-being of the person in the news into account. The question for the photographer goes to the heart of the tension between journalistic excellence and moral dictates, in that he is pulled by his duty to report the human drama, on the one hand, and his duty (as a human being) to take an active part in the action which he covers, on the other.

As is sometimes pointed out, photographers have been trained *not to experience* the same feelings which other people feel when faced with particular situations. The problem is not something which involves only the consideration of how photographers have appeared to be insensitive to the human suffering of those they film; such insensitivity also characterizes their own attitudes toward their own presence in dangerous situations. Their training demands such detachment; and if there is something wrong with such detachment, then the problem lies with the profession which permits and even encourages such an attitude.

II. GIVING EXPLANATIONS AND REASONS

To say that the journalist or photographer engages in actions which can be explained in terms of standards of excellence within the profession does not, of course, justify the actions or the standards. An explanation for some action is not a reason why it should be done. Knowing why someone does a particular action (i.e., why something is the case) does not suffice in giving reasons why someone should do it (i.e., why something ought to be the case).

A more formal way of expressing this principle might be to indicate how *cultural or personal relativism* (the belief that moral values differ among cultures or individuals) is *not* the basis for justified claims for *moral relativism:* the sheer fact that persons differ in their beliefs about values does not imply that they should or should not see some things as definitely better than others (no matter what they in fact see). Factual differences are no firm basis for value or moral differences.

Two considerations influence the thrust of these preceding remarks. First, there is a moral-philosophic justification for not identifying *facts* with *values:* facts indicate what is the case but in no way indicate anything about obligations. If values were purely personal or cultural, and if facts were not purely personal or cultural, then to say that someone is "wrong" could only apply to something factual or to one's own set of values. The task of moral philosophy is to indicate how the notions of right and wrong and moral obligation in general can make sense in more than purely relativistic ways.

Second, there is a practical, way-we-live justification for not identifying facts and moral values: we simply do not live and deal with people assuming that their decisions about moral right and wrong are of equal value with our own. To say that we do may be an attempt to appear tolerant; but practically we do not (if we are honest with ourselves) act with such toleration.

Words like "good" and "moral," of course, are defined within particular language groups; and in order that members of the language group might be able to communicate with one another, they must adopt standard uses of the terms. This does not mean, however, that they have to adopt patterns of behavior consistent with the usage. For example, I might adopt a particular meaning of the concept of a "good conscience"—a meaning consistent with others in my language group. (Why would I adopt one meaning rather than another?—In order to communicate with other members of a group to which I want to belong or which I see as affecting me.) Though I use the concept of "good conscience" in speaking to other members of the group in order to communicate with them, I might still choose to develop (and want to keep) what I recognize is a bad conscience.

In short, there are two ways in which moral discourse can be used: *linguistically* (i.e., in communicating with others within a particular language "game"), and *normatively* (i.e., in trying to affect one's own behavior or the behavior of others).

In examining topics in mass media ethics—particularly problems relating to questionable behavior inherent to the profession of journalism—we at times find individuals who claim that certain activities are "morally wrong" but are consistent with the standards of journalistic excellence. The above remarks would seem to indicate that the standards of ordinary morality and journalistic excellence embody characteristics of two different language games. Some within the journalistic community might be able to explain the causes for lapses in behavior (i.e., "lapses" as far as the outside community is concerned) by showing that the behavior does not result from the journalist's conscious choice to mislead, distort, or harm; rather, the behavior might be explained in terms of unconscious, non-directional, non-purposive or antecedent forces within the structure of modern journalism. As such, the journalist would not be personally responsible for his actions; if anything is at fault, it would be the way that the profession itself has been structured to handle an extraordinary task. Only those actions which are end-oriented and purposive—that is, only those actions done for *reasons*—can be actions for which individuals can be held responsible. An action done for a reason is one in which a conscious agent acts so as to attain or bring about an event's occurrence, and expects that his action will at least contribute to the event's occurrence.

III. THE PERSONAL NATURE OF ETHICS

Ethics is primarily concerned with the personal *duties* of an individual to himself and to others. The concern for ethics assumes an attitude of personal responsibility and freedom. What the journalist says when he

writes is an expression of himself and a means of defining himself as a
person and as a journalist. The highest good of the journalist as journalist
is the same as that of the journalist as human being—the development
of authenticity (i.e., the definition of one's self in terms of what one
does and in terms of one's willingness to take responsibility for the
person that one becomes through one's actions). Not to commit oneself
to a consistent life-plan is to choose not to engage in the ethics game—
that is, to choose not to become authentically and responsibly a human
self.[6] This is what is meant when it is often said that ethics deals with
self-enforced and self-legislated conduct; not to enforce or legislate a
code of personal behavior for which one will take complete responsibility
is to choose not to become a self, a human person.

Though this might appear to contradict what I have already said about
the differences between the standards of journalistic excellence and
general morality, it does not. Put in terms of the concepts already considered, the above remarks can be understood in the following way. The
linguistic function of moral discourse is *not* personal; rather it is social
and public. Law and social convention define the *meanings* of the moral
terms we use, and they allow us to be able to communicate with one
another about matters which are important to us. The *normative* function
of moral discourse, on the other hand, concerns how personal behavior
is affected by the adoption of publicly regulated meanings. To the extent
that this normative (i.e., one *ought* to do X) function is ignored or
superceded by the social/linguistic function of moral discourse, individuals will not be able to define themselves through their actions as anything other than products of social forces (and therefore are not
personally responsible for their actions). To say that ethics is primarily
personal is *not* to say that what is good or bad is decided by the individual; what is *meant* by "good" and "bad" is determined by a community of language-users. To say that ethics is personal means that one's
behavior defines him as a person: one is ethical only insofar as he is
willing to accept responsibility for the person he becomes and expresses
through his actions.

Insofar as the journalist engages in actions for which he is unwilling
or unable to take responsibility (due to pressures from sources outside
of himself or due to his inclinations which have been instilled in him as
part of his training as a journalist), his actions are not voluntary and
therefore cannot be considered as moral or immoral. Insofar as his
actions as a journalist exempt him from normal moral standards, his
behavior cannot be considered as contributing to the development of a

moral personality or of a self, deserving the respect accorded to individuals under the constraints of general moral principles.

Insofar as journalistic ethics is concerned with the *personal* duties of an individual to himself and to other specific individuals, and insofar as it presumes an attitude of personal responsibility and freedom, it highlights the journalist's activities as expressions of himself and means of defining himself as a person. Insofar as journalistic ethics is concerned with the *social* duties of the journalist toward his community in general, it highlights the positive or negative contributions and effects of the journalist's work.

In order to understand the journalist's position within these different focal points of personal and social duties, we must note one final characteristic of journalistic ethics, namely, its potential for a reflexive clarifying impact on the general study of ethics. Because the *social* duties of the journalist do not have as their focal concern his development as a distinct self or person (and, in fact, discourage his appearance as a self in his reporting), they do not provide him with any vindication for morally good behavior. Instead, they indicate how words like "good" or "moral" are used within a community of language-users (e.g., the journalistic community, or the larger community of viewers or readers). This social and linguistic regulation of moral discourse, however, does not have an overwhelmingly convincing effect on the journalist. For, the journalist as journalist does not see himself as a personal being as much as a being of society. Insofar as he is a social tool or a conduit of information, he is not an *ethical* being—that is, he is not a personally responsible being; his concern is not so much with ethical behavior as much as it is with professional excellence.

In this context, the social aims of the journalistic profession stipulate its operative moral assumptions as teleological: it defines excellence in behavior in terms of a response to the question "What is recognized socially and linguistically as moral?" In this teleological view of morality, we (as a community of language-users concerned with having the press perform a socially beneficial function) begin with asking "What is moral behavior for the press?" Seen from within a *personal* ethics of journalism, however, such a question misses the more fundamental question of "Why should I, a journalist, be moral in a socially regulated and teleologically determined way, when that very same teleology mitigates against my acting as and developing into a personally responsible self?"

This final characteristic of journalistic ethics—namely, its recognition of the tension between personal and social ethics—acts as a basis for examining broader ethical questions such as are found in legal and medical ethics. My purpose has been to indicate how the contrast between personal and social ethics parallels the journalist's appreciation of the contrast between a personal motivation for being moral and the social definition of what is meant by calling something moral.

NOTES

1. On the codes, see John L. Hulteng, *The Messenger's Motives: Ethical Problems of the News Media* (Englewood Cliffs: Prentice-Hall, 1976), pp. 14–24.

2. Quoted in Hulteng. op. cit., p. 141.

3. See Hulteng, op. cit., pp. 145–48; and Editors of the *Wall Street Journal,* "Unethical Newspaper Practices," in *Ethics and the Press,* ed. by John C. Merrill and Ralph D. Barney (New York: Hastings House, 1975), pp. 149–54.

4. See Hulteng, op. cit., pp. 148–156.

5. See William B. Blankenburg and Richard L. Allen, "The Journalism Contest Thicket: Is It Time for Some Guidelines," in *Ethics and the Press,* pp. 303–17; also see Hulteng, op. cit., pp. 159–84.

6. See John C. Merrill, *The Imperative of Freedom: A Philosophy of Journalistic Autonomy* (New York: Hastings House, 1974), ch. 8.

DISCUSSION QUESTIONS

1. Is what is moral always determined by each society? For example, suppose you lived in a society that practiced cannibalism. Would such a practice then be moral? Defend your answer.

2. Klaidman and Beauchamp claim that "morality cannot be purely a personal policy or code" and that morality must always consist of rules that are "acknowledged and shared by a culture." Are they correct in your estimation? Defend your answer.

3. Klaidman and Beauchamp maintain that "morality is absolutely essential to social stability and the preservation of human decency." Do you agree with this claim? Defend your answer.

4. What, according to Klaidman and Beauchamp, is the role of moral philosophy, especially as it relates to journalism? Is this, in your estimation, a worthwhile function? Defend your answer.

5. What, according to Klaidman and Beauchamp, is the difference between a morality of duties and rights and one of virtues? Which of these concepts do these authors prefer? For what reasons? Do you agree? Defend your answer.

6. Assuming a virtue-based approach to morality, what moral virtues (if any) do you think are most important to journalistic practice? Defend your selections.

7. What is the difference between a professional virtue and a moral virtue? Give examples of each. Can a professional virtue also be a moral virtue? Explain.

8. Klaidman and Beauchamp discuss a case in which some photographers risked their lives in order to film colleagues who, under a hail of machine gunfire, were dragging an injured man from a car wreck. In your estimation, did the photographers who took the pictures display professional virtue? Did they display moral virtue? Defend your answer.

9. Klaidman and Beauchamp distinguish between general and specific competence in journalism. Describe each of these forms of competence.

10. Klaidman and Beauchamp claim that "incompetence in journalism . . . often results from moral failure, not merely a lack of professional rigor or experience." Discuss the merit of this claim.

11. What do Klaidman and Beauchamp mean when they say that moral qualities are *intrinsic* to journalistic competence? What implications does this statement have for the sort of policies newspapers adopt? Do you agree with these authors? Defend your answer.

12. According to Daniel, "journalists often are torn between a set of ethical values which is intended to be applied to all morally responsible beings and a set of professional standards which assumes a special calling for journalists." Discuss the meaning and merit of this claim.

13. What, according to Daniel, is the difference between the *linguistic* use of moral discourse and its *normative* use?

14. Daniel argues that "the journalistic community" defines terms such as "moral" differently than the larger community of language-users. In other words, what is moral from the perspective of journalism may not be moral from the perspective of ordinary morality. Discuss the merit of this claim.

15. Suppose you worked in a professional climate in which journalists routinely engaged, and were taught and encouraged to engage in such behavior as blackmail, theft, and even homicide in order to obtain a story. According to Daniel, would such behavior then be regarded as "moral" by the journalistic community? Would you, as a practicing journalist, go along with such practices? Defend your answer, and compare it to the answer you have given to question 1 above.

16. Daniel states that "there are numerous practical ways in which the integrity of the journalistic profession is compromised." Mention and discuss some of the pressures that exist within journalism that might encourage conformity to behavior ordinarily considered to be immoral.

17. At one point in his essay, Daniel stresses the importance of "authenticity" as a human and journalistic value, by which he means "the definition of one's self in terms of what one does and in terms of one's willingness to take responsibility for the person that one becomes through one's actions." Discuss the importance of this value in the practice of journalism. How, according to Daniel, can this value be forfeited by a journalist in his quest for journalistic excellence?

3

Publication and Free Speech

The First Amendment of the United States Constitution declares that Congress shall make no law abridging freedom of speech or of the press. However, governmental censorship is not the only manner in which freedom of thought and expression may be limited in a free society. Indeed, even in a society that is relatively unhampered by government interference with the expression of opinions, the possibility of unjustified encroachments upon freedom of speech and of the press by the community at large, special interest groups, and other nongovernmental agents, still exists. In this chapter, the latter concern is explored from two contrasting philosophical perspectives.

In the first selection, drawn from his classical essay *On Liberty,* John Stuart Mill discusses the untoward consequences of suppressing the opinions of others. According to Mill, if the opinion in question is right, then we lose "the opportunity of exchanging error for truth"; and if it is wrong, then we lose "the clearer perception and livelier impression of truth, produced by its collision with error." Either way, according to Mill, humankind is a loser when an opinion is suppressed.

In the second selection, entitled "Censorship: Some Distinctions," Judith Andre argues, in contrast to Mill, that at least some "Attempts" by private individuals or interest groups at keeping some things from being published or made available to others by media sources (newspapers, magazines, TV, radio, etc.), can be morally justified. Moreover, she argues that such Attempts (as she refers to them) should not be confused with "censorship," as understood in its ordinary sense of legal or government actions preventing the publication of material by nongovernmental agents.

Andre grants that Attempts at preventing the publication of items are always *prima facie* morally wrong. Nevertheless, she maintains that there are relevant considerations which, while not constituting a precise calculus, can help to determine whether or not a given Attempt, within a

60

given context, is morally justified. Such determinations may depend upon (1) the kind of tactics used by the individuals seeking to block publication, for example, the making of political threats; (2) the particular obligations of the specific "Decision-Makers," for example, the obligation of news editors to provide all sides of a debate; (3) the nature of the material objected to, for example, whether the material is truthful or well argued; and (4) the certainty about the value of the targeted material, for example, how likely it is that the targeted material is false.

A major contention of Andre is that, even in "uncensored" societies, not all opinions will be published. For example, people who have money and influence are most likely to be given a forum. Moreover, since competition for limited space requires that some items will be selected over others, the beliefs and values of publishers will inevitably enter into the selection process.

According to Andre, it is against such a background that Attempts should be viewed. When so viewed, criticisms and accusations of censorship, and appeals to free speech in general, lose much of their force. Attempts emerge, not always as mere impediments to free speech, but instead, as possible ways of augmenting the regulatory dimension of the selection process of publishers, which is already in place. While many of these Attempts will nevertheless remain morally unacceptable, others, as judged by the previously mentioned considerations, will be morally justified.

On the other hand, if Mill is correct, then, insofar as Attempts are viewed as measures aimed at preventing opposing opinions from being heard, they are objectionable, whether or not the opinion being proffered is true or false, and no matter *how certain* one is of its truth or falsehood. For example, regardless of the veracity of "creation science," any Attempt by defenders of the latter view to silence the opposing evolutionary view would be objectionable.

In support of his position, Mill argues that, by virtue of being *fallible,* a human being can never be certain that his own beliefs are true and that the opposing ones are false. Moreover, there can be no *degree* of assurance that, for practical purposes, justifies one in suppressing an opposing opinion, for it is the "complete liberty of contradicting and disproving our opinion" that constitutes the very condition which "justifies us in assuming its truth for purposes of action." It would therefore be self-defeating for one to use the truth of his own opinion as a basis for silencing a contradictory opinion, since, by silencing such opposition, he destroys the credibility of his own opinion.

Second, even if one's opinion is true, by suppressing an opposing opinion, one fails to comprehend and appreciate its deeper meaning and rational grounds, holding it, instead, in the form of a mere dogma or prejudice. Moreover, even knowing the reasons for one's own opinion is not sufficient since there may be equally good reasons on the other side; and, if, as a result of suppressing the other side, one does not even know what these reasons are, then "he has no ground for preferring either opinion."

Finally, in the usual case, neither the prevailing opinion nor any opposing one is apt to contain the *whole* truth; rather each is more likely to contain only different parts of the truth. Therefore, by silencing the opposing opinion, one sacrifices the opportunity to learn the whole truth.

In the light of Mill's previously mentioned points, Andre's (limited) defense of Attempts may be brought into question. However, in response to Mill, it might be argued that it is plainly utopian thinking to insist that all opinions always be given an equal public hearing. As Andre has argued, there are unavoidable practical constraints on what can and will be published. Given such constraints, it is only reasonable to try to publish those opinions that are the truer, more useful, or morally superior opinions. As Andre points out, even if Attempts are typically "one-sided," the latter term is not synonymous with "unwise," "unfair," or "unbalanced." That is, even though Attempters may see things from one perspective, they may still see things from the true or morally right perspective. Indeed, it could be argued that some opinions, such as those of Satanists and child molesters, are not even worthy of consideration. In any event, such views have *already* been given enough of a hearing to warrant dismissing them. There are, after all, rational limits to *how much* of a hearing a view should be allowed to enjoy before it is rejected.

The above rejoinder to Mill, however, appears at least to some extent to make a straw man of his position. Mill does not claim that all opinions are equally true, useful or morally justified. First, the toleration of opposing opinions is, for him, a mode of verification, not a concession to a radical form of relativism according to which any opinion is as true as the next.

Second, Mill does not hold that there are no *moral* or *utility* constraints upon free speech. While Mill's defense of free speech is quite thoroughgoing, it does not appear to be absolute. In comparing actions to belief, Mill maintains that "opinions lose their immunity, when the circumstances in which they are expressed are such as to constitute their expression a positive instigation to some mischievous act." According to Mill, opinions which, through their expression, are apt in particular instances to cause serious harm to others can therefore be silenced without moral impunity. For example, on this principle a newspaper editor in a community already marked by racial unrest might be morally justified in deciding not to publish the racially inflamatory remarks of a local racist organization.

Third, even if publishers, guided by their own beliefs and values, must make decisions about which items to publish, and which ones not to publish, this does not mean that Attempters have a moral warrant to suppress the opinions of others in an effort to make their own side known. Indeed, if Mill is correct, then such Attempters are, in effect, undermining the validity of their own claims in the very process of trying to silence their opposition. On these terms, a more coherent stance for such objectors to take would be to seek a public forum for their own opinions without, at the same time, destroying that of their opposition. For instance, instead of attempting to silence the evolutionist, the creation scientist could simply demand equal time in media coverage or in the classroom.

Finally, Mill recognizes a "real morality of public discussion" the most serious offenses against which are "to argue sophistically, to suppress facts, or argument, to misstate the elements of the case, or misrepresent the opposite opinion." According to Mill, while it is often difficult or impossible to indict individuals on such grounds, such transgressions "may be very objectionable and may justly incur severe censure." When Mill defends free speech, his intentions are not, therefore, to defend the right to express or publish such distortions of the truth.

While Mill's defense of free speech is not wholly without qualification, the views of Mill and Andre on the moral status of Attempts to suppress the free speech of those who hold contrary opinions stand in fundamental opposition. Whereas Andre is prepared to argue that such Attempts are, on some occasions, morally legitimate, Mill sees them as self-defeating and unfair. While, for Andre, a publisher's willingness to concede to an Attempt may, under certain conditions, constitute an acceptable form of "editing," such Attempts would, for Mill, constitute, by their nature, a serious form of assalt upon freedom of speech.

In any event, the nature and scope of free speech in an "uncensored" society is no settled, simple matter. As Andre suggests, unqualified appeals to freedom of speech may serve merely to obscure the complexity of the underlying issues. But, as a reflective study of both essays also suggests, just what these issues are, and how they are to be assessed, are themselves subjects of significant philosophical controversy.

Liberty of Thought and Discussion

JOHN STUART MILL

The time, it is to be hoped, is gone by, when any defense would be necessary of the "liberty of the press" as one of the securities against corrupt or tyrannical government. No argument, we may suppose, can now be needed, against permitting a legislature or an executive, not identified in interest with the people, to prescribe opinions to them, and determine what doctrines or what arguments they shall be allowed to hear. This aspect of the question, besides, has been so often and so triumphantly enforced by preceding writers, that it needs not be specially insisted on in this place . . . Let us suppose, therefore that the government is entirely at one with the people, and never thinks of exerting any power of coercion unless in agreement with what it conceives to be their voice. But I deny the right of the people to exercise such coercion, either by themselves or by their government. The power itself is illegitimate. The best government has no more title to it than the worst. It is as noxious, or more noxious, when exerted in accordance with public opinion, than when in opposition to it. If all mankind minus one, were of one opinion, and only one person were of the contrary opinion, mankind would be no more justified in silencing that one person, than he, if he had the power, would be justified in silencing mankind. Were an opinion a personal possession of no value except to the owner; if to be obstructed in the enjoyment of it were simply a private injury, it would make some difference whether the injury was inflicted only on a few persons or on many. But the peculiar evil of silencing the expression of an opinion is, that it is robbing the human race; posterity as well as the existing generation; those who dissent from the opinion, still more than those who hold it. If the opinion is right, they are deprived of the opportunity of exchanging error for truth: if wrong, they lose, what is almost as great a benefit, the clearer perception and livelier impression of truth, produced by its collision with error.

It is necessary to consider separately these two hypotheses, each of which has a distinct branch of the argument corresponding to it. We can never be sure that the opinion we are endeavoring to stifle is a false opinion; and if we were sure, stifling it would be an evil still.

First: the opinion which it is attempted to suppress by authority may possibly be true. Those who desire to suppress it, of course deny its truth; but they are not infallible. They have no authority to decide the question for all mankind, and exclude every other person from the means of judging. To refuse a hearing to an opinion, because they are sure that it is false, is to assume that *their* certainty is the same thing as *absolute* certainty. All silencing of discussion is an assumption of infallibility. Its condemnation may be allowed to rest on this common argument, not the worse for being common.

Unfortunately for the good sense of mankind, the fact of their fallibility is far from carrying the weight in their practical judgment, which is always allowed to it in theory; for while every one well knows himself to be fallible, few think it necessary to take any precautions against their own fallibility, or admit the supposition that any opinion, of which they feel very certain, may be one of the examples of the error to which they acknowledge themselves to be liable. Absolute princes, or others who are accustomed to unlimited deference, usually feel this complete confidence in their own opinions on nearly all subjects. People more happily situated, who sometimes hear their opinions disputed, and are not wholly unused to be set right when they are wrong, place the same unbounded reliance only on such of their opinions as are shared by all who surround them, or to whom they habitually defer: for in proportion to a man's want of confidence in his own solitary judgment, does he usually repose, with implicit trust, on the infallibility of "the world" in general. And the world, to each individual, means the part of it with which he comes in contact; his party, his sect, his church, his class of society: the man may be called, by comparison, almost liberal and large-minded to whom it means anything so comprehensive as his own country or his own age. Nor is his faith in this collective authority at all shaken by his being aware that other ages, countries, sects, churches, classes, and parties have thought, and even now think, the exact reverse. He devolves upon his own world the responsibility of being in the right against the dissentient worlds of other people; and it never troubles him that mere accident has decided which of these numerous worlds is the object of his reliance, and that the same causes which make him a Churchman in London, would have made him a Buddhist or a Confucian in Pekin. Yet it is as evident in itself, as any amount of argument can make it, that ages are no more infallible than individuals; every age having held many opinions which subsequent ages have deemed not only false but absurd; and it is as certain that many opinions, now general, will be rejected by future ages, as it is that many, once general, are rejected by the present.

The objection likely to be made to this argument would probably take some such form as the following. There is no greater assumption of infallibility in forbidding the propagation of error, than in any other thing which is done by public authority on its own judgment and responsibility. Judgment is given to men that they may use it. Because it may be used erroneously, are men to be told that they ought not to use it at all? To prohibit what they think pernicious, is not claiming exemption from error, but fulfilling the duty incumbent on them, although fallible, of acting on their conscientious conviction. If we were never to act on our opinions, because those opinions may be wrong, we should leave all our interests uncared for, and all our duties unperformed. An objection which applies to all conduct, can be no valid objection to any conduct in particular. It is the duty of governments, and of individuals, to form the truest opinions they can; to form them carefully, and never impose them upon others unless they are quite sure of being right. But when they are sure (such reasoners may say), it is not conscientiousness but cowardice to shrink from acting on their opinions, and allow doctrines which they honestly think dangerous to the welfare of mankind, either in this life or in another, to be scattered abroad without restraint, because other people, in less enlightened times, have persecuted opinions now believed to be true. Let us take care, it may be said, not to make the same mistake: but governments and nations have made mistakes in other things, which are not denied to be fit subjects for the exercise of authority: they have laid on bad taxes, made unjust wars. Ought we therefore to lay on no taxes, and, under whatever provocation, make no wars? Men, and governments, must act to the best of their ability. There is no such thing as absolute certainty, but there is assurance sufficient for the purposes of human life. We may, and must, assume our opinion to be true for the guidance of our own conduct: and it is assuming no more when we forbid bad men to pervert society by the propagation of opinions which we regard as false and pernicious.

I answer, that it is assuming very much more. There is the greatest difference between presuming an opinion to be true, because, with every opportunity for contesting it, it has not been refuted, and assuming its truth for the purpose of not permitting its refutation. Complete liberty of contradicting and disproving our opinion, is the very condition which justifies us in assuming its truth for purposes of action; and on no other terms can a being with human faculties have any rational assurance of being right.

. . . The whole strength and value then, of human judgment, depending on the one property, that it can be set right when it is wrong, reliance can be placed on it only when the means of setting it right are kept constantly at hand. In the case of any person whose judgment is really deserving of confidence, how has it become so? Because he has kept his mind open to criticism of his opinions and conduct. Because it has been his practice to listen to all that could be said against him; to profit by as much of it as was just, and expound to himself, and upon occasion to others, the fallacy of what was fallacious. Because he has felt, that the only way in which a human being can make some approach to knowing the whole of a subject, is by hearing what can be said about it by persons of every variety of opinion, and studying all modes in which it can be looked at by every character of mind.

. . . There are, it is alleged, certain beliefs, so useful, not to say indispensable to well-being, that it is as much the duty of governments to uphold those beliefs, as to protect any other of the interests of society. In a case of such necessity, and so directly in the line of their duty, something less than infallibility may, it is maintained, warrant, and even bind, governments, to act on their own opinion, confirmed by the general opinion of mankind. It is also often argued, and still oftener thought, that none but bad men would desire to weaken these salutary beliefs; and there can be nothing wrong, it is thought, in restraining bad men, and prohibiting what only such men would wish to practice. This mode of thinking makes the justification of restraints on discussion not a question of the truth of doctrines, but of their usefulness; and flatters itself by that means to escape the responsibility of claiming to be an infallible judge of opinions. But those who thus satisfy themselves, do not perceive that the assumption of infallibility is merely shifted from one point to another. The usefulness of an opinion is itself matter of opinion: as disputable, as open to discussion, and requiring discussion as much, as the opinion itself. There is the same need of an infallible judge of opinions to decide an opinion to be noxious, as to decide it to be false, unless the opinion condemned has full opportunity of defending itself. . . .

[T]he dictum that truth always triumphs over persecution, is one of those pleasant falsehoods which men repeat after one another till they pass into commonplaces, but which all experience refutes. History teems with instances of truth put down by persecution. If not suppressed for ever, it may be thrown back for centuries. To speak only of religious opinions: the Reformation broke out at least twenty times before Luther, and was put down. Arnold of Brescia was put down. Fra Dolcino was put down. Savonarola was put down. The Albigeois were put down. The Vaudois were put down. The Lollards were put down. The Hussites were put down. Even after the era of Luther, wherever persecution was persisted in, it was successful. In Spain, Italy, Flanders, the Austrian empire, Protestantism was rooted out; and, most likely, would have been so in England, had Queen Mary lived, or Queen Elizabeth died. Persecution has always succeeded, save where the heretics were too strong a party to be effectually persecuted. No reasonable person can doubt that Christianity might have been extirpated in the Roman Empire. It spread, and became predominant, because the persecutions were only occasional, lasting but a short time, and separated by long intervals of almost undisturbed propagandism. It is a piece of idle sentimentality that truth, merely as truth, has any inherent power denied to error, of prevailing against the dungeon and the stake. Men are not more zealous for truth than they often are for error, and a sufficient application of legal or even of social penalties will generally succeed in stopping the propagation of either. The real advantage which truth has, consists in this, that when an opinion is true, it may be extinguished once, twice, or many times, but in the course of ages there will generally be found persons to rediscover it, until some one of its reappearances falls on a time when from favorable circumstances it escapes persecution until it has made such head as to withstand all subsequent attempts to suppress it. . . .

Let us now pass to the second division of the argument, and dismissing the supposition that any of the received opinions may be false, let us assume them to be true, and examine into the worth of the manner in which they are likely to be held, when their truth is not freely and openly canvassed. However unwillingly a person who has a strong opinion may admit the possibility that his opinion may be false, he ought to be moved by the consideration that however true it may be, if it is not fully, frequently, and fearlessly discussed, it will be held as a dead dogma, not a living truth.

There is a class of persons (happily not quite so numerous as formerly) who think it enough if a person assents undoubtingly to what they think true, though he has no knowledge whatever of the grounds of the opinion, and could not make a tenable defense of it against the most superficial objections. Such persons, if they can once get their creed taught from authority, naturally think that no good, and some harm, comes of its being allowed to be questioned. Where their influence prevails, they make it nearly impossible for the received opinion to be rejected wisely and considerately, though it may still be rejected rashly and ignorantly; for to shut out discussion entirely is seldom possible and, when it once gets in, beliefs not grounded on conviction are apt to give way before the slightest semblance of an argument. Waiving, however, this possibility—assuming that the true opinion abides in the mind, but abides as a prejudice, a belief independent of, and proof against, argument—this is not the way in which truth ought to be held by a rational being. This is not knowing the truth. Truth, thus held, is but one superstition the more accidentally clinging to the words which enunciate a truth.

... If the cultivation of the understanding consists in one thing more than in another, it is surely in learning the grounds of one's own opinions. Whatever people believe, on subjects on which it is of the first importance to believe rightly, they ought to be able to defend against at least the common objections. But, some one may say, "Let them be *taught* the grounds of their opinions. It does not follow that opinions must be merely parrotted because they are never heard controverted. Persons who learn geometry do not simply commit the theorems to memory, but understand and learn likewise the demonstrations; and it would be absurd to say that they remain ignorant of the grounds of geometrical truths, because they never hear any one deny, and attempt to disprove them." Undoubtedly: and such teaching suffices on a subject like mathematics, where there is nothing at all to be said on the wrong side of the question. The peculiarity of the evidence of mathematical truths is, that all the argument is on one side. There are no objections, and no answers to objections. But on every subject on which difference of opinion is possible, the truth depends on a balance to be struck between two sets of conflicting reasons. Even in natural philosophy, there is always some other explanation possible of the same facts; some geocentric theory instead of heliocentric, some phlogiston instead of oxygen; and it has to be shown why that other theory cannot be the true one: and until this is shown, and until we know how it is shown, we do not understand the grounds of our opinion. But when we turn to subjects infinitely more complicated, to morals, religion, politics, social relations, and the business of life, three-fourths of the arguments for every disputed opinion consist in dispelling the appearances which favor some opinion different from it. The greatest orator, save one, of antiquity, has left it on record that he always studied his adversary's case with as great, if not with still greater, intensity than even his own. What Cicero practiced as the means of forensic success, requires to be imitated by all who study any subject in order to arrive at the truth. He who knows only his own side of the case, knows little of that. His reasons may be good, and no one may have been able to refute them. But if he is equally unable to refute the reasons on the opposite side; if he does not so much as know what they are, he has no ground for preferring either opinion. The rational position for him would be suspension of judgment, and unless he contents himself with that, he is either led by authority, or adopts, like the generality of the world, the side to which he feels most inclination. Nor is it enough that he should hear the arguments of adversaries from his own teachers, presented as they state them, and accompanied by what they offer as refutations. That is not the way to do justice to the arguments, or bring them into real contact with his own mind. He must be able to hear them from persons who actually believe them; who defend them in earnest, and do their very utmost for them. He must know them in their most plausible and persuasive form; he must feel the whole force of the difficulty which the true view of the subject has to encounter and dispose of; else he will never really possess himself of the portion of truth which meets and removes that difficulty. . . .

If, however, the mischievous operation of the absence of free discussion, when the received opinions are true, were confined to leaving men ignorant of the grounds of those opinions, it might be thought that this, if an intellectual, is no moral evil, and does not affect the worth of the opinions, regarded in their influence on the character. The fact; however, is, that not only the grounds of the opinion are forgotten in the absence of discussion, but too often the meaning of the opinion itself. The words which convey it, cease to suggest ideas, or suggest only a small portion of those they were originally employed to communicate. Instead of a vivid conception and a living belief, there remain only a few phrases retained by rote; or, if any part, the shell and husk only of the meaning is retained, the finer essence being lost. . . .

It still remains to speak of one of the principal causes which make diversity of opinion advantageous, and will continue to do so until mankind shall have entered a stage of intellectual advancement which at present seems at an incalculable distance. We have hitherto considered only two possibilities: that the received opinion may be false, and some other opinion, consequently, true; or that, the received opinion being true, a conflict with the opposite error is essential to a clear apprehension and deep feeling of its truth. But there is a commoner case than either of these; when the conflicting doctrines, instead of being one true and the other false, share the truth between them; and the nonconforming opinion is needed to supply the remainder of the truth, of which the received doctrine embodies only a part. Popular opinions, on subjects not palpable to sense, are often true, but seldom or never the whole truth. They are a part of the truth; sometimes a greater, sometimes a smaller part, but exaggerated, distorted, and disjoined from the truths by which they ought to be accompanied and limited. Heretical opinions, on the other hand, are generally some of these suppressed and neglected truths, bursting the bonds which kept them down, and either seeking reconciliation with the truth contained in the common opinion, or fronting it as enemies, and setting themselves up, with similar exclusiveness, as the whole truth. The latter case is hitherto the most frequent, as, in the human mind, one-sidedness has always been the rule, and many-sidedness the exception. Hence, even in revolutions of opinion, one part of the truth usually sets while another rises. Even progress, which ought to superadd, for the most part only substitutes, one partial and incomplete truth for another; improvement consisting chiefly in this, that the new fragment of truth is more wanted, more adapted to the needs of the time, than that which it displaces. Such being the partial character of prevailing opinions, even when resting on a true foundation, every opinion which embodies somewhat of the portion of truth which the common opinion omits; ought to be considered precious, with whatever amount of error and confusion that truth may be blended. No sober judge of human affairs will feel bound to be indignant because those who force on our notice truths which we should otherwise have overlooked, overlook some of those which we see. Rather he will think that so long as popular truth is one-sided, it is more desirable than otherwise that unpopular truth should have one-sided asserters too: such being usually the most energetic, and the most likely to compel reluctant attention to the fragment of wisdom which they proclaim as if it were the whole. . . .

In politics, again, it is almost a commonplace, that a party of order or stability, and a party of progress or reform, are both necessary elements of a healthy state of political life; until the one or the other shall have so enlarged its mental grasp as to be a party equally of order and of progress, knowing and distinguishing what is fit to be preserved from what ought to be swept away. Each of these modes of thinking derives its utility from the deficiencies of the other; but it is in a great measure the opposition of the other that keeps each within the limits of reason and sanity. Unless opinions favorable to democracy and to aristocracy, to property and to equality, to cooperation and to competition, to luxury and to abstinence, to sociality and individuality, to liberty and discipline, and all the other standing antagonisms of practical life, are expressed with equal freedom, and enforced and defended with equal talent and energy, there is no chance of both elements obtaining their due; one scale is sure to go up, and the other down. Truth, in the great practical concerns of life, is so much a question of the reconciling and combining of opposites, that very few have minds sufficiently capacious and impartial to make the adjustment with an approach to correctness, and it has to be made by the rough process of a struggle between combatants fighting under hostile banners. On any of the great open questions just enumerated, if either of the two opinions has a better claim than the other, not merely to be tolerated, but to be encouraged and countenanced, it is the one which happens at the particular time and place to be in a minority. That is the opinion which, for the time being, represents the neglected interests, the side of human well-being which is in danger of obtaining less than its share. I am aware that there is not, in this country, any tolerance of differences of opinion on most of these topics. They are adduced to show, by admitted and multiplied examples, the universality of the fact, that only through diversity of opinion is there, in the existing state of human intellect, a chance of fair play to all sides of the truth. When there are persons to be found, who form an exception to the apparent unanimity of the world on any subject, even if the world is in the right, it is always probable that dissentients have something worth hearing to say for themselves, and that truth would lose something by their silence. . . .

I do not pretend that the most unlimited use of the freedom of enunciating all possible opinions would put an end to the evils of religious or philosophical sectarianism. Every truth which men of narrow capacity are in earnest about, is sure to be asserted, inculcated, and in many ways even acted on, as if no other truth existed in the world, or at all events none that could limit or qualify the first. I acknowledge that the tendency of all opinions to become sectarian is not cured by the freest discussion, but is often heightened and exacerbated thereby; the truth which ought to have been, but was not, seen, being rejected all the more violently because proclaimed by persons regarded as opponents. But it is not on the impassioned partisan, it is on the calmer and more disinterested bystander, that this collision of opinions works its salutary effect. Not the violent conflict between parts of the truth, but the quiet suppression of half of it, is the formidable evil; there is always hope when people are forced to listen to both sides; it is when they attend only to one that errors harden into prejudices, and truth itself ceases to have the effect of truth, by being exaggerated into falsehood. And since there are few mental attributes more rare than that judicial faculty which can sit in intelligent judgment between two sides of a question, of which only one is represented by an advocate before it, truth has no chance but in proportion as every side of it, every opinion which embodies any fraction of the truth, not only finds advocates, but is so advocated as to be listened to.

We have now recognized the necessity to the mental well-being of mankind (on which all their other well-being depends) of freedom of opinion, and freedom of the expression of opinion, on four distinct grounds; which we will now briefly recapitulate.

First, if any opinion is compelled to silence, that opinion may, for aught we can certainly know, be true. To deny this is to assume our own infallibility.

Secondly, though the silenced opinion be an error, it may, and very commonly does, contain a portion of truth; and since the general or prevailing opinion on any subject is rarely or never the whole truth, it is only by the collision of adverse opinions that the remainder of the truth has any chance of being supplied.

Thirdly, even if the received opinion be not only true, but the whole truth; unless it is suffered to be, and actually is vigorously and earnestly contested, it will, by most of those who receive it, be held in the manner of a prejudice, with little comprehension or feeling of its rational grounds. And not only this, but fourthly, the meaning of the doctrine itself will be in danger of being lost, or enfeebled, and deprived of its vital effect on the character and conduct: the dogma becoming a mere formal profession, inefficacious for good, but cumbering the ground, and preventing the growth of any real and heartfelt conviction, from reason or personal experience.

Before quitting the subject of freedom of opinion, it is fit to take some notice of those who say, that the free expression of all opinions should be permitted, on condition that the manner be temperate and do not pass the bounds of fair discussion. Much might be said on the impossibility of fixing where these supposed bounds are to be placed; for if the test be offense to those whose opinion is attacked, I think experience testifies that this offense is given whenever the attack is telling and powerful, and that every opponent who pushes them hard, and whom they find it difficult to answer, appears to them, if he shows any strong feeling on the subject, an intemperate opponent. But this though an important consideration in a practical point of view, merges in a more fundamental objection. Undoubtedly the manner of asserting an opinion, even though it be a true one, may be very objectionable, and may justly incur severe censure. But the principal offenses of the kind are such as it is mostly impossible, unless by accidental self-betrayal, to bring home to conviction. The gravest of them is, to argue sophistically, to suppress facts or argument, to misstate the elements of the case, or misrepresent the opposite opinion. But all this, even to the most aggravated degree, is so continually done in perfect good faith, by persons who are not considered, and in many other respects may not deserve to be considered, ignorant or incompetent, that it is rarely possible on adequate grounds conscientiously to stamp the misrepresentation as morally culpable; and still less could law presume to interfere with this kind of controversial misconduct. With regard to what is commonly meant by intemperate discussion, namely invective, sarcasm, personality, and the like, the denunciation of these weapons would deserve more sympathy if it were ever proposed to interdict them equally to both sides: but it is only desired to restrain the employment of them against the prevailing opinion: against the unprevailing they may not only be used without general disapproval, but will be likely to obtain for him who uses them the praise of honest zeal and righteous indignation. Yet whatever mischief arises from their use, is greatest when they are employed against the comparatively defenseless; and whatever unfair advantage can be derived by any opinion from this mode of asserting it, accrues almost exclusively to received opinions. The worst offense of this kind which can be committed by a polemic, is to stigmatize those who hold the contrary opinion as bad and immoral men. To calumny of this sort, those who hold any unpopular opinion are peculiarly exposed, because they are in general few and uninfluential, and nobody but themselves feels much interested in seeing justice done them; but this weapon is, from the nature of the case, denied to those who attack a prevailing opinion: they can neither use it with safety to themselves, nor, if they could, would it do anything but recoil on their own cause. In general, opinions contrary to those commonly received can only obtain a hearing by studied moderation of language, and the most cautious avoidance of unnecessary offense, from which they hardly ever deviate even in a slight degree without losing ground: while unmeasured vituperation employed on the side of the prevailing opinion, really does deter people from professing contrary opinions, and from listening to those who profess them. For the interest, therefore, of truth and justice, it is far more important to restrain this employment of vituperative language than the other; and, for example, if it were necessary to choose, there would be much more need to discourage offensive attacks on infidelity, than on religion. It is, however, obvious that law and authority have no business with restraining either, while opinion ought, in every instance, to determine its verdict by the circumstances of the individual case; condemning every one, on whichever side of the argument he places himself, in whose mode of advocacy either want of candor, or malignity, bigotry, or intolerance of feeling manifest themselves; but not inferring these vices from the side which a person takes, though it be the contrary side of the question to our own: and giving merited honor to every one, whatever opinion he may hold, who has calmness to see and honesty to state what his opponents and their opinions really are, exaggerating nothing to their discredit, keeping nothing back which tells, or can be supposed to tell, in their favor. This is the real morality of public discussion: and if often violated. I am happy to think that there are many controversialists who to a great extent observe it, and a still greater number who conscientiously strive towards it.

Such being the reasons which make it imperative that human beings should be free to form opinions, and to express their opinions without reserve; and such the baneful consequences to the intellectual, and through that to the moral nature of man, unless this liberty is either conceded, or asserted in spite of prohibition; let us next examine whether the same reasons do not require that men should be free to act upon their opinions—to carry these out in their lives, with out hindrance, either physical or moral, from their fellow men, so long as it is at their own risk and peril. This last proviso is of course indispensable. No one pretends that actions should be as free as opinions. On the contrary, even opinions lose their immunity, when the circumstances in which they are expressed are such as to constitute their expression a positive instigation to some mischievous act. An opinion that corn-dealers are starvers of the poor, or that private property is robbery, ought to be unmolested when simply circulated through the press, but may justly incur punishment when delivered orally to an excited mob assembled before the house of a corn-dealer, or when handed about among the same mob in the form of a placard. Acts, of whatever kind, which, without justifiable cause, do harm to others, may be, and in the more important cases absolutely require to be, controlled by the unfavorable sentiments, and, when needful, by the active interference of mankind. The liberty of the individual must be thus far limited; he must not make himself a nuisance to other people. But if he refrains from molesting others in what concerns them, and merely acts according to his own inclination and judgment in things which concern himself, the same reasons which show that opinion should be free, prove also that he should be allowed, without molestation, to carry his opinions into practice at his own cost. That mankind are not infallible; that their truths, for the most part, are only half-truths; that unity of opinion, unless resulting from the fullest and freest comparison of opposite opinions, is not desirable, and diversity not an evil, but a good, until mankind are much more capable than at present of recognizing all sides of the truth, are principles applicable to men's modes of action, not less than to their opinions.

"Censorship": Some Distinctions

JUDITH ANDRE

The cry of "censorship" is abroad in the land; censorship itself—or rather attempts at it—may also be prevalent, but the cry is made so indiscriminately that it's hard to tell. The charge of censorship is used against any attempt to keep something from being published or broadcast, or once published or broadcast, from being available to some audience.

The following are typical examples: a letter to the editor protesting movie ads which glorify violence against women; a phone call to a radio station about a racist song being played; a boycott of products manufactured by a company which sponsors a sexually explicit television show; the picketing of a movie offensive to gays; parents protesting textbooks which omit "creation-science"; townspeople requesting that the city library not buy anti-Semitic tracts.

For brevity's sake I will call each of these actions an "Attempt." I will also use "publishing" to represent all the ways of making material public: broadcasting, film-making, film projection, and so on. Finally, "Decision Makers" will refer to people whose jobs are to decide what will and what will not be published: editors, publishers, producers, disk jockeys, school boards, and so on.

I will argue that Attempts are not a form of censorship; that they are better described as efforts to change which materials are made publicly available by influencing those who ordinarily make such decisions. I will argue that Attempts are at times morally justified, and will identify several factors relevant to their moral assessment.

Attempts are not a form of censorship.[1] Ordinarily "censorship" refers to laws or other governmental action preventing the publication of material by non-governmental agents. Attempts are quite different. None is an effort to have *government* forbid publication. Only the last two of the examples given earlier are aimed in any way at government action, and even these share with the others this crucial aim: they want to change the minds of people who are already, and necessarily—by virtue of their jobs—deciding not to publish some things.

77

The overly simple popular debate not only obscures *differences* among the kinds of things called "censorship," it also obscures *similarities* between what we call censored or uncensored societies. The simple dichotomy of "censored" or "uncensored" keeps people from paying much attention to what they know: that even in "uncensored" societies some opinions are more likely to be heard than others.

In our "uncensored" society, anyone can *say* almost anything, but only those with money can print or produce—make their opinions widely known. The market, and the preferences of those favored by the market, decide which opinions receive public scrutiny. Editors, librarians, and television station managers—among others—constantly make decisions about what other people will see.[2]

The more facile objections against Attempts, then, can easily be met. "No one else has the right to decide what I read" may work against governmental censorship; it will not work in areas where others are already and necessarily deciding among competitors for limited space. A similar slogan objects to others "imposing their values"—but of course the Decision-Makers are and must be guided by their beliefs and values. Standards of taste, judgements of importance, assessments of truth claims, enter into every selection.

Another common objection appeals to justice. Is it unfair for a few to decide what the rest shall see? Without these Attempts, however, the decisions are made by even fewer. The claim that pressure groups seek unfair power assumes that it is more just for individual Decision-Makers[3] to have this power, unconstrained by anything except the law and the market. Such a claim must assume that the allocation of power produced by the market is just, since it is responsible for those Decision-Makers having the power they do. This claim is debatable at best, and in this case self-defeating, since pressure groups simply use the market in legal ways. The fear of injustice sometimes takes a different form: the belief that present deciders voluntarily takes into account the needs and desires of the entire public in ways which Attempts undermine. Obviously an Attempt brings more attention to its proponents than they would otherwise have—but such attention may simply correct an unfair past lack of it.

A broader version of this question of fairness must be taken more seriously and will be dealt with later: does a *climate* of regular protest impede reasonable decision-making?

For the time being, however, our question is simply this: are attempts to alter the decisions being made wrong *qua* attempts?

Since no governmental censorship is involved, some traditional arguments fall by the wayside: those which claim governmental power cannot be limited if only the government controls the press, for instance.[4] Others still have a point: democracy depends on an informed electorate, and a group could pressure the local paper to suppress important information. Nevertheless, these traditional concerns fall within a broad category which remains unarticulated until we distinguish governmental censorship from non-governmental decisions: Is it wrong to try to change the criteria of selection which others (editors, producers, and so on) are already using?

I will argue here that the answer depends upon several factors: the tactics used; the specific obligations of the target Decision-Maker; the objectionableness of the targeted material; and one's certainty about that objectionableness.

KINDS OF TACTICS

The kind of persuasion used matters: blackmail or physical threats, for instance, could not be fairly described as trying to change someone's mind. Most of the Attempts listed earlier involved morally neutral or even good means of persuasion. Providing information, reasons, or arguments usually makes thoughtful decisions more possible and correct decisions more likely. There could be an ethical problem even here, however, if the action recommended is wrong—say, a violation of the Decision-Maker's duty.

Techniques other than rational argument need closer attention. People who engage in Attempts often organize into "pressure groups." What kind of pressure, considered in itself and apart from its purpose, is wrong? Three kinds most often used are political (threats to vote against school board members), emotional (constant and public expression of displeasure), and economic (boycotts). Each is an attempt to make someone uncomfortable and each limits the freedom of its target (who can still choose as before, but at greater cost; this is the usual way in which freedom is limited). Each, therefore, is *prima facie* wrong and needs justification. But this means that, the specific content of the demand must enter the moral calculus. If what is sought is wrong, then using pressure will make it doubly wrong. If what is sought is of substantial moral worth, then the tactics may be justified.

THE OBLIGATIONS OF DECISION-MAKERS

It is wrong even to suggest that someone misuse her or his power. What counts as a misuse of Decision-Making power depends on the forum being controlled. Public libraries, school libraries, and corporation libraries differ. News pages and editorial pages differ. The ethical principles binding each type of editor and librarian are complex, and I will not attempt to work them out in detail. Several likely-looking candidates for such principles, however, need to be ruled out. One is the claim mentioned earlier: that decision-makers should not use their personal opinions about what is true or what is right as selection guides. But of course they should—and must. A more careful principle would run something like this: When substantial dispute exists about the truth of a claim or the rightness of an action, those Decision-Makers whose responsibility is to make possible an informed public (news editors, city librarians) should make available all sides of the debate. Other Decision-Makers have a lesser obligation: not to mislead, in matters of truth or in matters of value. A right-wing journal has no obligation to publish the work of socialists—but the editors may not, ethically speaking, try to convince their readers that socialists and communists are identical.[5] Producers select scripts in great ethical freedom, but have reasons in conscience not to produce one which they think would instigate a lynching.

Are the Attempts listed earlier efforts to persuade people to violate these principles? For the most part, no. Editors have no obligation to accept all movie ads,[6] nor radio stations to play all music; manufacturers naturally choose among programs which they will sponsor, and film houses select a personal mix of shows to screen. School textbooks, however, are a different matter. They must be written and chosen so as to present the truth, when that is known, and the degree of certainty attaching to a claim should be described as accurately as possible. Parents wishing "creation science" to be included in textbooks may be acting "out of respect" for this principle but not necessarily "in accord" with it. Their actions should be resisted if their beliefs are mistaken—but *not* simply because the actions fall under the description, "trying to prevent certain textbooks from being read by children." The other more complex case involves a public library. When citizens protest its buying of certain books, are they suggesting that the librarians act unethically? Like the textbook case, this one depends on the content of the books. Public libraries have special obligations; let me venture some suggestions about what they are. If a book is important to historical or literary research, then (*ceteris paribus*) it should be on the shelves, even if it makes false or evil claims. If the book presents an unpopular position, but one with substantial (sizeable and/or respectable) support, then it too should be on the shelves. But librarians are surely ethically free to choose among other books according to such criteria as "likely to be correct" and "unlikely to instigate violence."

Attempts, then, are not as such efforts to have some Decision-Maker misuse power. Cases differ as the nature of the forum differs.

THE NATURE OF THE MATERIAL
OBJECTED TO

Protesters have different kinds of targets; movies and ads make their points differently than do opinion claims. Is this relevant to evaluating the protest? The target may be a reasoned discussion or an emotionally powerful picture. Other things being equal, is the reasoned discussion privileged, since attempts to help people think are obviously good? (Even so, attempts to block publication could still be justified: there may be worthier ways to use space than for a reasoned defense of Nazism.)

It *is* good to help people think; this, however, gives no privilege to argument over depiction. Evocative pictures (and movies, and dance, and words) cannot be dismissed as non-rational nor as subversive of rationality, for they give us insight that no argument could provide. They help us understand what it is like to live and feel in new ways—understanding which is important in ethical choices.

Differences in the form of their targets, then, do not help us evaluate Attempts to block them. They do, however, suggest that differences in the content of the targeted material may matter. For both art and argument vary in quality. There is a spectrum from "sound argument" through "interesting argument that fails" to "bad argument" and finally "no argument." The higher on the spectrum, the more worthy of space. Art can also be evaluated: honest or dishonest, cheap or challenging.

Separable from the quality of the argument or the art is the quality of what it recommends: the truth of the argument's conclusion, the goodness of the art's suggestion. These—truth and goodness—are central to any decision about what material deserves publication. Ignorance of their rightful presence in the decision is the most dangerous element in the popular debate. No human choice is value-free, and the illusion that they are is a serious mistake.

Attempts need greater justification, then, if their targets are (1) interesting (these encourage thinking and lead toward the truth); (2) true claims (these encourage knowledge of the truth); (3) good art (these help people understand); or (4) depictions of good ways of life.

Since these qualities can rarely be assigned with complete certainty, Attempters must also take into account the degree of their certainty. As the tactics move from persuasion toward force, an especially honest effort to separate reflective convictions from unreasoned reactions is called for.

If the preceding discussion is correct, then, attempts to block publication are not wrong as such—as attempts to change decider's minds about what to reject. The tactics used, special obligations of the targeted Decision-Maker, the value of the targeted material (and uncertainty about that value) may make specific Attempts wrong.

One final question arises. Are the principles I've been suggesting generalizable?

GENERALIZABILITY

Is there nothing to be feared, nothing to be objected to, in the rising number of pressure groups influencing the contents of textbooks, advertisements, and movie houses? Is there not a danger of organized minorities dictating what the rest of us shall see? Two kinds of danger might be claimed: one, that the content of what survives is worse than what would otherwise be published; two, that a proliferation of such attempts degrades public life. The first fear is valid only if there's some connection between a tendency to make such attempts and intellectual or moral inferiority—at least inferiority relative to the Decision-Makers.

Editors and librarians are trained for their jobs. Fallible, of course, they nevertheless rise above personal taste and try to make choices according to principles: balance is one. Librarians try to build a balanced collection, one which will meet a great variety of needs. Editors balance their coverage, although the range within which they seek variety may itself be narrow, if the publication has a narrow purpose. As a general rule, then, those professionals are likely to choose more wisely than someone chosen at random would.

Attempters aren't quite random members of society—they are self-chosen, women and men with an intense interest in some subject. They are likely to know a lot about an issue—one side of it, at least. The phrase "one-sided" is loaded and readers may immediately conclude that Attempters would ordinarily choose less wisely than the professional Decision-Makers would.

'One-sided', however, is not synonymous with 'unwise', 'unfair', or even 'unbalanced'. Children, for instance, need to know that some people enjoy hurting others, but they don't need to spend as much time learning it as they do learning other things. No time at all should be spent encouraging them to fantasize about the joys of sadism.

The example reminds us that 'balance' is a loaded term, too. It means something like "the right amount of what's right to have"—a formal principle, not a material one. The balanced curriculum, obviously, does not give equal weight to all truth and value claims; less obviously, neither does the balanced library or newspaper.

Given this definition, let us return to the issue. Are pressured Decision-Makers less likely to decide wisely? There seems no way to answer this *a priori;* although they may be especially trained for their positions, these Decision-Makers are still subject to cultural blinders.

Pressure groups may be blinder yet—or, on the contrary, may see something which others have not.

The final fear—of social disharmony—suggests an instructive comparison with civil disobedience. "Attempt to block publication of that which (you are convinced) is dangerously false or promotes serious evil." "Disobey those laws which (you are convinced) create serious injustice." If everyone followed these principles, would anarchy result?

One person's discord is another's vitality. *Engagement* is preferable to unquestioning acceptance. On the other hand, although everyone must finally do what he or she thinks right, the verb is *think*—not feel. The response of Rawls[7] and others to those who fear anarchy is helpful here: breaking the law is *prima facie* wrong; there is no calculus to tell us when other moral factors outweigh the obligation to obey; but useful questions can be formulated—questions which identify morally relevant factors. Similarly for Attempts to block publication: they are *prima facie* wrong; no calculus is available for determining which factors outweigh others; but useful questions can be asked.

If this paper is correct, those questions include the following: what tactics are being used? What specific obligations do the Decision-Makers have? How sure are you that the target material is objectionable? And finally, how objectionable is that material: how false, how evil, and how persuasive?

Although this paper is entitled " 'Censorship': Some Distinctions" its conclusion is that "censorship" is the wrong word for most Attempts. 'Censor' is an ambiguous word; we use it of many acts of suppression, especially of self-censorship and of governmental censorship. When we describe the actions of private individuals dealing with the work of others, however, we use "censorship" only to criticize. Otherwise we use "editing" or "selection." Since the kind of Attempt discussed here is often not morally objectionable, the word "censorship" is inappropriate.

CONCLUSION

These Attempts are more accurately described as efforts to change *which* materials are made publicly available, by influencing those who ordinarily make decisions. The rhetoric of "censorship" arises in a public which fails to notice two facts: that decisions not to print (produce, broadcast, etc.) are and must constantly be made; and that such decisions justifiably—even necessarily—arise from the decider's beliefs and values. The refusal to face the first fact arises partly, perhaps, from a need not to see economic forces as limiting freedom. The refusal to face the second arises partly from the popular relativism which equates "beliefs and values" with the arbitrary and subjective. When what I have called Attempts are morally objectionable it is because of the specific beliefs and values being suppressed, or because of a relationship between the contents and the nature of the forum, or because of a disproportionate use of political, economic, or psychological force—where the correct proportion is a function of the moral importance of the issue. This means that ethical objections to these Attempts must address the specific beliefs and values whose publication is at issue. Appeals to freedom of speech merely obscure the issue.

NOTES

I am grateful for the suggestions of Steve McCleary and of an anonymous referee (Sept. 12, 1983).

1. I criticize a related misuse of the word "censorship" in "Poole, Obscenity, and Censorship," *Ethics* 94, no. 3 (April 1984).

2. Laws against libel, slander, and obscenity constrain these decisions slightly; fairness regulations make stiffer requirements, but only of broadcast materials.

3. These could of course be groups—committees and such. I'm assuming for convenience what seems to be true: that successful pressure groups will have more members than the editorial staffs, etc., which they influence.

4. Frederick Schauer's recent *Free Speech: A Philosophical Enquiry* (New

York: Cambridge University Press, 1982) analyzes these arguments in great and thorough detail.

5. There are many cases, of course, which don't fit any of these categories precisely. What are the obligations of a right-wing newspaper in a one-newspaper town?

6. It might be argued, though, that editors are not free to reject ads arbitrarily, that they must have a policy. That is a complex question.

7. John Rawls, *A Theory of Justice.* (Cambridge: Belknap Press of Harvard University Press, 1971), pp. 363–91.

DISCUSSION QUESTIONS

1. According to Mill, a person can never be sure enough about the truth of what he thinks to warrant his silencing an opposing view. How does Mill justify this position? In your opinion, is there such a thing as "practical certainty" (in contrast to "absolute" certainty)? That is, can we ever be sure enough for *practical* purposes to warrant our silencing the opposing view of another person? Explain and defend your answer.

2. According to Mill, even if we could know for sure that our opinion is true, that alone could not justify us in silencing another's oposing opinion. How does Mill justify this position? In your opinion, is he correct? Defend your answer.

3. At one point Mill states that "he who knows only his own side of the case, knows little of that." What does Mill mean by this? Is he correct? Defend your answer.

4. Discuss Mill's view of the dictim that "truth always triumphs over persecution." Do you agree with Mill? Defend your answer.

5. According to Mill, most popular opinions on subjects not directly verifiable by sense perception are "one-sided." What does Mill mean by the term *one-sided?* What, according to Mill, would a "sober judge of human affairs" think desirable as a way of dealing with the one-sidedness of popular opinions?

6. Andre states that the term "one-sided" is "not synonymous with 'unwise,' 'unfair,' or even 'unbalanced'." What reasons does she give for this view? In light of your answer to question 5, how do you think Mill would respond to Andre on this issue?

7. What does Mill mean by "the real morality of public discussion"? In your opinion, are violations of this morality ever just grounds for suppressing another's opinion? Defend your answer.

8. What does Andre mean by an "Attempt"? Give some examples.

9. Mention and briefly discuss the four considerations Andre offers for determining whether an "Attempt" is morally justified.

10. Consider the following hypothetical case. An editor of a small town newspaper has recently published an editorial defending the virtues of sex between

adults and young children. While the editor personally considered such a proposal to be perverse, he did not think it was up to him to pass judgment on it. However, a number of local citizens have subsequently written the editor protesting his printing of the editorial and demanding that either he cease publication of such "trash" in the future or they will exert political pressure to have him removed from his position as editor. Applying Andre's four considerations, could this "Attempt" by the townspeople to stifle publication be morally justified? What would Mill argue in such a case? In your opinion, what should the editor do? Defend your answer.

11. Andre sets up the following comparison between the rationale behind Attempts and that behind civil disobedience: "Attempt to block publication of that which (you are convinced) is dangerously false or promotes serious evil." "Disobey those laws which (you are convinced) create serious injustice." What similarities, if any, do you see between these two cases? What differences, if any, do you see between them? In your opinion, is the analogy Andre is suggesting between civil disobedience and Attempts an instructive one? What do you think Mill would have said about Andre's analogy?

12. Discuss the difference between the meaning and usage of the term *editing* on the one hand and *censorship* on the other. That is, how does one distinguish between a case of "editing" and one of "censorship"?

13. Suppose the following. You are an editor of a new journal of political philosophy in the early 1980s. During this period, the Soviet Union declares martial law in Poland in an effort to quiet opposition to their rule. A professor at a major Polish university requests a copy of the inaugural issue of your journal. Unbeknownst to the professor, this issue contains an article entitled "Free Political Speech Ought to Be an Absolute." Realizing that this literature would most likely be viewed as subversive by the Soviets, you are fearful that sending the article might endanger the security of the professor and perhaps his family. On the other hand, you are strongly committed to the values of freedom of speech and of the press. What should you do? Does it matter that the professor has no knowledge of the contents of the issue? From your standpoint as an editor, do you have an obligation to first inform the professor about the article? What do you suppose Mill would say about the matter?

4

Privacy, News Sources, and the Refusal to Testify

Some of the difficult ethical questions news reporters confront in relations with their sources concern the notion of privacy. In particular, under what conditions, if any and to what extent, are reporters ethically justified in invading the privacy of their sources? How far should reporters go in protecting the privacy of their sources? For example, is a reporter ever on firm ethical ground in resisting a subpoena in order to protect his or her source's privacy? Such questions as these also presuppose even broader philosophical ones. For instance, what is meant by "privacy" in the first place? What *value* does privacy possess? What is the nature and status of the moral *right* to privacy? What *criteria* can be used to decide whether or not such a right has been violated? What is the relationship between the moral right to privacy and the *legal* right to privacy? In this chapter such ethical, legal, and broad philosophical concerns regarding privacy and news sources are raised.

In the first selection, "Privacy, Morality, and the Law," W. A. Parent defines the concept of "privacy," discusses the moral and legal implications of her definition, and defends it against alternative conceptions. According to Parent, "privacy" is "the condition of not having undocumented personal knowledge about one possessed by others." By "personal information" she means facts about oneself that most people (in a given society) do not ordinarily choose to disclose to persons other than close friends or relatives (for instance, marital problems, drinking habits, etc.); or else facts about which some people may be especially sensitive (for instance, weight or age). Moreover, by "documented" personal information she means such facts as "belonging to the public record," for instance ones that are found in court proceedings or ones that have been published in a newspaper. According to Parent, an invasion of an individual's privacy occurs when personal information about that individual is "documented."

Parent argues that privacy, so defined, is a significant value in people's lives. First, the possession of personal information by others can be used to exert power over that person, for instance to exploit or harm that person; second, it can be a source of embarrassment for the person; third, the possession of personal information by others is an afront to the status of the person as an "autonomous, independent being with unique aims to fulfill." Moreover, according to Parent, anyone who "deliberately and without justification contravenes our desire for privacy violates the distinctively liberal, moral principle of respect for persons." Finally, the *moral right* to privacy arises out of the need to protect this important human value.

In the light of Parent's remarks, it is easy to see how reporters can face difficult moral decisions in their efforts to gather and publicize "undocumented personal information." On the one hand, there is the need to get the facts. On the other, there is the source's serious right to privacy which may, in the process of acquiring and reporting the facts, be jeopardized.

Given a source's moral right to privacy, can a reporter ever be on firm moral ground in invading the source's privacy?

Parent proposes some "general criteria of wrongful invasion" which she hopes will be of some use in making such "difficult and controversial value judgments." These criteria include consideration of the "legitimacy and importance" of the purpose(s) for which the undocumented personal knowledge is sought; the *relevance* of such knowledge to the purpose(s) in question; whether an invasion of privacy is the least offensive means available for obtaining the knowledge; the kind of restraints placed on "privacy-invading techniques"; and the means used to protect the information once it has been obtained.

From the standpoint of the reporter, the above criteria may raise further thorny issues. For example, the question of the "legitimacy and importance" of the purposes for which the undocumented knowledge is sought would seem to presuppose some further criterion of the "newsworthy"—an issue considered in Chapter 1 of this volume. For example, on one view, a "legitimate and important" purpose of news gathering is to obtain a story that will satisfy the interests of the community at large. On such a view, therefore, invading the privacy of an interesting recluse whose very goal in life is to escape the eye of the media would not, other things being equal, constitute a violation of the subject's right to privacy. (Parent, for example, discusses the case of William Sidis, who sued the *New Yorker* for such an invasion of privacy and lost.) On the other hand, it might be argued by some that, if reporters routinely respected their subjects' right to privacy in gathering information about them, then their ability to report the news would be seriously impaired.

Moreover, while Parent intends the above criteria as considerations for determining "whether the right to privacy has been violated in a specific case," this may be to overlook an important distinction. There is a difference between saying that a subject's right to privacy has not been violated and saying that some "legitimate and important" purpose was more compelling than that right. While reporters may sometimes find some purpose to be more compelling than the right to privacy itself, it would seem disingenuous to say that this right was therefore not violated.

Finally, the criteria posed by Parent may be criticized as being incomplete. For instance, the criteria cited fail to take account of whether the personal information acquired was "documented" with the *consent* of the subject. That is, has the subject about whom personal information is being published given his or her (fully informed and uncoerced) consent for (the entirety of) the information to be published? While Parent's phrase "wrongful invasion of privacy" may imply violation of the latter standard, the standard in question would seem to merit explicit mention among her several criteria.

In any event, whether or not the sense of "privacy" defined by Parent is the primary sense of that term (as she does, indeed, argue in her essay), it would appear to be a sense that is quite relevant within the context of journalistic practice.

In the second selection of this chapter, "The Reporter's Refusal to Testify," Philip Meyer examines possible rationales that reporters have for refusing to reveal information about their sources in court cases in which the reporters are called as witnesses. Beginning with the paradoxical case of a newspaper photographer who refused to disclose information about his source, even though subpoenaed on behalf of the source herself, Meyer argues against the view that journalists should enjoy an absolute professional exemption from testifying in court.

As Meyer indicates, one reason journalists tend to give for their refusal to testify involves the First Amendment. According to this rationale, "the freedom to impart the truth must include the freedom to discover the truth." If reporters were to disclose information about their sources, then their sources would stop talking and, consequently, the search for truth would be destroyed or greatly impaired. Therefore, reporters should not be required to disclose information about their sources.

According to Meyer, while the above argument has merit, it has been carried to extremes by some journalists. For example, according to one "absolutist" extension of the argument, the First Amendment should take precedence over any other amendment inasmuch as the process by which people are informed about their government is presupposed by all other constitutional rights. Thus, for example, when the the Sixth Amendment (providing a right to compel testimony) conflicts with the First Amendment, the latter is to be "preferred" to the former.

However, the above argument trades upon the assumption that the disclosure of information about sources will, in all instances, have a damaging effect (a so-called "chilling effect") upon the journalist's information-gathering function. Behind such a position is the further premise that, while some disclosures may have no direct effect upon the information-gathering process, it will nevertheless mark a first step in a progressive "slide down the slippery slope" whereby, at bottom, no one will be willing to talk to reporters. Meyer argues, however, that such logic is not universally supportable. For example, he argues that, in cases where sources have given their consent to disclosure (and may even request it), reporters' refusal to testify is unwarranted.

Given the questionable character of the above logic, Meyer examines other possible reasons, beyond the appeal to the First Amendment, which he thinks might underlie journalists' unconditional reluctance to testify. For example, among other practical considerations, he points to the inconvenience and expense involved in having to testify.

While Meyer's examination of possible journalistic motives behind the refusal to testify is provocative, it may also be incomplete from an ethical perspective. At the outstart he states that "to many news people, the silence itself is the virtue, not any underlying concern for the people who make the news." Yet, the concern for the source's *privacy* would appear to constitute an important ethical basis for journalists' refusal to testify, one that Meyer does not examine. Indeed, even if this is not the underlying concern of many journalists, it is arguable that it *should* be at least part of their motivation.

First, it is the sources' concern for privacy, in Parent's sense, that appears to undergird the reluctance of sources to talk to reporters without assurance that what they say will be held in confidence. The value of privacy is therefore fundamental, at least from the perspective of the source.

Second, if reporters are not to treat sources as mere instruments, or means, to the gathering of news, then they too would need to value the sources' privacy for its own sake. In Parent's terms, respect for sources as "autonomous, independent beings with unique aims to fulfill" would seem to require that journalists have intrinsic regard for their sources' privacy. Thus, it might be argued that journalists who respect their sources' privacy, *only insofar as* doing so can be justified by professional interests, have missed an important ethical justification for their conduct.

Finally, Meyer does not consider the role that general criteria of "wrongful invasion of privacy," such as those proposed by Parent, might play in journalistic decisions regarding disclosure of information about sources. For example, instead of insisting on nondisclosure, the photographer in the case discussed by Meyer might have taken account of the "legitimacy and importance" of the purpose for which the source's personal information was being sought. Since, in the latter case, this purpose was the vindication of the source herself, no charge of "wrongful violation of privacy" could reasonably have been advanced on the criterion in question. In any event, such a solution to the problem at hand points to the importance of considering Meyer's concerns against the background of Parent's philosophical analysis of privacy and its value.

Privacy, Morality, and the Law

W. A. PARENT

I. THE DEFINITION OF PRIVACY

Defining privacy requires a familiarity with its ordinary usage, of course, but this is not enough since our common ways of talking and using language are riddled with inconsistencies, ambiguities, and paradoxes. What we need is a definition which is by and large consistent with ordinary language, so that capable speakers of English will not be genuinely surprised that the term "privacy" should be defined in this way, but which also enables us to talk consistently, clearly, and precisely about the family of concepts to which privacy belongs. Moreover the definition must not usurp or encroach upon the basic meanings and functions of the other concepts within this family. Drawing useful and legitimate distinctions between different values is the best antidote to exploitation and evisceration of the concept of privacy.

Let me first state and then elaborate on my definition. Privacy is the condition of not having undocumented personal knowledge about one possessed by others. A person's privacy is diminished exactly to the degree that others possess this kind of knowledge about him. I want to stress that what I am defining is the condition of privacy, not the right to privacy. I will talk about the latter shortly. My definition is new, and I believe it to be superior to all of the other conceptions that have been proffered when measured against the desiderata of conceptual analysis above.

A full explication of the personal knowledge definition requires that we clarify the concept of personal information. My suggestion is that it be understood to consist of *facts* about a person[1] which most individuals in a given society at a given time do not want widely known about themselves. They may not be concerned that a few close friends, relatives, or professional associates know these facts, but they would be very much concerned if the information passed beyond this limited circle. In contemporary America facts about a person's sexual preferences, drinking or drug habits, income, the state of his or her marriage and health belong to the class of personal information. Ten years from now some of these facts may be a part of everyday conversation; if so their disclosure would not diminish individual privacy.

This account of personal information, which makes it a function of existing cultural norms and social practices, needs to be broadened a bit to accommodate a particular and unusual class of cases of the following sort. Most of us don't care if our height, say, is widely known. But there are a few persons who are extremely sensitive about their height (or weight or voice pitch).[2] They might take extreme measures to ensure that other people not find it out. For such individuals height is a very personal matter. Were someone to find it out by ingenious snooping we should not hesitate to talk about an invasion of privacy.

Let us, then, say that personal information consists of facts which most persons in a given society choose not to reveal about themselves (except to close friends, family, . . .) or of facts about which a particular individual is acutely sensitive and which he therefore does not choose to reveal about himself, even though most people don't care if these same facts are widely known about themselves.

Here we can question the status of information belonging to the public record, that is, information to be found in newspapers, court proceedings, and other official documents open to public inspection. (We might discover, for example, that Jones and Smith were arrested many years ago for engaging in homosexual activities.) Should such information be excluded from the category of personal information? The answer is that it should not. There is, after all, nothing extraordinary about public documents containing some very personal information. I will hereafter refer to personal facts belonging to the public record as documented.

My definition of privacy excludes knowledge of documented personal information. I do this for a simple reason. Suppose that *A* is browsing through some old newspapers and happens to see *B*'s name in a story about child prodigies who unaccountably failed to succeed as adults. *B* had become an obsessive gambler and an alcoholic. Should we accuse *A* of invading *B*'s privacy? No. An affirmative answer blurs the distinction between the public and the private. What belongs to the public domain cannot without glaring paradox be called private; consequently it should not be incorporated within our concept of privacy.

But, someone might object, *A* might decide to turn the information about *B*'s gambling and drinking problems over to a reporter who then publishes it in a popular news magazine. Isn't *B*'s privacy diminished by this occurrence?[3] No. I would certainly say that his reputation might well suffer from it. And I would also say that the publication is a form of gratuitous exploitation. But to challenge it as an invasion of privacy is not at all reasonable since the information revealed was publicly available and could have been found out by anyone, without resort to snooping or prying. In this crucial respect, the story about *B* no more diminished his privacy than would have disclosures about his property interests, say, or about any other facts concerning him that belonged to the public domain.

I hasten to add that a person does lose a measure of privacy at the time when personal information about him first becomes a part of the public record, since the information was until that time undocumented. It is also important not to confuse documented facts as I define them here with facts about individuals which are kept on file for special purposes but which are not available for public consumption, for example, health records. Publication of the latter does imperil privacy; for this reason special precautions are usually taken to ensure that the information does not become public property.

I believe the personal knowledge definition isolates the conceptual one of privacy, its distinctive and unique meaning. It does not appropriate ideas which properly belong to other concepts. Unfortunately the three most popular definitions do just this, confusing privacy with quite different values.

1. *Privacy consists of being let alone.* Warren and Brandeis were the first to advocate this broad definition.[4] Brandeis movingly appealed to it again in his celebrated dissent to the U.S. Supreme Court's majority ruling in *Olmstead* v. *U.S.*[5] Objecting to the Court's view that telephone wiretapping does not constitute a search and seizure, Brandeis delivered an impassioned defense of every citizen's right to be let alone, which he called our most cherished entitlement. Several other former U.S. Supreme Court Justices have endorsed this conception of privacy, among them Douglas, Fortas, and Steward.[6] And a number of distinguished law professors have done likewise.[7]

What proponents of the Brandeis definition fail to see is that there are innumerable ways of failing to let a person alone which have nothing to do with his privacy. Suppose, for instance, that *A* clubs *B* on the head or repeatedly insults him. We should describe and evaluate such actions by appeal to concepts like force, violence, and harassment. Nothing in the way of analytical clarity and justificatory power is lost if the concept of privacy is limited, as I have suggested that it be, to cases involving the acquisition of undocumented personal knowledge. Inflationary conceptions of privacy invite muddled reasoning.

2. *Privacy consists of a form of autonomy or control over significant personal matters.* "If the right to privacy means anything, it is the right of the individual, married or single, to be free from unwarranted government invasion into matters so fundamentally affecting a person as the decision whether to bear or beget a child."[8] With these words, from the Supreme Court case of *Eisenstadt* v. *Baird,* Mr. Justice Brennan expresses a second influential theory of privacy.

Indeed, definitions of privacy in terms of control dominate the literature. Perhaps the most favored among them equates privacy with the control over personal information about oneself. Fried, Wasserstrom, Gross, and Beardsley all adopt it or a close variation of it.[9] Other lawyers and philosophers, including Van Den Haag, Altman, and Parker,[10] identify privacy with control over access to oneself, or in Parker's words, "control over when and by whom the various parts of us can be sensed by others."

All of these definitions should be jettisoned. To see why, consider the example of a person who voluntarily divulges all sorts of intimate, personal, and undocumented information about herself to a friend. She is doubtless exercising control, in a paradigm sense of the term, over personal information about herself as well as over (cognitive) access to herself. But we would not and should not say that in doing so she is preserving or protecting her privacy. On the contrary, she is voluntarily relinquishing much of her privacy. People can and do choose to give up privacy for many reasons. An adequate conception of privacy must allow for this fact. Control definitions do not.[11]

I believe the voluntary disclosure counterexample is symptomatic of a deep confusion underlying the thesis that privacy is a form of control. It is a conceptual confusion, the mistaking of privacy for a part of liberty. The defining idea of liberty is the absence of external restraints or coercion. A person who is behind bars or locked in a room or physically pinned to the ground is unfree[12] to do many things. Similarly a person who is prohibited by law from making certain choices should be described as having been denied the liberty or freedom to make them. The loss of liberty in these cases takes the form of a deprivation of autonomy. Hence we can meaningfully say that the right to liberty embraces in part the right of persons to make fundamentally important choices about their lives and therewith to exercise significant control over different aspects of their behavior. It is clearly distinguishable from the right to privacy, which condemns the unwarranted acquisition of undocumented personal knowledge.[13]

3. *Privacy is the limitation on access to the self.* This definition, defended by Garrett and Gavison[14] among others, has the virtue of separating privacy from liberty. But it still is unsatisfactory. If we understand "access" to mean something like "physical proximity," then the difficulty becomes that there are other viable concepts which much more precisely describe what is at stake by limiting such access. Among these concepts I would include personal property, solitude, and peace. If, on the other hand, "access" is interpreted as referring to the acquisition of personal knowledge, we're still faced with a seemingly intractable counterexample. *A* taps *B*'s phone and overhears many of her conversations, including some of a very intimate nature. Official restraints have been imposed on *A*'s snooping, though. He must obtain permission from a judge before listening in on *B*. This case shows that limitation of cognitive access does not imply privacy.

A response sympathetic with the Garrett-Gavison conception to the above criticism might suggest that they really meant to identify privacy with certain kinds of limitations on access to the self. But why then didn't they say this, and why didn't they tell us what relevant limitations they had in mind?

Let us suppose that privacy is thought to consist of certain normal limitations on cognitive access to the self. Should we accept this conception? I think not, since it confuses privacy with the existential conditions that are necessary for its realization. To achieve happiness I must have some good luck, but this doesn't mean that happiness is good luck. Similarly, if I am to enjoy privacy there have to be limitations on cognitive access to me but these limitations are not themselves privacy. Rather privacy is what they safeguard.

II. THE VALUE OF PRIVACY

Is privacy a basic human value? There are many unpersuasive arguments that it is. Consider one of the most well-known, that given by Fried: "to respect, love, trust, feel affection for others, and to regard ourselves as the objects of love, trust, and affection is at the heart of our notion of ourselves as persons among persons, and privacy is the necessary atmosphere for these attitudes and actions, as oxygen is for combustion."[15] Privacy is essential for intimate relationships because, in Fried's view, their defining mark is the sharing of information about oneself that is not shared with others, and without privacy this would be impossible.

The difficulty with Fried's argument is that it relies on a skewed conception of intimacy. Intimacy involves much more than the exclusive sharing of information. It also involves the sharing of one's total self—one's experiences, aspirations, weaknesses, and values. This kind of emotional commitment, and concomitant giving, is entirely overlooked by Fried. He furnishes no argument for the claim that it cannot survive the loss of privacy.

Several so-called functional arguments on behalf of privacy also fail. Thus it is sometimes said that privacy is needed for relaxation, emotional release, self-reflection and self-analysis,[16] but this account confuses privacy with solitude, that is, the condition of being physically alone. Granted *A* might not be able to relax or think about her life unless she is left by herself, we are still not being told why *privacy* is important. Of course *A* might have to believe that her privacy is being respected if she is to relax and reflect successfully, but this still doesn't show that privacy itself (as opposed to the belief that we have it) is necessary to do these things.

Nor should we buy the thesis that privacy is necessary for individuality and freedom.[17] It is easy to imagine a person who has little or no privacy but who nonetheless possesses the determination and strength of will to think and act individually. Even those lacking in such determination might still be able to think and act for themselves so long as they believe (rightly or wrongly) that their privacy is intact. Similarly, persons without privacy might still enjoy considerable freedom. This will be true in cases where *A* is not aware of and has no reason for thinking that someone else is watching her every move and so is not deterred from pursuing various activities. It will also be true in cases where *A* simply doesn't care whether anyone else is watching her.

Lest you now begin to wonder whether privacy has any value at all, let me quickly point to several very good reasons why people in societies like ours desire privacy as I have defined it. First of all, if others manage to obtain sensitive personal knowledge about us they will by that very fact acquire power over us. Their power could then be used to our disadvantage. The possibilities for exploration become very real. The definite connection between harm and the invasion of privacy explains why we place a value on not having undocumented personal information about ourselves widely known.

Second, as long as we live in a society where individuals are generally intolerant of life styles, habits, and ways of thinking that differ significantly from their own, and where human foibles tend to become the object of scorn and ridicule, our desire for privacy will continue unabated. No one wants to be laughed at and made to feel ashamed of himself. And we all have things about us which, if known, might very well trigger these kinds of unfeeling and wholly unwarranted responses.

Third, we desire privacy out of a sincere conviction that there are certain facts about us which other people, particularly strangers and casual acquaintances, are not entitled to know. This conviction is constitutive of "the liberal ethic," a conviction centering on the basis thesis that individuals are not to be treated as mere property of the state but instead are to be respected as autonomous, independent beings with unique aims to fulfill. These aims, in turn, will perforce lead people down life's separate paths. Those of us educated under this liberal ideology feel that our lives are our own business (hence the importance of personal liberty) and that personal facts about our lives are for the most part ours alone to know. The suggestion that all personal facts should be made available for public inspection is contrary to this view. Thus, our desire for privacy is to a large extent a matter of principle.[18]

For most people, this desire is perfectly innocent. We are not seeking to hurt or disadvantage anyone by exercising it. Unquestionably some people at times demand privacy for fraudulent purposes, for example, to hide discreditable facts about themselves from future employers who are entitled to this information. Posner emphasizes this motive for privacy.[19] But not everyone values privacy for this reason and, even for those who do, misrepresentation is most often not the only or the overriding motive.

So there are several good reasons why we hold privacy to be an important value, one worth arguing for, and defending from unwarranted invasion. Now. I want to suggest that anyone who deliberately and without justification frustrates or contravenes our desire for privacy violates the distinctively liberal, moral principle of respect for persons. Let us say that A frustrates B's desire for privacy if he invades B's privacy and B know it. A acts in contravention of B's desire for privacy if he invades B's privacy without B's knowing it. Assuming that A has no justification for doing either, we can and should accuse him of acting in disregard of B's own desires and interests. A's action displays contempts for *B* in the sense that it is undertaken with no effort to identify with her life purposes or to appreciate what the fulfillment of these purposes might mean to her. Specifically by gratuitously or indiscriminately invading *B*'s privacy (I will explain these terms shortly) *A* manifests disrespect for *B* in the sense that he ignores or counts as having no significance *B*'s desire, spawned and nurtured by the liberal values of her society, not to have personal facts about herself known by ingenious or persistent snooping.[20]

III. THE MORAL RIGHT TO PRIVACY

The above argument establishes that privacy in indeed a moral value for persons who also prize freedom and individuality. That we should seek to protect it against unwarranted invasion should come, then, as no surprise. Advocating a moral right to privacy comprises an integral part of this effort. It expresses our conviction that privacy should only be infringed under exigent circumstances and for the most compelling reasons, for example, law enforcement and health care provision.

The moral right to privacy does not embody the rule "privacy may never be invaded." It is important to emphasize that there are such things as justifiable invasions of privacy. Our concern is not to condemn invasions but to declare our right not to become the victims of wrongful invasions (see Section IV). Discussion of a right to privacy presupposes that privacy is a good, vulnerable to loss by human contrivance. It does not presuppose that such is always bad. . . .

IV. CRITERIA OF WRONGFUL INVASION

Which invasions of privacy are justifiable and which are not? A complete conception of the right to privacy must address this question, providing general criteria of wrongful invasion, which will then have to be applied to specific cases. Whether the right to privacy has been violated in a specific case can often only be answered through a process of making difficult and controversial value judgments. No conception of the right to privacy, no matter how detailed and sophisticated will allow us to eliminate or bypass this process.

The following questions are central to assessing alleged violations of the right to privacy:

1. For what purpose(s) is the undocumented personal knowledge sought?
2. Is this purpose a legitimate and important one?
3. Is the knowledge sought through invasion of privacy relevant to its justifying purpose?
4. Is invasion of privacy the only or the least offensive means of obtaining the knowledge?
5. What restrictions or procedural restraints have been placed on the privacy-invading techniques?
6. What protection is to be afforded the personal knowledge once it has been acquired?

The first four questions all have to do with the rationale for invading privacy. We can say that the right to privacy is violated by *gratuitous* invasions and that these occur when: there is no purpose at all to them; when the purpose is less than compelling; when the personal facts sought have nothing to do with the justifying purposes; when the personal information could have been obtained by less intrusive measures. Among the legitimate purposes for acquiring undocumented personal information are efficient law enforcement, confirmation of eligibility criteria set forth in various government welfare programs, and the compilation of statistical data concerning important behavioral trends.

Question 5 pertains to the actual invasion of privacy itself. We can say that the right to privacy is violated by *indiscriminate* invasions and that these occur when insufficient procedural safeguards have been imposed on the techniques employed so that either: all sorts of personal information, some germane to the investigation but some totally irrelevant thereto, is obtained; or persons with no business knowing the personal facts acquires are allowed to gain cognitive access to them. One can argue against a proposed invasion of privacy on the grounds that it is too likely to be indiscriminate in either of these two senses.

Question 6 pertains to postinvasion safeguards. We can say that the right to privacy is violated when the undocumented personal information acquired is not adequately protected against unwarranted cognitive intrusion or unauthorized uses. It is also violated, of course, by actual instances of such intrusions and uses.

Let us look at the concrete example. Suppose a large city is faced with the growing problem of welfare fraud. It decides that to combat this problem an elaborate system of surveillance must be initiated. Personal information regarding welfare recipients' income, family status, sexual habits, and spending habits is to be obtained. Search warrants are obtained permitting unlimited surveillance and specifying the kind of information being sought. Once obtained the information is to be stored on magnetic tapes and kept in the welfare department.

Any person who takes the right to privacy seriously will raise the following questions and make the following observations about this city's (*C*'s) action:

i. *C* presents no arguments or evidence in support of its belief that the problem of welfare fraud can be solved by restoring to large-scale surveillance. We should demand that *C* do so.

ii. *C* presents no arguments or evidence showing that surveillance is the only way to acquire the relevant personal information. Did it first try to obtain knowledge of welfare recipients' life style by asking them about it or sending them questionnaires? Were there other, less intensived measures available for acquiring this knowledge?

iii. Search warrants permitting unlimited surveillance are insufficiently discriminating. So are warrants which do not particularly describe the places to be observed and the facts to be gathered. *C* should have insisted that the warrants place restrictions on the time periods of surveillance as well as on its scope.

iv. Why is it necessary to acquire information about welfare recipents' sexual habits? How is this knowledge relevant to the object of eradicating fraud?

v. What kind of security does *C* intend to provide for the magnetic tapes containing the acquired information? Who will enjoy access to these tapes? Will they eventually be erased or destroyed? *C* has the duty to guard against the potential abuse of the stored facts.

I hope this brief analysis is helpful in isolating some of the crucial issues and difficult questions that must be confronted when applying the right of privacy to particular cases. Often there will be strong disagreement over whether proposed programs of physical, psychological, and data surveillance are gratuitous or indiscriminate. This is to be expected. The results of these disputes will determine the contours of the privacy right.

V. THE LEGAL RIGHT TO PRIVACY

One final inquiry remains regarding how the moral right to privacy has fared in the law. To what extent is it receiving legal protection, and should it be receiving more? The account that follows is largely descriptive. My purpose is to show how contemporary privacy jurisprudence could have benefited from the use of disciplined philosophical analysis.

We must begin with the well-known U.S. Supreme Court case of *Griswold* v. *Connecticut*,[21] for this decision more than any other is responsible for the jurisprudential notoriety that now attends the right to privacy. In *Griswold* the Court struck down a law that made it a criminal offense to married couples to use contraceptives. Writing the majority opinion, Justice Douglas argued that even though the Constitution does not explicitly mention a right to privacy, one can still justifiably infer its existence from examining the penumbras or emanations of various specific constitutional provisions. The contraceptive law under challenge, according to Douglas, violates this right.

Unfortunately Douglas never explained why it did. Of course there is an obvious reason why the law's enforcement would invade privacy, but the Court made only passing reference to this problem. What precisely did Douglas mean by the expression "right of privacy"? *Eisenstadt* v. *Baird* provided an answer. In that case, decided seven years after *Griswold,* a majority of the Court equated the right to privacy with the right to make fundamentally important choices free from unwarranted government intrusion.[22] They went on to find a Massachusetts law forbidding the use of contraceptives among unmarried persons in violation of this right.

Since *Eisenstadt* the Supreme Court has invoked the right to privacy, conceived of as a species of the right to choose, in voiding several state laws which prohibited women from choosing an abortion except when necessary to save their lives.[23] And several state supreme court have embraced this conception of the right to privacy and have applied it in cases involving euthanasia,[24] the use of marijuana,[25] and the prescription of laetrile as a cancer cure.[26]

All of these cases conflate the right to privacy with the right to liberty. I won't repeat my critique of the *Eisenstadt* definition set out in Sectional I. Suffice it to say that laws preempting the choice of citizens are coercive in an obvious sense of the term. Consequently they involved a denial of liberty and must therefore be evaluated against the Fourteenth Amendment's guarantee that citizens shall not be deprived of liberty without due process of law.[27] For years the U.S. Supreme Court decided cases like *Griswold* by Fourteenth Amendment interpretation. Thus legislation interfering with prospective employees' choice of work,[28] with students' choice whether to study foreign languages in private or public elementary schools,[29] and with parents' choice whether to send their children to public or private schools[30] was properly seen as implicating liberty interests and was assessed accordingly. That some of these decisions (I am thinking particularly of *Lochner*) met with severe criticism from later scholars and were even repudiated by later courts does not justify judicial indulgence in conceptual legerdemain. Confusing liberty with privacy only severs to impugn the intellectual integrity of the judiciary.

Another class of spurious privacy cases needs to be exposed. Consider the question whether a "music as you ride" program on buses and streetcars violates passengers' right to privacy; or whether solicitors and peddlers who go on private property and disturb homeowners infringe the latters' right to privacy; or whether sound trucks that emit loud and raucous noises in residential neighborhoods violate homeowners' right to privacy. The U.S. Supreme Court has had to consider such questions, and it has treated them as raising bona fide privacy interests.[31] This was a mistake. Unwanted or excessive solicitation or noise imperil homeowners' peace and their right to property, understood in the broad but widely accepted sense of the right to enjoy what one owns. Being exposed to music on buses might rattle the nerves and thereby threaten our peace. It certainly preempts the choice whether to listen or not while riding. But that is all. The concept of privacy has no useful role to play in any of these cases. Indeed, its introduction only obscures the gravamen of petitioners' complaints.

Invasion of privacy must consist of truthful disclosures about a person. Occasionally aggrieved parties will forget or ignore this. The case of *Paul* v. *Davis* will illustrate: The police distributed a five-page flyer to some 800 store owners in the Louisville, Kentucky, area which contained the names and photographs of persons identified as "known shoplifters." Davis's picture and name appeared there. He had been arrested for shoplifting but the charges against him were dropped shortly after the flyer's distribution. Davis brought an invasion of privacy suit against the police. He ought not to have done so, for the flyer did not reveal any personal facts about him. His only legitimate course would have been to bring a cause of action for defamation. Justice Rehnquist said precisely this in his majority opinion.[32]

The unfortunate view that cases like this can be argued in terms of privacy finds support in William Prosser's extraordinarily influential 1960 essay.[33] Prosser maintained that the law of privacy comprises four distinct torts, the third of which he identified with placing the plaintiff in a false light in the public eye. This false light categorization displays an egregious misunderstanding of privacy.

Are Prosser's remaining three torts similarly confused? The first form of privacy invasion he distinguishes is intrusion upon the plaintiffs seclusion or solitude, or into his private affairs. My personal knowledge definition shows that privacy is invaded by certain kinds of intrusions, namely those of a cognitive nature that result in the acquisition of undocumented personal facts. Other kinds of intrusion, for example, those involving causal access (see definition 3 discussed in Section I) and environmental disturbances, are more exactly and perspicuously described by concepts like trespass, nuisance, and peace.

Prosser's second privacy tort, the public disclosure of embarrassing private facts, is legitimate provided the facts are undocumented. The fourth tort, appropriation for the defendant's advantage of the plaintiff's name or likeness, should not be subsumed under privacy for the simple reason that such appropriation does not result in the obtaining of undocumented personal knowledge about the plaintiff. It does however, preempt the choice whether or not to have one's name or likeness used (usually for advertising purposes) and could therefore be challenged on liberty grounds. It could also be challenged on property grounds, particularly in circumstances where the plaintiff is seeking financial remuneration for the use of his name or likeness.

Some First Amendment cases involving the disclosure of personal information implicated genuine privacy interests, others do not. Two well-known cases which ought not to have been decided in terms of privacy are *Cox Broadcasting Co.* v. *Cohn* and *Briscoe* v. *Reader's Digest.* In *Cohn* a newspaper published the name of a rape victim.[34] In *Briscoe,* the identity of a former truck hijacker was disclosed.[35] Because these facts belonged to the public record their disclosure cannot plausibly be condemned on privacy grounds.

However, the press sometimes does gratuitously invade privacy. One former case comes immediately to mind. William Sidis was a child prodigy (at the age of eleven he lectured to Harvard professors on the Fourth Dimension) who in his later years sought solitude and privacy. *The New Yorker* decided to do a story on him. The article focused on Sidis's life as a recluse. Sidis sued for invasion of privacy and lost.[36] In my judgment he should have won. Granted there is the First Amendment guarantee of a free press, but this has never been interpreted to mean that the press can publish anything it wants. There are limitations (for example, pornography, libel), and invasions of privacy which serve no useful purpose should be included among them. The pubic had no need to know about Sidis's later life.

Other First Amendment–privacy cases are more difficult to decide.

Much depends on the particular facts of the situation and the plaintiff's status. Public officials are not entitled to the same degree of protection as are private citizens. Warren and Brandeis took note of this many years ago when they wrote: "to publish of a modest and retiring individual that he suffers from an impediment of his speech or that he cannot spell correctly is an unwarranted, if not unexampled, infringement upon his privacy, while to state and comment on the same characteristic found in a would-be congressman would not be regarded as beyond the pale of propriety."[37]

Thus far our conclusion must be that privacy is not receiving significant legal protection. It is only when we look at Fourth Amendment cases that privacy enthusiasts can begin to take heart. In having to formulate criteria for unreasonable searches and seizures the Supreme Court has been slowly evolving a conception of the right to privacy.[38] In many of these cases the Court has povided substantial protection to privacy interests.[39]

Moreover, the Court may be sympathetic to privacy grievances not related to searches and seizures. Consider the recent and important case of *Whalen* v. *Roe*.[40] The State of New York required that the names and addresses of all persons obtaining schedule II drugs—opium, cocaine, amphetamines, and other drugs for which there is both a lawful and an unlawful use—be kept on record in a centralized computer file. This information was put on magnetic tapes which were then stored in a vault. After five years the tapes would be destroyed. A locked fence and alarm system provided security for the information-processing system. Public disclosure of the patient's identity was prohibited.

The Court unanimously agreed that this legislation did not infringe the patient's right to privacy. But in reaching this (reasonable, I believe) conclusion, the judges exhibited a genuine sensitivity to the privacy interests at stake. Thus Justice Stevens wrote:

> We are not aware of the threat to privacy implied in the accumulation of vast amounts of personal information in computerized data banks or other massive government files. The collecting of taxes, the distribution of welfare and social security benefits, the supervision of public health, the direction of our armed forces, and the enforcement of the criminal laws all require the orderly preservation of great quantities of information, much of which is personal in nature and potentially embarrassing or harmful if disclosed. The right to collect and use such data for public purposes is typically accompanied by a concomitant statutory or regulatory duty to avoid unwarranted disclosures.[41]

So the *Whalen* decision should not be a source of despair for privacy advocates. Privacy might yet come to occupy a significant place in American jurisprudence.

NOTES

1. The spreading of falsehoods or purely subjective opinions about a person does not constitute an invasion of his privacy. It is condemnable in the language of libel or slander.

2. I know a recently divorced man who doesn't want anyone to know the fact. He and his former wife still live together, so it is possible for him to conceal their martial status from most everyone.

3. I owe this example, as well as other useful comments and suggestions, to an Editor of *Philosophy & Public Affairs*.

4. Samuel Warren and Louis Brandeis. "The Right to Privacy." *The Harvard Law Review*, 4, (1890): 205–07.

5. Olmstead v U.S. 2–U.S. 438 (1928): 475–76.

6. See William Douglas, *The Rights of the People* (Westport. CT: Greenwood Press, 1958). See Fortas's decision in Time v. Hill 385 U.S 374 (1967): 412; and in Gertz v. Robert Welch, Inc., 418 U.S. 323 (1974): 412–13. See Stewart's decision in Katz v. U.S., 389 U.S. 347 (1967): 350; and in Whalen v. Roe, 429 U.S. 589 (1977): 608.

7. For example, Edward Bloustein, in "Group Privacy: The Right to Huddle," from his *Individual and Group Privacy* (New Brunswick, NJ: Transaction Books, 1978), pp. 123–86; Paul Freund in "Privacy: One Concept or Many?" ed. J. Pennock and J. Chapman. *Nomos XIII: Privacy* (New York: Atherton Press, 1971). Pp. 182–98; Henry Paul Monagham, "Of Liberty and Property," *Cornell Law Review* 62 (1977): pp. 405–14; and Richard Posner, *The Economics of Justice* (Cambridge, MA: Harvard University Press, 1981), p. 123.

8. Eisenstadt v. Baird, 405 U.S. 438 (1972): 453.

9. Charles Fried, *An Anatomy of Values* (Cambridge, MA: Harvard University Press, 1970), chap. 9, p. 141; Richard Wasserstom, "Privacy: Some Assumptions and Arguments," in *Philosophical Law,* ed. Richard Bronaugh (Westport, CT: Greenwood Press, 1979), pp. 148–67; Hyman Gross, "Privacy and Autonomy," *Nomos XIII,* p. 170; Elizabeth Beardsley, "Privacy, Autonomy, and Selective Disclosure," *Nomos XIII,* p. 65.

10. Ernest Van Den Haag, "On Privacy," *Nomos XIII,* p. 147ff.: Irwin Altman, "Privacy—A Conceptual Analysis," *Environment and Behavior* 8 (1976): 8; and "Privacy Regulation: Culturally Universal or Culturally Specific?" *The Journal of Social Issues* 33 (1977): 67; Richard Parker. "A Definition of Privacy," *Rutgers Law Review* 27 (1974): 280

11. Proponents of a control definition might respond by saying that they are

really interested in identifying *the right of privacy* with the right to control personal information about our access to ourselves. But then they should have said so explicitly instead of formulating their contention in terms of privacy alone. And even if they had done so their position would still be confused, since the right to choose is an integral aspect of the right of liberty, not the right to privacy.

12. Here I use "unfree" to mean "lacking liberty." My concern is not with the metaphysical notion of free will.

13. I do not mean to ascribe to proponents of control definitions the view that every interference with liberty is by that very fact an infringement to privacy. I do mean to criticize them for failing to recognize that interferences with personal choice or control, taken by themselves and with no considerations given to undocumented personal knowledge that might be acquired from them, are not appropriately described or persuasively condemned in the language of privacy.

14. Roland Garrett, "The Nature of Privacy," *Philosophy Today* 18 (1974): 264; and Ruth Gavison, "Privacy and the Limits of the Law." *Yale Law Journal* 89 (1980): 428

15. Charles Fried, "Privacy," *Yale Law Journal* 77 (1968): 477

16. Westin, Bazelon, and Weinstein are among those who advance the relaxation argument. See, respectively: Alan Westin's *Privacy and Freedom* (New York: Atheneum Press, 1967), p. 34; David Bazelon, "Probing Privacy," *Georgia Law Review* 12 (1977): 588ff.; and Michael Weinstein, "The Uses of Privacy in the Good Life," *Nomos XIII,* p. 99. Westin (p. 36), Weinstein (p. 104), and Gavison (p. 449) are among those who defend the argument from query.

17. Westin (p. 33) and Bloustein, particularly in his essay, "Privacy as an Aspect of Human Dignity: An Answer to Dean Prosser," *The New York University Law Review* 39 (1964): 970, are among those who defend the argument from individuality.

18. This argument from liberalism invites rebuttal from socialists and communists, of course, who want to maintain that the "ideal" of privacy does nothing but encourage unnecessary (and unnatural) conflict among human beings.

19. Richard Posner, "The Right to Privacy," *The Georgia Law Review* 12 (1978): 491–522.

20. I don't mean to identify the liberal principle of respect for persons with Kant's conception of respect for hunanity. Kant does not formulate his conception in terms of what persons desire. Instead he focuses on the property of rationality that all persons possess and that, in his view, confers intrinsic worth upon them.

21. Griswold v. Connecticut, 381 U.S. 479 (1965).

22. Eisenstadt v. Baird, 405 U.S. 438 (1972): 453.

23. See, for example, Roe v. Wade, 410 U.S. 113 (1973).

24. In the matter of Quinlan, 355 A.2d 647 (1976). Here the New Jersey Supreme Court ruled that the right to privacy is broad enough to encompass a

patient's decision to decline life-sustaining medical treatment under certain circumstances.

25. Ravin v. State, 537 P.2d 494 (1975). Here Alaska's Supreme Court ruled that a law forbidding the possession of marijuana by adults for their personal use in their homes violated the right to privacy.

26. People v. Privitera, 74 C.A. 3d (1977), and People v. Privitera, 23 Cal. 3d 687 (1979). The California Court of Appeal ruled that the right to privacy protects the choice of cancer patients to use laetrile as a treatment. The California Supreme Court disagreed. It accepted the privacy conceptualization of the issue but contended that the right is not broad enough to legitimate the choice of laetrile.

27. The Fourteenth Amendment provides in part that no state shall "deprive any person of life, liberty, or property, without due process of law. . . . " The Fifth Amendment protects liberty against arbitrary infringement by the Federal Government.

28. Lochner v. N.Y., 198 U.S. 45 (1905). In this controversial case the Court ruled that legislation forbidding employees from contracting to work more than sixty hours a week or ten hours a day in bakeries gratuitously infringed the right to liberty.

29. Meyer v. Nebraska, 262 U.S. 390 (1923). Here the Court invalidated a law that barred the teaching of foreign languages in private and public elementary schools on the grounds that it constituted an arbitary infringement on the right to liberty.

30. Pierce v. Society of Sisters, 268 U.S. 510 (1925). In this case the Court invalidated a law that compelled children aged eight to sixteen to attend public schools on the ground that it unjustifiably abridged the right to liberty.

31. The cases are: Public Utilities Commission v. Pollack, 345 U.S. 451 (1952); Breard v. Alexandria, 341 U.S. 622 (1951); and Kovacs v. Cooper 336 U.S. 77 (1949).

32. Paul v. Davis, 424 U.S. 693 (1978).

33. William Prosser, "Privacy," *California Law Review* 48 (1960): 383–423.

34. Cox Broadcasting Co. v. Cohn, 420 U.S. 469 (1975). The U.S. Supreme Court correctly ruled that Cohn had no bona fide privacy complaint.

35. Briscoe v. Reader's Digest, 93 Cal. Rptr. 866 (1971). Briscoe won this case principally because so long a time had passed between his offense and the publication. The California Court should have realized, however, that personal information contained in official records which have not been destroyed is undeniably public.

36. Sidis v. F-R Publishing Corp., 34 F. Supp. 19 (1938).

37. Warren and Brandeis, "The Right to Privacy," p. 205.

38. The Fourth Amendment reads: "The right of the people to be secure in their persons, house, papers, effects, against unreasonable searches and seizures shall not be violated, and no warrants shall issue, but upon probable cause supported by oath or affirmation, and particularly describing the place to be

searched and the persons or things to be seized." One can plausibly argue that this Amendment presupposes a right to privacy.

39. I have the following cases in mind: Katz v. U.S. 389 U.S. 347 (1967), where the Court ruled that the police may not attach electronic listening devices to the outside of a telephone booth in order to record the conversations on bets and wagers without first obtaining a search warrant; Berger v. New York, 388 U.S. 41 (1967), where the Court invalidated a permissive eavesdropping statute authorizing the indiscriminate use of electronic surveillance devices: Stanley v. Georgia, 394 U.S. 447 (1969), in which the Court ruled that allegedly pornographic movies seized without a search warrant from the defendant's home could not be used as evidence in his trial; Lo-ji Sales, Inc. v. N.Y., 442 U.S. 319 (1979) in which the Court declared that a search of an adult bookstore resulting in the seizure of several films and magazines violated petitioner's Fourth Amendment rights because the warrant issued failed to particularly describe the things to be seized; and Steagold v. U.S., 101 S. Ct. 1642 (1981), where the Court ruled that the police may not search for the subject of an arrest warrant in the home of a third party without first obtaining a search warrant.

40. Whalem v. Roe, 429 U.S. 589 (1976).

41. Ibid., p. 605.

The Reporter's Refusal to Testify

PHILIP MEYER

Suppose for a moment that you have been accused of a crime—a crime that you sincerely believe you did not commit—yet here you are, on trial, and with a policeman testifying that he saw you perform the illegal act.

Now suppose further that an impartial witness saw what the policeman saw. Not only did this witness see it, he recorded it on film. Better yet, this impartial witness is a newspaper photographer, and his newspaper is well known for its integrity and devotion to uncovering and disclosing the truth.

You are home free, right? Wrong. If that newspaper photographer is your only witness, you may be in big trouble.

Strange as it may seem, many newspaper people consider it a violation of their ethical standards to testify in court about events they have heard and seen. You may get that photographer's evidence eventually, but you and the court may have to subpoena him, threaten him, place him in fear for his own liberty before he will make the slightest effort to help you.

This is not an issue of protecting confidential sources. A few reporters, in highly publicized cases, have gone to jail rather than identify sources whom they had promised to protect. Their tenacity in keeping their promises to those sources is admirable. But in this case the source needs disclosure, not silence, and is not likely to get it, at least not without a struggle. To many news people, the silence itself is the virtue, not any underlying concern for the people who make the news. What was once rational protection of sources has become a law of journalistic *omerta*.

Newspaper people today are ethically confused. Their attitudes toward the moral implications of their work range from humility to arrogance, from total insensitivity to hypersensitivity. Sometimes these conflicting attitudes are held simultaneously by the same individuals. On the one hand, they risk alienating their public through insistence on special privileges not available to the rest of us, and, on the other, they risk locking themselves into timorous paralysis, fearful of acting lest someone cry foul.

This book is an attempt to sort such ethical issues out. News people are good people, and the responsibility they face in bringing us a daily measure of truth out of the noise and confusion of events is an awesome one. Conflict is inevitable.

The example of the reluctant witness is based on a real case. It came to my attention in 1984, at a luncheon meeting of newspaper people who were swapping tales of the tribulations of their craft. The man from the *Dallas Morning News* reported that his paper had a legal problem on its hands. A photographer was being subpoenaed, and the court was determined to make him testify.

The case was straightforward. A woman had been arrested—unjustly, she believed—in a demonstration against nuclear power. She was charged with blocking a public passageway. The photographer had witnessed the event, recorded it on film, and was now being summoned to testify on her behalf and to provide prints of the shots made at the scene to support her claim of innocence. Some of the images had not been published in the newspaper.[1]

"Why are you fighting it?" the young editor was asked. He looked surprised.

"Because of the First Amendment," he said.

One of the troubles with newspapers is this tendency to invoke the First Amendment reflexively to justify their immediate self-interest or even their mere convenience. The First Amendment is such a powerful and integral part of our basic law that this practice is a little like invoking Holy Scripture to avoid taking out the garbage. Newspapers have also invoked the First Amendment to explain why they feel they must publish the names of rape victims, why they should reveal the circumstances of people which, if known, would make them potential victims of crime, and as justification for not allowing persons about whom disparaging things have been said to reply in their columns.

Our concern here is newspaper ethics, not press law. But because many decisions involving moral obligations are justified with First Amendment arguments, we need to start with an examination of those arguments. The legal outcome of a case and the ethical outcome are not always the same. Sometimes an action that is immoral will be within the law, and sometimes a moral action will violate the law. For newspaper people, however, the First Amendment involves an ethical principle as well as a legal one. Indeed, for many the First Amendment is the foundation of an ethical system, and to understand how news people think, it is necessary to understand the structure of that system.

The Texas case turned on a question of fact: whether the woman had or had not chained herself in the doorway. She argued that to prove she had not, she needed the photographer's testimony, his photographs, or both. Her argument, as much as his, was grounded in the Constitution. The Sixth Amendment states, "In all criminal prosecutions, the accused shall enjoy the right . . . to have compulsory process for obtaining witnesses in his favor." And bearing witness is a traditional duty of every citizen, regardless of his or her status. A trial applies the law to facts, and there must be procedures for making the facts known. The right is not absolute. It yields, for example, to the power of the national government to protect its military secrets.

But how does the First Amendment get involved? The First Amendment, of course, says that "Congress shall make no law . . . abridging the freedom of speech, or of the press . . . " The bridge from that language to the photographer's reluctance to be a witness involves an extrapolation from the freedom to speak to the freedom to discover the truth. Forcing a newsperson to give testimony, the argument goes, interferes with his or her ability to gather news. Protecting that ability is indeed important, as it has been since the birth of our republic. . . .

The Absolutist Position on Press Freedom

. . . The objection to the absolutist position is summed up in the aphorism that your freedom to swing your fist ends where my nose begins. An absolute freedom to swing your fist would place no protections around my nose. There has been a school of thought, never subscribed to by a majority of the Supreme Court, that the First Amendment freedoms are absolute and therefore must prevail in any conflict—and there will always be conflict—between a First Amendment claim and some other claim under the Constitution. Thus, the accused trespasser in Texas must yield her right to compel testimony on her behalf if the reluctant witness has a First Amendment claim.

The Preferred-Position Theory

Any First Amendment claim? If you think about it, you realize that pure absolutism is impossible, because you can always dream up a hypothetical First Amendment claim that even the most rigid fundamentalists would not accept. It would be absurd to argue, for example, that a reporter should be allowed, in the name of the First Amendment, to pistol-whip a source to make him talk. And refusing to come to the aid of a source who needs a witness is also pretty high on the scale of absurdity. However, we would be making a serious mistake if we were to leap from that judgment to an assumption that the underlying rationale used by a reluctant media witness is also absurd. There is a vital and essential truth at the bottom of it, and the great danger of trying to push this truth to its silliest limits is that the importance of the basic truth itself may be obscured or even lost.

The vital core of this argument is that the freedom to impart the truth must include the freedom to discover the truth. Therefore government should not only refrain from preventing or punishing speech, but it should also refrain from inhibiting the process of discovering and imparting information. There is much historical justification for this position. Following the social-contract theory of John Locke and its later elaboration by Jean Jacques Rousseau of France, the authors of the Constitution believed—as we still do today—that government exists with the consent of the governed, and that this consent must be informed consent.[2] The system can't work unless the public knows and understands what the government is up to. This was not idle theorizing. There were too many examples of despotic governments the world over, and even England, where the notion of individual liberty had been born, was on the edge of darkness under the corrupt Parliament of George III. America seemed the only hope for the future, and that hope lay in an enlighted and knowledgeable public. On these shores, wrote John Adams, must begin "the illumination of the ignorant and the emancipation of the slavish part of mankind all over the earth."[3]

Government, the Founders believed, was essentially selfish, grasping, and abusive of power. So an independent check in the form of the free transfer of information was essential to keep it in line. The connection with some of today's more difficult ethical and legal problems comes as soon as you decide that the free flow of information requires not only noninterference with speech and noninterference with the processes by which information is developed and distributed, but also a ban on any government action that might conceivably lead to such an interference. With each of those successive steps, the case for absolutism grows weaker. The legal and moral problem is one of where to draw the line.

In modern times the debate over just how far the First Amendment extends to protect the press has centered on a few key extensions of the basic need articulated by John Milton in the seventeenth century and written into the U.S. Constitution in the eighteenth. One such extension holds that when the First Amendment is in conflict with some other provision of the Constitution, the First Amendment should generally prevail. The case of the Texas photographer is just such a conflict because the accused person was invoking her Sixth Amendment right to compel testimony when she asked for the newspaper photographer's pictures. The theory that the First Amendment comes first is called the *preferred-position theory,* and it stems from a footnote, in a case about something totally different, that was written by Associate Justice Harlan F. Stone in 1938. Stone elaborated on the idea in later decisions and said that when constitutional provisions are in conflict, there should be special protection for "those political processes which make all other rights in our society possible."[4]

THE CHILLING EFFECT AND THE SLIPPERY-SLOPE PROBLEM

The process of getting the information out so that the people will know what their government is doing is certainly one that makes everything else possible. And if you walk far enough down that road, you can reach the justification for a photographer's refusal to testify in a criminal case. The justification has to do with avoiding a *chilling effect.*

A chilling effect can be almost anything that has an unfavorable effect on the reward system for journalists or their sources. It raises the cost or decreases the pleasure of discovering and imparting information and so discourages the free flow of information, without necessarily obstructing it outright. If a person responsible for gathering news is required to testify about the things that he learned in that process, the argument goes, it will make the people who tell him things or pose for the pictures less willing to do so in the future.

There was no such chill in the Texas case because the person who was arrested had invited the photographer to be there and hoped to benefit from his testimony. But, say the newspapers, the principle still applies. And here we have an encounter—the first of many in dealing with the way newspapers think about ethics—with the *slippery-slope problem.* Sure, editors will acknowledge, this case does not make any practical difference, but if we give in on this one, we'll have to do it in the next one, too. And that one will be a little bit different and before you know it, we will have slid all the way down the slippery slope to the point where no one will want to talk to or be photographed by a journalist.

In the view of those newspaper people who are First Amendment fundamentalists, the chilling effect begins at the top of that slippery slope. That's why the expression is used so much. "I sometimes think," wrote David Shaw of the *Los Angeles Times*, "that the phrase 'chilling effect'—as in 'This will have a chilling effect on the ability of the press to fulfill its First Amendment obligations'—is routinely administered to all journalists, by injection, along with their first press cards."[5]

The slippery slope is a recurrent theme in ethical thought. My grandmother, for one, believed in it. Consuming carbonated soft drinks from bottles, she warned, was a bad idea because it can lead you to sipping from bottles with wine or beer in them. From there, you may be tempted to try some of the hard stuff, and the next thing you know, you're lying in a gutter somewhere not knowing what day it is. She wasn't far wrong, at least for some people. But the existence of some slippery slopes in real life does not demonstrate either the immutability or the universal application of the theory. Yes, everybody who lands in a heap at the bottom of some slippery slope did indeed have to start with that first step. But lots of others take the first step with no harm at all. In real life, slippery slopes must have handholds, ledges, tree branches, or even golden staircases leading back up.

In application, the image of the slippery slope justifies various kinds of absolutism. "If I did this for you, I'd have to do it for everybody." Or "If we don't fight communism in Southeast Asia, we'll eventually be fighting it on the beaches of California." Or "If we admit one of those (insert any ethnic group, sex, or profession) into the club, they'll soon take over the place." Or Richard Nixon stating that he was worried about the effect on "future presidents" of his potential prosecution in the Watergate scandal.

The moral problem with an absolutist position is that it rejects compromise before discussion even begins. As Walter Lippmann observed, whenever you hold your positions to be "perfect examples of some eternal principle or other, you are not talking, you are fighting."[6] When there is conflict, the absolutist insists that all the adjustment must be made by other parties. In a world where nobody is perfect, that is a difficult position to sustain. Yet journalists sometimes behave as if theirs were the world's only perfect profession. The issue of refusing to take part in other people's legal proceedings is perhaps the clearest example of this claim to preferential treatment. How far will journalists go to defend their claim? Pretty far, it seems.

In 1982 *Washington Post* reporter Loretta Tofani wrote a three-part series about sexual assaults among prisoners in the Prince Georges County, Maryland, jail. She described 12 cases of jail rape. This story was reported at a time when the *Post* was in a mood for reform of its methods. In 1981 Janet Cooke, another *Post* reporter, had received a Pulitzer Prize for her gripping story about an 8-year-old heroin addict. It was later discovered that the story was fabricated and that the child did not exist; the Pulitzer was returned and Cooke was fired. After that episode . . . the *Post* was jumpy about printing dramatic disclosures that could not be traced back to specific sources. Tofani therefore went to more than the usual trouble to get her sources on the record. Many of them, including prisoners, did allow her to use their names. The series was published and led to a grand jury investigation of the county jail system. The grand jury, not illogically, decided that the place to start was by talking with Tofani—to verify her story, to find out what else she might have learned that didn't get into the paper, and to learn who else might have been present to verify her conversations with the inmates.

The *Post,* through Tofani, fought the subpoena even though no question of protecting the confidentiality of sources was involved here. There was at least the possibility of a chilling effect—modest here, perhaps, but maybe not so modest in future cases. How can there be a chilling effect when the sources allowed the use of their names? Well, it can be argued, they knew their names would be in the newspaper, but they didn't expect the reporter to repeat her information to a grand jury; if they had, they might not have talked. So, if Tofani were to testify, future subjects of jailhouse interviews would find out about it, and that would make them reluctant to talk, and the press's freedom to report would have been damaged.

That's a pretty faint chill, in light of what actually happened. While Tofani was resisting her subpoena, the grand jury went right ahead and indicated several people, and they were eventually convicted. To believe that a lawbreaker would weigh an equation so delicate that he would decide it is safe to admit misdeeds to a reporter and to allow use of his name—but that he won't cooperate if he thinks she might testify—is to stretch the argument awfully thin. It makes sense only on the slippery slope.

It is fear of sliding down the slippery slope that leads newspaper people to balk at giving testimony even in cases where there is absolutely no possibility of a chilling effect. Cases where newspaper people go undercover are a good example. If the source doesn't know he is talking to a reporter, then nothing he believes about the reporter's role can have any kind of effect, chilling or otherwise. Yet, even in undercover cases such as the *Chicago Sun Times*'s famous Mirage Bar operation, where reporters ran a bar in order to observe corrupt city inspectors, newspapers and broadcast media reflexively resist providing evidence when no chilling effect would result from doing so. Again, the slippery-slope argument is invoked—the claim that any instance of cooperation would be the first line in a long chain of events that would ultimately undermine the neutrality and independence of the media.

Leonard Downie, the managing editor of the *Washington Post,* paints a troubling scenario toward the bottom of that slippery slope. Individual instances of newspaper cooperation with law enforcement authorities could, he argues, add up to a public perception that the newspaper is a part of the law enforcement process. This could be true even if no single instance creates a practical chill. If news sources start to equate reporters with cops, they will stop talking. Downie told a meeting of Wisconsin newspaper people in 1984, "The *Post* refuses to cooperate with law enforcement authorities when they request or even when they subpoena testimony, photographs, notes, or documents from our reporters because we strongly believe a free press should not be an arm of the law."[7]

This stance is based less on eternal principle than on the kinds of situations that news people often faced in the 1960s and 1970s, when civil rights demonstrations and antiwar protests were major news. Many of the protesters used civil disobedience as a tactic, and repressive law enforcement was a common countertactic. Police officers were no longer automatically perceived as the good guys, as they had been in the past. Covering those movements, getting those viewpoints heard, was of overriding importance to journalists, and the tradition of cooperation between reporters and policemen was set aside. But the new tradition carried problems of its own, particularly when it was overgeneralized.

In the *Dallas Morning News* case, the photographer finally agreed to testify, but he balked at supplying photos that had not been printed in the paper. He would not even look at the photographs to refresh his memory. Some witnesses claimed that the defendant had chained herself in a doorway. She claimed she had not. The photographer said he couldn't be sure whether she was chained in the doorway, and he admitted that looking at his own photos might refresh his memory. But he refused to do so.

In general, the courts have had very little sympathy with these far-flung extensions of the chilling-effect argument. That newspapers keep fighting anyway suggests that they are being bad legal tacticians. It is never wise to press for a final decision on a legal point that you are going to lose: far better to preserve any ambiguity that might exist in the absence of a final decision. This was particularly true when the Supreme Court under Chief Justice Warren Burger had made a number of rulings against the press and, in the opinion of some observers, had gone out of its way to reach down for and examine lower court rulings that favor the press. If newspapers were truly interested in preserving their First Amendment privileges, they would try to dodge as many contests as possible, postponing final resolution until a more sympathetic majority is created among the nine justices. Sophisticated civil rights groups are very choosy about the issues they attack. They have sometimes—even in cases involving capital punishment—chosen to let an adverse ruling in a state court stand rather than take it to the Burger Court and risk losing and having that rule given national scope. The news media, in contrast, sometimes appear eager to strike out in all directions, litigating everything, even when it is clear that there is a high risk that more antipress decisions will be written into the record.

ARGUMENTS FOR PRESS PRIVILEGE BEYOND THE FIRST AMENDMENT

News people are not stupid, so some reasons other than refining and enhancing First Amendment law must lie behind their dogged refusals to testify. Indeed, there *are* other interests, more immediate and less noble, that journalists are protecting.

Inconvenience and Expense

One of their concerns is the sheer inconvenience and expense of having to provide evidence. By fighting subpoenas at every turn, they raise the cost to litigants of relying on evidence generated by news people— thereby, ironically, imposing a chilling effect of their own. In any community, a newspaper is just one of many power centers, and its place in the pecking order may depend on how it responds to what outsiders may consider perfectly reasonable requests. Perhaps to be free, strong, and independent, it has to be prickly as well. Yet if the newspaper were truly strong, perhaps it could afford to be more routinely helpful.

Ideally, a newspaper is seen as an honest and neutral chronicler of fact. Its agents would therefore be ideal witnesses because they would be readily believed. And because reporters and photographers always go where the interesting things are happening, they tend to be in those places where litigation arises. If there are 50 witnesses to a crime and one happens to be a newspaper reporter, the prosecutor may find it more convenient to call the reporter than any of the other 49. The reporter is easy to identify, is a trained observer, and is easy to track down. If newspapers did not routinely fight subpoenas, bearing witness in criminal and civil litigation would become a heavy overhead cost— one that they are not prepared to bear and for which they are not compensated.

Some editors make this argument without ever mentioning the First Amendment, and one has to admire their straightforwardness. An economic problem is more amenable to solution than one based on abstract principle. The case of newspaper clipping files or morgues suggests a precedent. Typically, newspapers have barred the public from their files simply because of the inconvenience and expense of maintaining a system accessible to the public. But with newspaper libraries converting to electronic data bases, the possibility suddenly exists of making money from lawyers, businesses, and members of the general public by providing nonintrusive access to those libraries. Some newspapers are following the example of the *Toronto Globe & Mail* and making their morgues available to the public on a fee-for-use basis.

Expert witnesses in civil cases sometimes command fees of $1000 a day or more. If newspapers could work out a way to charge for the time their staff members spend on the witness stand, if testifying were to become part of the revenue stream instead of a nuisance, some pressures on the First Amendment might disappear. But first, news people would have to discuss the issue frankly as a nuisance or as an economic problem, rather than package it in the First Amendment.

Emotional Reasons for Refusing to Testify

Once we set aside the First Amendment argument and look for practical considerations behind the reluctance of newspaper people to be witnesses in court, a number of others appear. An investigative reporter shares some of the methodology of the confidence artist, blind-siding sources with soothing talk, giving subtle psychological rewards for cooperation. A *Washington Post* editor's account of Tofani's method reveals an excellent example. As the editor described the process, Tofani

> warmed them up with softball questions. . . . She knew when to back off
> if she felt like her source was getting uncomfortable. . . . Then at some

point she would usually ask what Francis Bacon called 'the bold, unex-
pected question that lays a man open.' You wait for a time when they're
not expecting anything, then ask it point blank and 50 percent of the time
you're going to get an answer that amazes you.[8]

This makes it sound as if a reporter *likes* to "lay a man open" with
unseemly zest. But reporters are human, they have some humane reservations about such manipulative behavior, and they have ways of
dealing with these reservation. When a source is rendered vulnerable
in this way, a news person feels a moral responsibility to do no unnecessary harm, to get the facts as gently as possible, and to remain on as
good terms with the source as the circumstances will permit. In such a
situation, the reporter truly wants to believe that the information being
coaxed from the source will not bring the source undue harm. This is
perhaps a necessary side effect of the rapport that arises in the coaxing
process. For the confidence man, part of the swindling process is "cool-
ing out the mark," leaving the swindled person feeling as good and as
philosophical about being victimized as possible. This process has the
twin functions of assuaging the swindler's guilt and reducing the mark's
motivation for retribution. Reporters are not swindlers, but there are
some parallels in their relationships with sources. And to testify in court
against someone whom one has already manipulated and exposed to
painful publicity may seem unconscionable at worst and unpleasant at
best. The reporter's feeling that he or she should not be forced to do a
law enforcement agency's job is a very understandable and strongly felt
one. But it may be pushing the First Amendment too far to use it to
relieve reporters of such emotional burdens that go with the job.

Reluctance to Help Public Officials Get Off the Hook

There is yet another reason for the reluctance of news people to be
party to legal proceedings related to their investigative work. When a
newspaper uncovers specific instances of wrongdoing, it is often using
those cases to illuminate a more general problem. But public officials
will often ignore the general problem and respond to the illustrative
cases as though they were isolated incidents. In addition, these officials
sometimes behave as though they are more interested in punishing the
reporter for revealing the problem than they are in eliminating its causes,
and the main function of the subpoena is a punitive one.

In the Tofani case, it was perfectly clear that a general and ongoing
problem had been aired by the *Post* series. Nevertheless, according to

Downie, the grand jury went after only the people named by the reporter, not anybody else. The true moral of the story, that a reporter could walk in from outside and document a situation that had been ignored by officials inside the system, was lost amid the flurry of official attention to the specific instances. A reporter can't be blamed for not wanting to be a party to that kind of misdirection.

Tofani and her editors had a right to feel resentful. But not even justified resentment over the self-interested maneuverings of public officials is enough to make a First Amendment case. Overuse, particularly ineffectual use, can damage the First Amendment. To understand its particular fragility, we need to examine some other uses of the preferential arguments.

PRESS PRIVILEGE AND THE ISSUE OF PRIOR RESTRAINT

As we saw earlier, the preferred-position theory says that when First Amendment rights conflict with other constitutional guarantees, the First Amendment takes priority. It has been further argued that because freedom of speech and freedom of the press are mentioned separately in the Bill of Rights, the authors of the Constitution meant the press to receive special consideration. The latter argument has been received with even less sympathy than the former. And the question of just what the First Amendment basically protects remains to be resolved. Judicial precedents have given the amendment three levels of meaning, with decreasing levels of absolutism. At the most absolute level, the First Amendment means that there can be no prior censorship of the press. This tradition is rooted in English common law and was well known by 1787, the year of the Constitutional Convention. Sir William Blackstone, in his influential *Commentaries,* wrote: "Every freeman has an undoubted right to lay what sentiments he pleases before the public; to forbid this is to destroy the freedom of the press; but if he publishes what is improper, mischievous and illegal, he must take the consequences of his own temerity."[9]

But recent court cases have held that not even prior censorship is absolutely forbidden. In 1971 the *New York Times* was blocked from publishing Neil Sheehan's reports on the Pentagon Papers for 15 days until it received a go-ahead from a divided Supreme Court. In 1979 *Progressive* magazine was restrained for six months from publishing an article that the government said contained information that could be useful in constructing a hydrogen bomb. The government relented after another publication released the same information.[10]

There remains, however, a strong presumption against prior restraint. Other sanctions may chill free speech, the Supreme Court said in 1976, but censorship "freezes" it.

At the second level of restriction, it is claimed that the First Amendment prevents newspapers from being punished for whatever they print. And at the third level, the amendment is held to prevent any government interference with the editorial process—that is, with the activities of reporters and editors in gathering the news. It is at these two levels that exceptions are most often found and the issue of a chilling effect on free expression is most often raised. Among the exceptions are issues of obscenity, invasion of privacy, subversion, and—by far the most troublesome—libel.

The power of a civil litigant to collect damages for libel represents a very old form of restraint against freedom of speech and the press. A libel is publication that defames or damages the good name or reputation of someone. The main defense is also old: if you publish the truth *and* can prove it, nobody can collect libel damages from you. In 1964 the Supreme Court under Chief Justice Earl Warren handed the newspapers what appeared to be a marvelous gift in the form of a brand new and easier kind of protection. Recognizing the need in a democracy for "uninhibited, robust, and wide-open" debate about matters of public concern, it laid down tough new rules for public figures hoping to chill newspaper coverage through libel actions. The Court's ruling, in *New York Times Co.* v. *Sullivan,* removed from the newspaper the burden of proving the truth of what it had said and instead placed on the plaintiff the burden of proving that the newspaper had printed a falsehood with "actual malice," meaning that it had done so in the knowledge that the statement was false or "with reckless disregard of whether it was false or not."

This ruling removed some inhibitions from newspaper and broadcast reporting, and it helped news organizations become more aggressive in their investigative reporting where public figures were concerned. And how do you think newspapers reacted? Did they receive this gift with appropriate grace and humility, or did they scream for even more concessions from the Court? You guessed it. It's hard to be a humble journalist. When the *Sullivan* rule shifted the burden of proof from the news writer to the news maker, it gave the press a degree of freedom never enjoyed before, but a new set of burdens was part of that package. If plaintiffs were forced to prove knowing and reckless falsehood to win a case, they had to have some means of getting at the facts. And how do you prove that a reporter knew he or she was telling a falsehood? You can't read the reporter's mind, but you can ask the reporter to tell under oath what he or she was thinking about and what was in his or her notes and what was said in staff conversations about the story in question. In 1979 the Burger Court ruled that a libel plaintiff could inquire into the editorial process to ask such questions about a reporter's state of mind when the alleged libel was written.[11] Such a ruling follows logically enough from the *Sullivan* case, and by itself it seems a reasonable price to pay for the great extension of editorial freedom that the *Sullivan* ruling provided. But the news people's reaction was more than shrill—it was hysterical.

Some editorial writers said the Court had reversed the *Sullivan* ruling. Some said newspapers could not function without a special privilege to protect them from such inquiries. One even said that truth would no longer be a defense in libel suits. Associate Justice William Brennan, Jr., a champion of a free press and a partial dissenter on the Burger Court's ruling, was appalled. Invited to give a speech at the dedication of the S.I. Newhouse Center for Law and Justice at Rutgers University on October 17, 1979, he used the occasion to urge the press to abandon the absolutist tack and face the real world.

"This may involve a certain loss of innocence," he said, "a certain recognition that the press, like other institutions, must accommodate a variety of important social interests. But the sad complexity of our society makes this inevitable, and there is no alternative but a shrill and impotent isolation."[12]

One can argue—and some newspaper people do—that a shrill, nagging, tireless, always adversarial response is the only way to hold the forces of restriction and oppression at bay. Give an inch on the smallest point, in their view, and you start tumbling down the slippery slope toward the bottomless pit of regimented expression. Brennan's point was that such a rigid policy is bad legal strategy. If you raise every argument you can think of, the unsound along with the sound, the sound will go unnoticed amid all the noise. And, legal stratagems aside, the strategy is impossible to defend from an ethical point of view because it depends on a selfish insistence that journalists are so special as to require freedom from the inconveniences that civic duty imposes on ordinary people. This is a lonely and precarious position.

It is also ineffective. Journalists have not been successful in convincing the courts or the public that they should have such privileges, even though they have produced some impressive anecdotal evidence of the existence of chilling effects. The most efficient and effective way for journalists to improve the free flow of information may be to clean up some of their own bad habits—as the *Washington Post* did when Loretta Tofani demonstrated that even difficult sources can be put on the record. Tofani accomplished that with hard work, building her information from the outside in, talking to the most cooperative sources, defense lawyers first, then judges, prison guards, medical workers, and victims. Only when she knew what had happened and when it happened did she talk to the prison rapists. Seeing how much she knew already, they gave the details without any promise of confidentiality from her. In her case, the Pulitzer Prize was well earned.

Fighting to uphold claims of privileged status is also hard work, and it isn't getting the press very far. News people might be better off if they abandoned their claims of privilege and cast their lot with the general public, fighting for their rights as public rights, not for recognition as a privileged class. They might feel better about themselves, too.

NOTES

1. *Ex Parte Randy Eli Grothe,* in the Court of Criminal Appeals of Texas. Application for writ of habeas corpus denied July 1984.

2. See John Herman Randall, Jr., *The Making of the Modern Mind* (Boston: Houghton Mifflin, 1940).

3. Quoted in Bernard Bailyn, *The Ideological Origins of the American Revolution* (Cambridge, Mass: Harvard University Press, 1967).

4. Justice Stone's footnote may be found in *United States* v. *Carolene Products,* 1938.

5. David Shaw, *Press Watch* (New York: Macmillan, 1984).

6. *Public Opinion,* 1920.

7. Leonard Downie, remarks made at a seminar held by the Wisconsin Newspaper Association at Madison on March 15, 1984.

8. Tofani's reporting methods are described by Virginia Holcomb in "Surviving the Long Haul," *The Quill,* June 1984, p. 38.

9. Quoted in Edward S. Corwin, *The Constitution and What It Means Today* (New York: Atheneum, 1963).

10. *New York Times Co.* v. *United States,* 1971; *Nebraska Press Association* v. *Stuart,* 1976; *United States* v. *Progressive,* 1979.

11. *Herbert* v. *Lando,* 1979.

12. Quoted in *Editor & Publisher,* October 27, 1979.

DISCUSSION QUESTIONS

1. What does Parent mean by "privacy"? What does she mean by the related notions of "personal information" and "documented" facts? Does Parent regard personal information merely kept on file for specific purposes (for example, health records) as being "documented," and, therefore, as an invasion of privacy? Why or why not?

2. Parent argues that a reporter who published previously published personal information about somebody would not be invading that person's privacy. Why does she maintain this? Do you agree with her? Defend your answer.

3. Parent rejects three alternative definitions of privacy. They are: (1) privacy consists of being let alone; (2) privacy consists of a form of autonomy or control over significant personal matters; (3) privacy is the limitation on access to the self. What are Parent's main reasons for rejecting each of these definitions as the core meaning of privacy? Do you agree with each of her reasons for rejecting these definitions? In what ways, if any, are each of these three senses of privacy nevertheless relevant to the practice of journalism?

4. What, according to Parent, makes privacy (as she has defined it) an important human value?

5. Parent provides six criteria of "wrongful invasion" of privacy. Provide some illustrations of how journalists could, in practice, violate one or more of these standards. (Your examples may come from actual or hypothetical cases.) In each case that you cite, discuss the question of whether the violation would constitute a "wrongful" invasion.

6. What criticisms, if any, do you have of Parent's criteria of "wrongful invasion" of privacy as they relate to journalistic practice? Defend your answer.

7. Suppose a local newspaper printed the names of several persons who were allegedly found guilty of having committed misdemeanors. However, suppose one such individual on the list was not found guilty of any such offense so that the newspaper was in error. According to Parent, would this individual be justified in bringing a law suit against the newspaper for invasion of privacy?

8. Parent mentions that in one legal case (*Cox Broadcasting Co.* v. *Cohn*) a newspaper published the name of a rape victim. According to Parent, could the newspaper be justly sued for invasion of privacy? Do you agree with her? defend your answer.

9. Parent cites Warren and Brandeis as stating that "to publish of a modest and retiring individual that he suffers from an impediment of his speech or that he cannot spell correctly is an unwarranted, if not unexampled, infringement upon his privacy, while to state and comment on the same characteristic found in a would-be congressman would not be regarded as beyond the pale of propriety." Do you agree with the latter? In general, is the right to privacy stronger in the case of private individuals than in the case of public officials? Defend your answers.

10. Discuss the relevance of the First Amendment to reporters' refusal to disclose information about their sources.

11. What is the "preferred-position theory" and what bearing does this theory have on journalists' refusal to testify in criminal cases? Do you agree with this theory? Defend your answer.

12. What is meant by a "chilling effect"? What is "the slippery-slope problem"? How, according to Meyer, have some journalists used the slippery-slope problem to justify refusal to disclose information about their sources even in cases (such as the Texas case discussed by Meyer) in which there is no apparent "chilling effect"? Do you agree with these journalists? Defend your answer.

13. What other "practical" reasons, beyond the appeal to the First Amendment, does Meyer think journalists have for refusing to testify in court? Meyer suggests that journalists would be better off if they used these "practical" reasons, rather than "overusing" the First Amendment, as their rationale for refusing to testify. Do you agree with him? Defend your answer.

14. Meyer argues that journalists' absolute stand against testifying in court has been ineffective in convincing the courts that they should have such a privilege. What evidence does Meyer present for this claim?

15. Referring to journalists' absolute stand against testifying in court, Meyers states that "legal stratagems aside, the strategy is impossible to defend from an ethical point of view because it depends on a selfish insistence that journalists are so special as to require freedom from the inconveniences that civic duty imposes on ordinary people." Do you agree with Meyer? Are these journalists being "selfish"? Defend your answer.

16. In your opinion, what *ethical* reason(s), if any, exists for journalists' refusal to testify in court? Does this reason(s) support an *absolute* privilege to refuse (that is, one that is binding in *all* circumstances)? Defend your answers.

5

Political Power and the Media

Few would deny that the role of the media in a society committed to democracy is a central one. However, it is a less settled matter as to the nature of that role in regard to the formation of public policy. For instance, are the media primarily *passive* instruments through which the public is kept informed about government activities? On the other hand, are the media themselves a vital and *active* force in determining those activities? Moreover, if the media do have the power to determine public policy, what implications does this have for a democracy? Finally, what power can the mere *belief* in the power of the media to shape public policy have on the shaping of public policy? In this chapter, these questions will be investigated.

In the first selection, entitled "The Role of the Media in Shaping Public Policy: The Myth of Power and the Power of Myth," Charles Green examines the role of the media regarding public policy from 1964 through 1984. For example, Green explicitly addresses the role of the media in the early civil rights movement, the Vietnam War, "The War on Poverty," and Watergate.

Green argues that the media's role regarding public policy is analogous to that of an amplifier or public address system which "may increase the range of power of the speaker's words, but . . . has no control over what goes into it." That is, while the media has the power to choose which facts to promulgate, it is not the artificer of those facts—even if it sometimes helps to expose them. For example, in response to the argument that it was the media that drove Nixon from office, he rejoins that "the truth hounded Nixon from office. The media merely reported the truth."

Nevertheless, Green maintains that the actual power of the media in terms of its ability to set the public agenda (that is, the power to choose which facts are to be promulgated) can be considerable. For example, he states that "if every Israeli misdeed is to be analyzed in exhaustive detail and every atrocity of its most bitter foes is to be overlooked, it can be safely predicted that ultimately the U.S.–Israeli 'special relationship' will be undermined." Still, he contends that the media "in general do a fair job of setting that public agenda" especially since much of this agenda actually comes from "small journals of opinion" as well as liberal and conservative "think tanks" which serve to keep "the critical issues" from being neglected. The *actual* power of the media to shape public policy is, therefore, on this line of thinking, overrated.

However, according to Green, there is also power in the *perception* of power and "an enduring myth takes on a kind of reality of its own. . . . while the media's power in public policy is both misunderstood and overrated, the very fact that politicians and others themselves tend to believe in it tends to reinforce it." On this line of argument, the "myth" of the power of the media to influence public policy can itself influence public policy: If politicians believe in this myth, they may adjust their conduct according to their belief.

Nevertheless, Green's suggestion that it is the myth of the power of the media, and not the media itself, which has the power to influence public policy presupposes that such a power is, indeed, just a myth. This premise, however, may require more justification than that which Green himself provides. First, as mentioned earlier, Green does allow that the media has the power of agenda setting, which, by his own admission, can, at least in principle, negatively affect public policy. Second, Green's optimism that the media "in general do a fair job of setting that public agenda" appears to rest largely on his confidence in "small journals of opinion" and "think tanks" to keep the media's agenda focused upon "the crucial issues." However, it is far from clear how the readership of the latter media sources, which is relatively small, can generally offset any broader media tendency across a wider readership. For example, regardless of what the Brookings Institution may be saying about certain tension in the Middle East, a wider audience will most likely hear what CBS is saying. Third, Green assumes that there are "crucial issues" upon which an accurate portrayal of the news depends. However, what the media may regard as "crucial" may be colored by its own interests and values regarding public policy issues.

Finally, in arguing that the media is ordinarily passive in its "reporting" of the truth, Green fails to address the view of the media as *interpreters* of fact. Indeed, as will be discussed in the following chapter, the role of the reporter as a neutral messenger of "the facts" may itself be called into question.

In the second selection, "Network News Coverage of the Presidency:

Implications for Democracy," Fred Smoller calls into question Green's contention that the power of the media to influence public policy is just a myth. In particular, he argues that extensive television network news coverage of the presidency—"The Six O'Clock Presidency"—has contributed to a trend of declining public support for U.S. presidents, which, in turn, has had serious negative effects upon presidential policies and decisions, and upon democracy itself.

According to Smoller, largely due to the ease and inexpensiveness of covering the White House, presidents receive extensive network news coverage. However, this coverage, he maintains, is "organizationally slanted" against the Office of the Presidency, resulting in a negative image of a president regardless of his performance. According to Smoller, such factors as the brevity of television evening news items and the selective use of pictures (for example, Gerald Ford stumbling or bumping his head) inevitably contribute to an oversimplified and distorted view of the presidency.

Smoller contends that "The Six O'Clock Presidency" has serious negative effects upon the presidency and upon democracy. In particular, he argues that it leads to "the decline in residual public support for the Office and the political system"; to presidential ineffectiveness; to preoccupation of presidents with their public image; to abuses of public office; and to unnecessary and dangerous risks taken by presidents in order to secure a place for themselves in history.

Green's idea of the power of myth may, however, call into question the actual power of the media to produce negative results such as those mentioned above. According to this line of argument, it is not the media which lead a president to act rashly and unwisely, or to be preoccupied with his public image, but rather his own *perception* (or *mis*perception) that the media will otherwise portray him unfavorably. Paradoxically, when the media then report such presidential indiscretion, it is the media that are blamed for the president's subsequent loss of public support.

Conversely, Smoller's view of the power of network news to negatively affect the presidency may also call into question Green's commitment to the mythical status of such power. Nevertheless, Green does not share Smoller's skepticism about the ability of a president to withstand a negative media image. For example, Green states, "the power to stereotype and to ridicule has a potent effect on the course of public policy. Once again, however, a media image need not in itself be decisive to a politician who carefully tends his base. Jesse Helms has certainly received a generous dose of such treatment, yet he succeeded in his 1984 race for Senate reelection."

For Green, a politician who does his job well ("carefully tends his base") presumably has less reason to fear the media than one who does not. According to this line, Nixon's distrust of the media was warranted due to his own incompetence in executing his presidential duties, and not because of any inherent power of the media to destroy public support for presidents irrespective of their performances. Again, Green is here assuming that the media generally do a "fair job in setting the public agenda" and that they are primarily passive in their role in "reporting the truth." However, for Smoller, who apparently does not share these two (optimistic) media assumptions, the case is otherwise.

Smoller prefers that the extensive media coverage of the presidency be relaxed in order to guard against harmful social consequences. He sees the latter measure as offering some protection against the erosion of democracy. On the other hand, for those who share Green's outlook, the prosperity of democracy may require keeping such "watchdog" powers of the media intact. These latter individuals are, perhaps, more apt to see events like those in the unfolding of Watergate as signs of democracy at work, rather than as signs of its erosion.

The Role of the Media in Shaping Public Policy: The Myth of Power and the Power of Myth

CHARLES GREEN

"The role of the media in shaping public policy: 1964 to 1984" is, of course, an impossibly broad subject. It ranges from the flowering of the civil rights movement through the Vietnam War to the "Me Generation" era, and spans five presidents. There's an old author's trick that says when you're faced with an impossibly broad subject, the only safe course is to expand it still further. Thus, let's begin on 18 December 1917 by quoting a famous article published on that date in the *New York Evening Mail:*

A NEGLECTED ANNIVERSARY

On December 20 there flitted past us, absolutely without public notice, one of the most important profane anniversaries in American history—to wit: the seventy-fifth anniversary of the introduction of the bathtub into these states.... Bathtubs are so common today that it is almost impossible to imagine a world without them ... and yet the first American Bathtub was installed and dedicated so recently as December 20, 1842.

Curiously enough, the scene of its setting up was Cincinnati, [by] Adam Thompson.... [His] trade frequently took him to England, and in that country, during the 1830s, he acquired the habit of bathing.

The bathtub was then still a novelty in England. It had been introduced in 1828 by Lord John Russell and its use was yet confined to a small class of enthusiasts.

Moreover, the English bathtub, then as now, was a puny and inconvenient contrivance—little more, in fact, than a glorified dishpan—and filling and emptying required the attendance of a servant. Taking a bath, indeed, was a rather heavy ceremony, and Lord John in 1835 was said to be the only man in England who had yet come to doing it every day.

Thompson, who was of inventive fancy ... conceived the notion that the English bathtub would be much improved if it were made large enough to admit the whole body of an adult man, and if its supply of water, instead

131

of being hauled to the scene by a maid, were admitted by pipes from a central reservoir and run off by the same means. Accordingly, early in 1842 he set about building the first American bathroom in his Cincinnati home.

. . . In this luxurious tub Thompson took two baths on December 20, 1842—a cold one at 8 A.M. and a warm one some time during the afternoon. The warm water, heated by the kitchen fire, reached a temperature of 105 degrees. On Christmas day, having a party of gentlemen to dinner, he exhibited the new marvel to them and gave an exhibition of its use, and four of them, including a French visitor, Col. Duchanel, risked plunges into it. The next day all Cincinnati . . . had heard of it, and the local newspapers described it at length and opened their columns to violent discussions of it.

The thing, in fact, became a public matter, and before long there was bitter and double-headed opposition to the new invention.

. . . The noise of the controversy soon reached other cities, and in more than one place medical opposition reached such strength that it was reflected in legislation. Late in 1843, for example, the Philadelphia common considered an ordinance prohibiting bathing between November 1 and March 15, and it failed of passage by but two votes. . . .

. . . Dr. Oliver Wendell Holmes declared for the bathtub and vigorously opposed the lingering movement against it. . . . The American Medical Association held its annual meeting in Boston in 1859 and a poll of the members in attendance showed that nearly 55 percent of them now regarded bathing as harmless and that more than 20 percent advocated it as beneficial. At its meeting in 1850 a resolution was formally passed giving the imprimatur of the faculty to the bathtub. . . .

But it was the example of President Millard Fillmore that, even more than the grudging medical approval, gave the bathtub recognition and respectability in the United States . . . on succeeding to the presidency at Taylor's death, July 9, 1850, he instructed his secretary of war, Gen. Charles M. Conrad, to invite tenders for the construction of a bathtub in the White House. . . . This was installed early in 1851.[1]

Most of us are already familiar with most of these "facts" that were a staple of newspaper features and fillers for more than a half-century. Most of us also know that each "fact" was a total fraud generated by the beguiling mind of the article's author, H. L. Mencken.

As Mencken himself confessed in a 23 May 1926 article, his tongue-in-cheek article, buttressed by its rich if imaginary detail, lodged itself deeply in the popular culture:

It was reprinted by various great organs of the enlightenment. . . . Pretty soon I began to encounter my preposterous "facts" in the writing of other men. They began to be used by chiropractors and other such quacks as evidence of the stupidity of medical men. They began to be cited by medical men as proof of the progress of public hygiene. They got into learned journals. They were alluded to on the floor of Congress. . . . Finally, I began to find them in standard works of reference. . . .

I recite this history not because it is singular, but because it is typical. It is out of just such frauds, I believe, that most of the so-called knowledge of humanity flows. What begins as a guess—or, perhaps, not infrequently, as a downright and deliberate lie—ends as a fact and is embalmed in the history books.

As a practicing journalist for many years, I have often had close contact with history in the making. I can recall no time or place when what actually occurred was afterward generally known and believed. Sometimes a part of the truth got out, but never all.[2]

Mencken's article is a legend among journalists precisely because it illustrates the staying power of misunderstanding—as well as the chronic inability of corrections to catch up with error, whether deliberate or inadvertent. Let a story contain an erroneous assertion and it will be faithfully clipped and filed in newspaper morgues and public libraries throughout the country—from which it is resurrected by diligent researchers and incorporated anew into more articles, which in turn are filed away to await a new generation of researchers. The correction, or in more serious cases the debunking article, seems in contrast always destined to lie below the fold under someone's birdcage, its nagging presence unseen, unwanted, and unquoted.

It's worth remembering Mencken's hoax today for reasons that go beyond comic relief. Today's media myths have lost none of their power to endure, although they often today assume less amusing forms. Today the prevalent myth is of the Imperial Media, an awesome force that somehow bestride the republic like a colossus, working their will and whim upon a passive populace.

I do not deny that the news media collectively played an important, even a vital role in the unfolding of public policy in the last two decades. But however important that role was, I suggest it was also primarily though not wholly passive. How can we be both powerful and passive? You need look no further than the nearest public address system for an analogy. The amplifier may increase the range of power of the speaker's words, but it has no control over what goes into it.

In a nutshell, we did our job, and generally, we did it very well. We recorded and sometimes catalyzed the great events of these two decades. But we did not cut them from whole cloth.

Let's begin with the most obvious myth, one that even sometimes finds adherents within the communications industry itself: that the news media drove President Richard Nixon from office. This is no place to recount in detail the sordid history of Watergate. But the belief that the news media were somehow the decisive actors in the events that by and large they faithfully recorded flourishes with a strength directly proportional to the believer's misunderstanding of the constitutional process.

It was, after all, federal judge John Sirica who struck the first decisive blow against the Watergate cover-up by sentencing the original burglary defendants to long prison sentences, then commuting them when they broke their conspiracy of silence about the instigators of their squalid caper. The next great acts were the hearings of the House and Senate judiciary committees. While these televised hearings made folk heros of the likes of Senator Sam Ervin and Representative Elizabeth Holtzman, they were not media events devoid of a broader power. They were acts of the most profound constitutional meaning, which the media were privileged to attend and report.

Finally, the U.S. Supreme Court cast the decisive blow by unanimously ruling against President Nixon on the question of the tapes. That set off the final act in this drama in which two of the coequal branches of the federal government, Congress and the judiciary, exercised their classic "checks and balances" role to terminate an unlawful act within the executive branch.

Admittedly, this is one occasion where the notion that the media's role is primarily passive seems contradicted by their own exertions. Obviously, the *Washington Post* exposed many of the early lies with which the White House had tried to sweep the burglary and cover-up under the rug. *Time* magazine and the *New York Times* reported on the wiretapping. The *Baltimore Sun* unearthed irregularities within the Internal Revenue Service. The Dita Beard–ITT connection received considerable attention in our own *Denver Post,* among other outlets. The television networks, while plowing little new ground themselves, did keep the nation's attention riveted on the unfolding events.

But all this activity only highlights the true power of the much-misunderstood "power of the press" on major public policy issues. The media do have power to focus public attention on a problem, to put a subject on the national agenda. But this is distinctly not a power to punish the wicked or to reward the just, save for what good or ill feeling the subjects of a story may privately derive from it. Such punishment or reward must come from other persons and institutions making their independent judgment upon those media revelations. We do not indict, we do not acquit. Newsrooms do not write laws, and paperboys do not enforce them.

Thus it is simply silly to say the media hounded Nixon from office. That gives us far too much credit. The truth hounded Nixon from office. The media merely reported the truth. Congress did not grovel before the pens of outraged editorial writers. It acted because its own investigations, however much they may have been spurred by media revelations, had stirred its own outrage.

The story of the news media and public policy throughout the rest of the 1964–1984 period is much the same—as indeed it was for centuries before and will doubtless be for generations to come. Our power, and it is a great one, is basically the power to put an issue on the public agenda. We are not the sole possessors of that power. But even when we do not initiate the discussion of an item on the public agenda, our decisions as to the reporting of that item can greatly shape its direction, amplifying or diminishing its importance.

That becomes clear if we turn back to the beginning of the era in question, when the great civil rights movement was stirring. The media did not instigate its seminal protest, the Montgomery bus boycott. That began when a black woman, Rosa Parks, had had enough of indignity one day and refused to move to the back of a bus. The media merely reacted, rather laggardly when one considers the scope and duration of the underlying social policies, to a great event already unfolding.

The institution most responsible for putting the question of black dignity on the national agenda was one with which we share the first amendment, the church. Beginning with black religious leaders such as the Reverend Martin Luther King but swiftly spreading to those of white Christian and Jewish groups, ministers and rabbis began denouncing a system of laws and customs violently at war with our Judeo-Christian tradition.

Obviously, the coverage in print and on television of the protests at Selma, Birmingham, and Ole Miss, of such martyrdoms as those of Goodman, Chaney, and Schwerner, and above all the impassioned dignity of King helped arouse the conscience of the American people.

But it's worth noting again that our role was essentially passive. However strongly we might sympathize editorially with their goals and however far we might spread their words, we did not create the Selma marchers. Moreover, victory was theirs only after the other great institutions of American public opinion—the church, the academy, business, labor unions, and political parties—had weighed their message, found it just, and marched by their side.

In debunking the myth that the media exercise awesome power in public affairs, I do not wish to belittle the role we do play. But it is quite clear that however effectively we may serve as amplifiers, and occasionally as catalysts, we are generally not leading actors in the dramas we report and have very little power to determine their outcome.

The contrast between the power to focus public attention on an issue and the power to influence the outcome of the resulting political process is vividly apparent in the very different outcomes of the black civil rights movement and the similar quest a decade later by homosexuals for equal rights. It can be argued that the media gave comparable and fairly respectful coverage to the demands of gay and lesbian leaders. But with the exception of a few scattered local ordinances, homosexuals have had much more limited success in changing their standing in either the law or public opinion than blacks did. In the latter case, our reporting and commentary have simply not convinced the other opinion-molding institutions of society or the public at large to embrace the gay cause. The media can lead the public policy horse to water, but we can't make it drink.

Oddly, the myth that the media somehow determine the outcome of the public agenda hides and obscures just how great our real power is in terms of forming that agenda itself. The power to put an item on the public agenda—or to keep it off—is more than enough power for any one institution in a free society.

Mussolini once mused, "If you give me the power to nominate, you can vote for whomever you please." We similarly tell our readers that we can't tell them what to think. But we have a great deal of influence in deciding what they think or don't think about.

That power is at its most absolute when exercised in the negative. Every day in the newsrooms of print and broadcast media in this country thousands of stories come in begging for a few seconds of airtime or a few inches of print. We select only a small fraction of them. You may disagree vigorously with the opinions or purported facts we do present— but you have little means of knowing about the more numerous items we did not transmit. The latter may well have been the more critical.

As a very simple example, consider the coverage given to the massacre of Moslem refugees in Beirut by Christian Phalangists. Much criticism was vented upon Israel for not acting more decisively to prevent such slaughter. The day the Israelis released their own official report on the massacre—one that sharply criticized their own government for its in-direct complicity—our wire services at the *Post* bulged with nearly seventy different accounts of that report.

I don't think we really need to write editorials and columns saying that the Beirut massacres were bad. People in general don't like massacres and if the question, "Should we stop massacres in Beirut?" is put on the public agenda, then the answer is inevitable. But why was there no similar outcry over the massacres at Ad Judayl or Hama?

Ad Judayl is—or more precisely, was—a town in Iraq where, on July 11, 1982, someone made an assassination attempt on Iraqi dictator Saddam Hussein. According to a five-inch article in the London magazine *The Economist* five months later, Hussein responded much as Hitler did in destroying the village of Lidice, Czechoslovakia, after the assassination of Reinhard Heydrich.

The British newsmagazine reported: "There were about 150 casualties in the two hours of fighting that followed the attempted assassination. After that, 150 families simply disappeared. The remaining men were sent off to northern Iraq, the women and children were sent south. Bulldozers then demolished the town."

A check of *Post* wire services and a computerized data-base search of American newspapers and magazines produced absolutely nothing about this event. We did base an editorial on the *Economist* article and what little we were able to learn from our own independent sources about the Ad Judayl massacre. But it is clear that the general decision to regard the massacre in Iraq as non-news and the massacre in Beirut as news had a profound effect on U.S. foreign policy in the region.

Little more attention was given in American media to a far worse massacre in Hama, a city in Syria where the Moslem Brotherhood had mobilized opposition to the rule of Hafez Assad. Assad surrounded the city with troops and opened fire with artillery rather indiscriminately. Reports that reached us through Japanese newspapers later indicated that between 5,000 and 10,000 people died—mostly innocent people caught in the crossfire. Yet U.S. media paid very little attention to the event.

Such events are not suppressed as a result of a conscious conspiracy. But they do reflect a sense of what journalists think is important in selecting items for the public agenda, and those choices do influence the outcome of public policy. If every Israeli misdeed is to be analyzed in exhaustive detail and every atrocity of its most bitter foes is to be overlooked, it can be safely predicted that ultimately the U.S.–Israeli "special relationship" will be undermined.

Paradoxically, it is the fairly open societies, such as Israel, that receive the often unwelcome microscopic examination. Reporters can get into the country, talk to victims and survivors, film with only a minimum of censorship, and report in voluminous detail. Contrast that to the fact that it took five months for even the most minimum account of the Ad Judayl massacre to leak out of the tightly closed Iraqi society. When such facts do emerge, they are difficult to verify and have lost much of their timeliness.

Still, I think the media in general do a fair job of setting that public agenda. It is fortunate that the media in this country are quite numerous and diverse. Thus critical issues have a way of being thrust upon us by our own brethren. Much of the intellectual agenda actually comes from small journals of opinion, such as the *National Review, Commentary, The New Republic,* or the numerous outpourings of liberal and conservative think tanks such as the Brookings Institution or the Heritage Foundation. Their readership is small but highly concentrated within the mass media.

To a substantial degree the initiatives of the Great Society were a success. But because the media used its agenda power in a negative way, the public was left with an overriding impression that they failed. That, in turn, may have profoundly influenced the political climate to usher in the so-called "Reagan revolution" of the 1980s.

Let me quote from John Schwarz, associate professor of political science at the University of Arizona, in *The New Republic:*

> The War on Poverty decisively changed the living conditions facing the poor. Programs such as food stamps virtually eliminated serious malnutrition among low-income children and adults in America. Medicaid and Medicare greatly increased the access of low-income Americans to health care. In turn, the enlargement of both the nutritional and medical programs led to a decline in the infant mortality rate among minority Americans of 40 percent between 1965 and 1975, a drop that was eight times larger than the decline that had taken place in the ten years prior to 1965. The expansion of governmental housing programs helped to reduce the proportion of Americans living in overcrowded housing from 12 percent in 1960 to 5 percent in 1980. Those living in substandard housing declined from 20 percent to 8 percent.
>
> If that's true, then how did the popular impression emerge that the War on Poverty was a failure? That impression did much to aid the success of Reagan's attack on what he called "the failed policies of the past."[3]

To a great extent, such success stories just did not make good copy. Editors and reporters did not aggressively pursue them. The negative side of our policy role showed its power because people were not made aware of these successes.

Of course, it must be said that one reason the media did not declare a victory in the War on Poverty is because its own generals were so busy crying defeat. The Pentagon doesn't march into a congressional budget hearing and loudly proclaim that the Red Army couldn't fight its way out of a wet paper bag. The administrators of the War on Poverty were no less canny in the bureaucratic infighting, trying to bestir Congress to increase their budgets by focusing on the magnitude of yet unsolved problems. Many minority leaders, fueled by a sense of frustration over what remained undone, similarly belittled the genuine progress that had been made. Once again we see the media's role in public policy being essentially the passive one of transmitting the ideas of others—even when exercising our greatest power of deciding what stories to ignore.

Let's close by discussing issues great and issues small: the tragedy of Vietnam and Gerald Ford's tendency to bump his head. Taking the latter first, we get a small glimpse of the fairly inadvertent exercise of media power.

Ford was actually our most athletic president since Teddy Roosevelt. It's a fact that even the best skiers fall down occasionally, let alone one of his age. The rule that the exceptional tends to make news dictated that those pictures would be given disproportionate play—and that the public would pay more attention to them than to shots showing the president gliding smoothly down a slope. Thus an impression was created of clumsiness—which then led photographers and the public to watch eagerly for more such inevitable incidents, which reinforced the erroneous stereotype. The image became a kind of metaphor for his administration.

The same rule applies, of course, to the verbal "faux pas." James Watt actually did say some sensible things in his stormy tenure. But his love for the vivid and polarizing remark soon had everyone waiting to pounce upon further controversial remarks. A public figure who gets into too many controversies simply reaches a point where he can't avoid them because he's subjected to an intense scrutiny by journalists looking for a "there he goes again" story.

The power to stereotype and to ridicule has a potent effect on the course of public policy. Once again, however, a media image need not in itself be decisive to a politician who carefully tends his base. Jesse Helms has certainly received a generous dose of such treatment, yet he succeeded in his 1984 race for Senate reelection.

What then of the seminal media issue of this turbulent period: Vietnam. Its complex history shows evidence of all the issues we have discussed so far. Obviously, the news media didn't put the war itself on the agenda. Presidents Kennedy and Johnson deployed the troops. By and large, the media didn't begin the chorus of protest either, though that protest was often carefully crafted to attract the attention of the press.

But the power of setting agenda still showed at key points. The Viet Cong and North Vietnamese terror campaigns that killed thousands of local leaders and their families received scant attention in American media. But the picture of General Loan executing the Viet Cong suspect went worldwide. The My Lai massacre was intensely reported, as it should have been. But once again, a relatively open society found its warts displayed before the world while a closed one basically limited the message of its atrocities to those they were intended to terrorize. The power of stereotype and ridicule showed clearly in coverage of the inept South Vietnamese regimes, particularly in the era of frequent coups that followed the assassination of Ngo Dihn Diem.

In retrospect, it is clear that the Tet offensive of 1968 was an enormous military defeat for the Viet Cong which lost so much of its cadre that it had to turn over the main battlefield role to North Vietnamese main force units. But it was a tremendous psychological victory for the National Liberation Front and North Vietnamese and broke the back of American public support for the war. Many media critics have used this as a key example of how ignorance of military history, sensationalism, and the rush to deadlines in the media can distort the path of public policy.

Even more basic, many thoughtful analysts argue that the U.S. defeat in Vietnam stemmed from its being the first war fought in the living room. Advances in technology made it very easy to cover the war and plaster ugly images across the nineteen-inch color screen.

Yet even the lessons of Vietnam are at least ambiguous. It's worth noting that even before the Tet offensive the United States had been involved in Vietnam longer than our entire fighting role in World War II. And Tet was hardly the first time we'd been caught with our pants down by a supposedly beaten enemy. Remember the Battle of the Bulge? Yet the Nazi Ardennes offensive only served to stiffen American resolve to destroy the Hitler regime. Why did Tet weaken our resolve in Vietnam?

One of the best analysts of that war, Colonel Harry Summers, Jr., has argued,

Our failure in Vietnam mostly grew out of a lack of appreciation of military theory and military strategy, and especially the relationship between military strategy and national policy.

By failing to mobilize the national will behind the Vietnam War, our national leaders ignored Clausewitz's precept that war is a continuation of national policy by other means.

American leaders deliberately excluded people from their role in selecting the political object—the reason for fighting the war. Not only did the Johnson administration fail to declare war; it sought to commit American troops to combat as imperceptibly as possible, lulling the American people into forgetting that a war was on. It was not surprising that Washington's resolve collapsed after Tet–68. What is surprising is that it did not collapse much earlier. We must relearn that public support is critical to American military strategy.[4]

Former secretary of state Dean Rusk has stated that President Johnson deliberately forswore stirring up patriotic sentiment over Vietnam because he was afraid of arousing a conservative political tide that would hinder his liberal Great Society programs domestically. Whether that would have happened is debatable. What is not debatable is that the president called the people to arms with an uncertain trumpet. The media did not create this ambiguity in public policy. They could not and should not have avoided reporting it.

After all, technological flourishes aside, the media today aren't really so different from their predecessors in their power to inform and arouse emotion. Someone once quipped that "Marshall McLuhan says the printed word is obsolete. He wrote eighteen books to prove it."

Can it really be said that it took television to expose the horror and ugliness of war? Did Stephen Crane write *The Red Badge of Courage* for nothing? Didn't *All Quiet on the Western Front* and other works expose the stupidity and slaughter of World War I? Didn't Emie Pyle and a generation of combat reporters expose all too vividly the horror of Guadalcanal, of Tarawa, of Omaha Beach? Yet the public bore the burden of those wars because the same media that reported their horror were used by their political leaders to justify their necessity.

In summation, I should say that as the Mencken piece shows an enduring myth takes on a kind of reality of its own. It is an overstatement to say that in politics the perception of power is power, because there can be power in the unperceived as well. But while the media's power in public policy is both misunderstood and overrated, the very fact that politicians and others themselves tend to believe in it tends to reinforce it. They may overrate our ability to influence public opinion, as distinct from reporting it, but they do assign some weight to our opinions.

But in the end, it is the broader reality that we try to report that decides the outcome of public policy, not reporting itself. Just ask President Thomas E. Dewey.

NOTES

1. The original Mencken article and Mencken's later comments upon it are quoted from H. L. Mencken, *The Bathtub Hoax,* edited by Robert McHugh (New York: Knopf, 1958), pp. 4–9.

2. Ibid.

3. John Schwarz, *New Republic,* June 18, 1984.

4. Harry G. Summers, *On Strategy: A Critical Analysis of the Vietnam War* (New York: Dell, 1982).

Network News Coverage
of the Presidency: Implications
for Democracy

FRED SMOLLER

Every few weeks the Gallup organization poses the following question to a sample of the American public: "Do you approve or disapprove of the way (name of the incumbent) is handling his job as president?" The percentage of "yes" responses makes up what is called the president's approval rating. This approval score matters: It is a crucial determinate of presidential effectiveness. Presidents who have high public support scores have an easier time getting their programs passed by the Congress and implemented by the Bureaucracy. Presidents who are high in the polls have a much better chance of influencing domestic elites and foreign leaders. In addition, the Gallup index has been found to be a good predictor of the vote share Congressmen and Senators from the president's party receive during midterm elections, and a very good predictor of how well a first term president will do in the general election.[1]

Because presidents need public support to govern effectively, political analysts are disturbed by an unmistakable pattern in these evaluations. With the exception of the Eisenhower Administration, and for the time being the Reagan Administration, public support has declined systematically over the course of a presidential term. Many analysts have argued that in terms of the president's ability to get things done—that we are moving from an eight year presidency to a six month presidency, and that presidents and their aides are forced to push untested legislative programs, programs whose consequences have not been well thought out, through the Congress, for fear that they will not have the support necessary to do so later in the term. The question arises, then, why do presidents lose support?

Several explanations have been offered by scholars: Some suggest that the men we elect are at fault, that they lack the ethical, intellectual, or political attributes—in Tom Wolfe's words, "The Right Stuff"—that the presidency requires. Others have argued that presidents have lost support because their policy initiatives have not been successful, due to the complexity of the modern world and the intractable nature of modern social and economic problems, solutions to which require sacrifices by large sectors of society. The Office of the Presidency is simply too much for any one mortal: the psychological and physical demands of the job invariably wear presidents down to the point where they are no longer effective, and in some cases "self destruct" either politically or emotionally, or both.[2]

The declining support trend is a complex phenomenon that has no one single cause, but instead many factors are involved. In this paper, I would like to highlight one of those factors: the television networks and their nightly news programs.

THE THESIS

The television networks are not provided for in the Constitution. Nevertheless they are major actors in American politics. They are the primary source from which the public gains its information both about the state of the nation and the conduct of the nation's public officials in promoting its general welfare.

The great power of the network news programs, and their special attention to the presidency, enable them to play a major role in determining the fate of modern presidents. I believe, in fact, that the networks, seeking to realize their own goals, set in motion a dynamic pattern that can unravel the career of individual presidents and the public's support for the Office of the Presidency.

Thus, the era of televised news coverage has produced a tendency for the modern presidency to be defined by, and systematically destroyed by, the image of presidential performance presented on the evening news.

In the same way that a roulette wheel slanted in a certain direction produces unfair results, regardless of the honesty and integrity of the croupier, I believe the television networks are organizationally "slanted" against the Office of the Presidency, and that a negative image of the president is the result, regardless of the political ideology of the incumbent or his performance in office.[3] I call this phenomenon the "Six O'Clock Presidency" because its origins are the needs of the commercial networks rather than the values implicit in the Constitution.

This research is based on in-depth interviews with executives, correspondents, and technicians who work for the three major networks and observations made as a participant observer in the White House, in addition to the coding and analysis of over 5,500 news stories which appeared in the CBS Evening News from 1969 through 1985.

THE "CORE" ASSUMPTIONS

Two core assumptions lie at the heart of the Six O'Clock Presidency thesis. The first assumption is that commercial and logistical concerns contribute to policies which favor extensive coverage of the president.

The second assumption is that news judgement decisions, the needs of the technology of television, and the work routines of White House reporters contribute over time to a negative portrayal.

Let's examine these assumptions in turn:

1. Extensive Coverage

Virtually one-fifth of a typical evening news broadcast concerns presidential activities and policies. The White House is the only beat in Washington to which reporters, crew, and equipment are permanently assigned because the presidency is the single biggest continuing news story that the network news presents. As a matter of fact, since the assassination of John Kennedy, a crew referred to as the "death watch" made up of technicians and correspondents from the three networks record every step the president takes that can be recorded. The networks have several important economic and political incentives for covering the president extensively: First, by focusing on the president the network is able to deliver to its affiliates a news program which focuses on national news and therefore does not compete with local news programs. Second, extensive coverage of the president allows affiliates to meet the Federal Communications Commission's requirement to serve the public interest. Third, news coverage of the president legitimates the network's role in American politics and elevates network prestige, thus offsetting criticisms of prime time programming.

Most importantly, though, the news division focuses intensely on the activities of the president because doing so is logistically easy and inexpensive. Direct communication between the bureau and the White House is possible virtually 24 hours a day. No advance ordering of satellites or coaxial lines is necessary, nor is the transmission of Washington news stories to New York charged against a producers's budget.

Finally, yards, perhaps miles of videotape collected by the "death watch" pool are readily available. These are strong incentives for a cost conscious producer to use Washington stories. The point here is that because news coverage of the president is comparatively inexpensive and convenient to produce, the evening news has a major organizational incentive to broadcast news stories about the president other than the fact that the president may inherently be deserving of that coverage. Former White House correspondent Robert Pierpoint put it this way to me:

> When you are a producer putting together a news show for 15 million Americans every night, you want to be sure that you are going to have stories that look and sound like news. But if you are facing court decisions that may not come down in time or satellites that aren't working or available, or if your correspondent trying to get from the Beirut airport to the transmission point doesn't make it, you are in deep trouble. But you can always count on a piece from the White House that looks and sounds like news.

2. The Negative Bias of Washington News

Extensive coverage is not by itself detrimental to the presidency. I believe that a further examination of the way the news is collected reveals a built in bias toward the incumbent. Here are a few of those built in biases:

Format of the Evening News

Unlike a newspaper whose number of pages can be increased or decreased depending on the amount of news to be covered, the time limit of the evening news program is fixed—22 minutes, without commercials. This means that the actual amount of news delivered in a typical evening news program is relatively small when compared to the amount of news which appears in a typical newspaper. For example, the entire transcript of an evening news program would barely fill the front page of the Los Angeles Times. This means that individual reports must be short and therefore uncomplicated, producing in Walter Cronkite's words, "inadvertent and perhaps inevitable distortion." This also means that the complexity of the presidency is rarely captured in news reports. Dan Rather put it this way:

> There is no way a White House correspondent . . . can come out there in a minute and 15 seconds and give the viewer even the essence, never mind

the details or the substance [of a president's policies] . . . One of the great difficulties of television is that it has a great deal of trouble dealing with any subject in depth.

The Need for Pictures

Television news uses its technology ("pictures") to compete with other news media. The need for pictures affects news coverage of the president in three ways. First, it makes the reporting of complicated stories that focus on complex issues more difficult. Second, it highlights those aspects of the Office that are amenable to pictures and ignores those that are not. Finally, the need for "interesting" pictures reinforces journalism's penchant for the novel and the unusual (e.g., presidential faux pas).

The need for pictures contributes to the distortion of the presidency because pictures capture, condense, simplify and exaggerate complex political phenomena. Pictures often portray politics in "black" and "white," "good" or "evil" terms. The "grays" the qualifications, the nuances, are often lost. News pictures, like political cartoons, are effective devices for symbolic communication (which is why television is ideally suited to political compaigning). When presidents or candidates control media access, they have a formidable political tool at their disposal. But because pictures present complex political phenomena in symbolic terms reality is often exaggerated. This is how a producer for ABC's "World News Tonight," who was a deputy White House press secretary during the Carter Administration, explained it to me:

> Basically, when things aren't going well at the White House, the evening news' portrayal is worse than in fact the reality is. And then when things are going well for an Administration the stories suggest that things are far better than they are. There is a tendency to extremes because television is so dependent on pictures. The Camp David peace agreement between Israel and Egypt is a good example. Those pictures of Carter and Begin and Sadat embracing are just wonderful visuals. The impression they leave is that what occurred was 100 percent positive. A newspaper reporter, however, might go on for two-thirds of his story about what a great achievement it was. But might for the last third talk about the history of the problem and certainly how insurmountable it has been up to this point. He might also add that this achievement hasn't been as great as it may appear. A negative example would be hecklers at an event who threw tomatoes at the president. This is so visually compelling that the resulting story will be a one minute spot that says, yes, the president spoke, but he was heckled throughout, and following his speech the crowd threw three tomatoes. The visuals of the tomatoes splattering on the secret

service agent would be the lasting impression that you would come away with. It would have to be, arguably, ten times more dramatic to come across in print. So in print you would talk about what was said in the speech and so forth, that he was heckled throughout, and then three tomatoes were thrown.

The need for pictures also biases news coverage toward those aspects of the presidency that are amenable to visual portrayal. Many times this is due to White House restrictions. For example, President Carter's efforts to get the hostages released could not be shown in pictures. Instead descriptions of the president's actions had to compete with visually and emotionally engrossing pictures of angry Iranian students burning the American flag. Presidential actions such as the ordering of troops on a mission to free the hostages will receive more coverage than stories concerning the evolution of that policy decision, or, more important, the constraints which inhibit the exercise of presidential power. Because actions (e.g., ceremonies, bill signing, a firing of air traffic controllers, a presidential tour of a disabled nuclear power plant) receive more attention and have greater impact than "processes" (such as the development of policy options, negotiations, the evolution of ideas, the structure and functioning of the office, the constraints on presidential power) the power, purpose, and functioning of the Office is systematically exaggerated and distorted. This is a direct consequence of the environmental constraints affecting television coverage of the president.

Finally, the need for interesting pictures reinforces journalism's penchant for the unusual, the departure from the norm. Thus, network news coverage of presidential faux pas and clumsiness (e.g., presidents falling down stairs, dropping their election ballot, bumping their head on a helicopter door) and visually compelling but often gratuitous, trivial, and unrepresentative stories containing compelling visuals receive more coverage than they might otherwise merit solely because of their value in pictures.

Does it matter? Former President Gerald Ford thinks so:

> Every time I stumbled or bumped my head or fell in the snow, reporters zeroed in on that to the exclusion of almost everything else. The news coverage was harmful... [This] helped create the impression of me as a stumbler. And that wasn't funny.[4]

In addition, the need for pictures encourages coverage of conflict and controversy and other melodramatic events rather than the plain, routine functioning of government, which is not amenable to interesting pictures. This is how one producer for the CBS Evening News explained it to me:

> There is a real big mandate for pieces to not be boring; no standup, no bland looking stuff. [CBS News] wants it to be more visually enticing. So you try to be more creative. People are not going to watch if it is just a standup. And audience polls show that they like what we are doing, which is pepping up the news. I covered President Reagan when he went to Pittsburgh. There were the angriest demonstrators in the two years that I have been travelling with him. However, if I just had the two crews that was the normal standard on the road I couldn't have gotten good pictures of those demonstrators. I had another crew sent in from New York just to cover them, and that became the main focus of the story.

Recapitulation

On the one hand, we have a complex and multifaceted Office that is based on persuasion and the subtle exercise of power and influence, an office in which most significant activities are conducted in private; an institution with limited formal power that must struggle to reach and maintain consensus; an institution in which the execution of routine governing chores is offered as one measure of competence; and an institution that depends on public support for success.

Yet, on the other hand, we have a medium which requires simplistic, visible indicators of presidential performance, a medium which is ideally suited to the portrayal of conflict; and a medium whose stated purpose is to report, interpret, as well as critically analyze the news.

The extensiveness of televisions's commitment as well as the factors which contribute to negative portrayal produce a dynamic which has contributed to an increase in negative coverage of the modern presidency, and the erosion of public support. This coverage is not due to evil or disloyal persons politically opposed to the president occupying positions of power within the broadcasting industry; instead, it is simply a natural function of the nature of television news and its needs. Though some Administrations may transcend the dire consequences of the Six O'Clock Presidency, each Administration must contend with them.

IMPLICATIONS FOR DEMOCRACY

Because the dynamic results in lost public support, I shall first consider its effect on the standards used to judge presidents. I will then consider how modern presidents have responded to this erosion of public support and how they have attempted to manipulate network news to serve their own ends.

Effect on Public Opinion

I believe that the Six O'Clock Presidency phenomenon has led to the cumulative erosion of the standards used by the public to judge presidents and, for this reason, recent presidents have been judged more harshly and more quickly. Because citizens rely almost exclusively on network news for information about national affairs, they are inclined to judge the president on the basis of his portrayal on the evening news. Network needs, we have seen, lead to a premature evaluation of the president. Thus, the erosion of public support for presidents would not take place as quickly if television news did not cover the president extensively. Repeated disillusionment with successive regimes also leads to the decline in residual public support for the Office and the political system.

Effect on the Presidency

The Six O'Clock Presidency impacts on the presidency in three ways, along the lines of three sets of value clusters Bruce Buchanan says are used to judge presidents.

> The first value cluster can be termed 'effectiveness values.' By this is meant the expectation that presidents will devise pragmatic ways to solve any and all problems that confront the nation. The premium from this perspective is on getting the job done, with questions of the appropriateness of means and methods distinctly in second place. The second cluster, 'moral values' combines precepts of democracy and constitutional propriety. Presidents have been expected to implement and embody such virtues as respect for the constitutional order, for the rights and liberties of individual citizens, and increasingly for maintenance of the international moral order . . . The third cluster, 'survival values,' involves the preservation and ultimately the very survival of the social and political order in more-or-less recognizable form.[5]

Buchanan believes that these values can be reduced to a single judgmental query, "Is the presidential action in question effective? Is it morally right? Is it dangerous?" Let's examine how the Six O'Clock Presidency influences each of these value clusters.

Effectiveness Values

The Six O'Clock Presidency obviously makes the president's job more difficult. Recent administrations have devoted increasing resources to public relations efforts.[6] High level aides and the president himself also appear to spend an inordinate amount of time on image making and image enhancing activities with the result being less time spent on substantive issues. In the beginning of a president's term, the White House attempts to use the media to marshall support for its legislative program. Later, however, these efforts are much more defensive in nature, and are aimed primarily at keeping the level of negative news coverage to a minimum.

Most important, the erosion of support has made it more difficult for the president to govern—to get his programs through the congress, to bargain effectively with foreign and domestic leaders, and to mediate conflicts among conflicting social and economic and political interests. Because presidents lose support so quickly, new Administrations have only a few short months to devise and implement their legislative agenda. This has led presidents and their staffs to grasp at often ill-conceived but broadly based policies (e.g., "supply-side economics"). An all-out effort is then exerted to drive these policies through the congress. Such efforts invariable antagonize Members of Congress who believe that the legislature's role in the policy process has been preempted, and who become bent on retaliation.

Moral Values

In an effort to recapture lost support, however, presidents often abuse their office, engage in covert activities, disregard the rights and liberties of individuals, and trample on the roles of other Constitutional actors, most notably the Congress. In recent years the presidency has been at the center of national scandal and national disgrace. Many of the abuses which originated here, however, can be attributed partly to a belief by presidents and their staffs that they could not maintain enough support to achieve their goals through legal channels.

In recent years we have seen how well-intentioned reforms have contributed to the weakening of the House of Representatives. Ironically, just when younger and less parochial members were moving to positions of power within the Chamber, those positions were considerably weakened in response to the abuses of an entrenched elite. A weakened chamber has not facilitated the attainment of social and economic justice. In a similar vein, those who look to the presidency for widescale social change have an interest in maintaining an effective and strong institution—one which, however, adheres to and promotes democratic values.

Survival Values

It is the psychological effect brought on by lost public support, however, that is of greatest concern. The erosion of public support arguably places additional psychological pressures on the president. Four psychological exposures have been associated with the presidency—frustration, dissonance, deference, and stress.[7] The Six O'Clock Presidency exacerbates each of these debilitating psychological experiences. Presidents become increasingly frustrated because they are unable to get the "real" story of their adminstration to the American people. Because presidents may come to believe that their administration, their family, as well as themselves have been falsely and unfairly portrayed on the evening news, the internal moral barriers which may have prevented them from being less than truthful with the media (and therefore with the public) become lowered. Thus, the temptation to justify deceptive and illegal activities and outright lies is increased. All of these factors invariably increase the stress the president experiences. In response to this stress, and in an often futile effort to secure their place in history, presidents have taken unnecessary and unwise policy risks which have not been successful (e.g., the failed hostage rescue mission). When they do so, especially in the nuclear age, they jeopardize the security, safety, and ultimately the survival of the nation.

WHAT CAN BE DONE?

What can be done? Potential solutions to the problems posed by the Six O'Clock Presidency must address the internal logic of the argument. This means altering one or both of the assumptions which drive the dynamic. Thus, possible reforms are of tow kinds: one set of reforms would address the extensiveness of news coverage of the president. The second set of reforms would address the way in which news about the president is gathered and produced. I shall address these possible reforms in reverse order.

Change the Nature of News Coverage

One way of altering the cycle of news coverage is to change the way that presidential news is gathered, produced and reported. For example, if more resources were to be assigned to news coverage of the president and the format of the evening news program was changed (lengthened, with longer reports), reporters could be given more lead time for the preparation of reports and more time in the program in which to air them. News stories about the president could be longer and more complex, detailing the nuances and subtleties that get lost when reports are limited to less than two minutes of air time. This course of action would also involve a redefinition of news and the altering of assumptions about the nature of the viewing audience (thus reducing the need for conflict, drama, simplicity, and pictures.) Consistent with this series of reforms would be the re-education of White House reporters with more formal training in history and political science.

Such a wholesale restructuring of the industry is highly unlikely and impractical given the fact that a much simpler and direct solution that would achieve the same result is at hand.

Turn the Cameras Off

The pattern of news coverage of the president that I have presented in this paper is partly a function of the scope of the network's commitment to news coverage of the president. Thus, covering the president less, according to the logic of the argument, would defuse the impact of the negative nature of presidential news. This reform would involve changes in network policies concerning the reliance on Washington news and the Washington bureau's reliance on presidential news. Covering the president less would involve some hard-headed thinking by the networks about the consequences of their coverage of the president, and the examination of some firmly entrenched assumptions about the inherent news value of the president. (Does he really warrant that much coverage?) Thus, it may be necessary to reassign, or assign on a temporary basis, one or both of the network news crews permanently stationed at the White House, and instead rely more on network pools. This would undercut the incentive to use White House news. White House reporters would not push for airtime (a minimum level of which is guaranteed to some in their contracts with the network); the network would not be collecting news it didn't use. If the resources were re-directed to other areas (e.g., coverage of the regulatory agencies) the incentive would be further reduced because stories from other sources would be available.

I believe the time has come for a serious examination of this proposal.

NOTES

1. See, for example, George C. Edwards *The Public Presidency: The Pursuit of Popular Support* (New York: St. Martin's Press, 1983).

2. See Bruce Buchanan, *The Presidential Experience* (New Jersey: Prentice Hall, 1978).

3. Edward J. Epstein used the "roulette wheel" metaphor to describe the negative organization bias of network news. See Edward J. Epstein, in "The Selection of Reality" *The New Yorker* (March 3, 1973): 41–61.

4. Gerald Ford, *A Time to Heal* (Harper & Row, 1979), p. 289.

5. Bruce Buchanan, "Appraising Presidential Performance," paper presented at the annual meeting of the American Political Science Association, 1981.

6. See, for example, Sidney Blumenthal *The Permanent Campaign* (New York: Dutton, 1981).

7. Bruce Buchanan, *The Presidential Experience* (New Jersey: Prentice Hall, 1978).

DISCUSSION QUESTIONS

1. Green thinks the power of the media to influence public policy is a "myth." What does he mean by calling it a myth. Why does he think it is a myth?

2. Green argues that even a myth can have power. How can a myth have power? Why, in particular, does Green think that the myth of the media's power to shape public policy has power?

3. Green cites the case of Mencken's fraudulent bathtub story in order to support his own view that the power of the media to influence public policy is a myth. Why does he think the case of Mencken supports his view? Could the case of Mencken also have been used to support the opposite view that the power of media to shape public policy is an *actual,* and not a mythical, media power? Defend your answer.

4. Green compares the media to an amplifier which "may increase the range of power of the speaker's words," but which "has no control over what goes into it." What does he mean by this? Do you agree with him? Defend your answer.

5. Green distinguishes between "the power to focus public attention on an issue and the power to influence the outcome of the resulting political process." In your estimation, is the actual role of the media primarily restricted to their power to focus public attention on issues (to set public agendas) without influ-

encing outcomes, as Green argues? Is this possible? Is this desirable? Defend your answers.

6. Green asserts that "I think that the media in general do a fair job of setting that public agenda." What explanation does Green offer for the ability of the media to do such a "fair job" in setting the public agenda? In your estimation, *do* the media do a fair job in setting the public agenda? Defend your answer?

7. Smoller argues that the trend toward declining public support for American presidents (as evidenced by the Gallup index) is largely a result of network news coverage of the president. What other possible explanations can be given for this trend? Which explanation do you favor? Defend your answer.

8. Why does Smoller think that the decline in presidential popularity is the fault of the networks? That is, what factors of network news coverage of the presidency does he claim are contributing to the decline? In your estimation, is Smoller overestimating the effects of any of these factors on the decline in presidential popularity? Defend your answer.

9. Smoller argues that the networks' coverage of the presidency (the so-called Six O'Clock Presidency) has serious negative repercussions for the presidency and for democracy itself. What are these repercussions? Do you agree with Smoller? Defend your answer.

10. What changes does Smoller think should be made in network news coverage of the presidency? In your estimation, are these changes justified? Could any of these changes themselves have any negative implications for democracy? What other changes, if any, do you think should be made? Defend your answers.

11. While Smoller focuses upon the influence of network news on the presidency, the converse influence can also be discussed. In what ways, if any, do you think the presidency might influence network news? Defend your answer.

12. In your estimation, should newspaper editors have a right to make political endorsements (for example, to explicitly and publicly support one presidential candidate over another) on behalf of their newspapers? Defend your answer.

13. Both Green and Smoller mention the media propensity for focusing on presidential faux pas, for example the photographing of President Ford stumbling or bumping his head. Why are such occurrences a focus of media attention in the first place? Do you think that they *ought* to be a focus of media attention? Defend your answer.

14. Green asserts that "a media image need not in itself be decisive to a politician who carefully tends his base." How might Smoller respond to this statement? What is your response to it? Defend your answer.

6

Objectivity and News Reporting

According to one popular current in journalism, a reporter is expected to be "objective" in his or her account of the facts. Ordinarily, this demand amounts to the demand that journalists keep their own personal biases, emotions, interpretations, and other "subjective" factors out of the news. On this conception, the job of the journalist is to "report the facts," not to "create" them. So understood, however, there are several philosophical questions that arise. In the first place, to what extent is it possible for journalists, or human beings generally, to transcend their own subjectivity in accounting for "the facts"? Does such a demand rest upon plausible philosophical assumptions about the nature of, and relations between, perception, the external world, facts, and values? Moreover, *how* should journalists comply with the demand for objectivity? That is, what procedures or "conventions" should they employ in pursuing objective accounts of the news? And, if journalistic objectivity is attainable, is it something journalists *ought* to pursue? In this chapter, these and related questions will be explored.

In the first selection, "Stereotypes, Public Opinion, and the Press," Walter Lippmann advances a conception of objectivity which challenges the epistemological assumption that reportable reality is independent of perceivers' subjective states. According to Lippmann, "a report is the joint product of the knower and the known, in which the role of the observer is always selective and usually creative. The facts we see depend on where we are placed, and the habits of our eyes."

Lippmann uses the term "stereotypes" to denote the "types and generalities" that human beings impose on the world. Stereotypes are not limited to ideals: "Our stereotyped world," he says, "is not necessarily the world we should like it to be. It is simply the kind of world we expect it to be." These stereotypes help us to substitute order for "the great blooming, buzzing confusion of reality" which otherwise confronts us in attempting to see all things "freshly and in detail." For example, seeing a black widow spider as "shiny, black, and very poisonous, some-times having a red hourglass marking on its underside" may be to ster-eotype this particular creature and would not be suitable to an entomologist whose purposes would require seeing in greater detail. But for many people, such a characterization may be to impose an order on this part of reality which may suffice for practical purposes.

For Lippmann, objectivity does not flatly demand that we give up all of our stereotypes. Rather, "what matters is the character of the ster-eotypes, and the gullibility with which we employ them." Whereas a dogmatist lacks the "critical power to separate truth from error," seeing his opinions as irrefutable according to his own stereotyped perspective, the objective individual takes a critical reflective attitude toward his own opinions: He is aware of his own stereotypes and the manner in which they operate upon his perception. Through this awareness, he remains open to alternative possibilities, seeing his own opinions, instead, as hypotheses that may be modified or relinquished in favor of alternative opinions in the light of further evidence. In embracing such a critical reflective outlook, one is nevertheless operating within a particular ster-eotypical framework, albeit one under the influence of science.

For Lippmann objectivity is a product of a process of philosophical thinking: "It is the Socratic dialogue, with all of Socrates' energy for breaking through words to meanings. . . . " It is by carrying on such a philosophical discussion in which meanings are clarified and underlying prejudices are exposed that beliefs are "objectified." "After it has been thoroughly criticized, the idea is no longer *me* but *that*. It is objectified, it is at arm's length. Its fate is not bound up with my fate, but with the fate of the outer world upon which I am acting." For example, through a Socratic line of inquiry, an investigator may break through the hastily drawn and highly emotionally charged generalization that "Labor is exploited" to the more accurate and emotionally enlightened statement that "Labor groups C and M, but not X, are underpaid."

Lippmann does not deny that this Socratic approach may be harnessed by newspaper reporters in their efforts to provide objective accounts of the news. However, his skepticism about the ability of the press to furnish all the knowledge that is needed adequately to fuel public opinion in a democratic society leads him to opt for leaving the primary Socratic chores to other social institutions. According to Lippmann, the press "can normally record only what has been recorded for it by the working of institutions." For example, it can record that "Labor groups C and M, but not X, are underpaid" after this information has been analyzed and recorded by a further institution that has the "machinery of knowledge" to mediate labor disputes. It is not itself equipped to supply public opinion with all such knowledge. "The press," Lippmann contends, "is no substitute for institutions."

However, such a press stance as that ultimately embraced by Lippmann can be challenged. In the second selection of this chapter, "Objectivity and News Bias," Theodore L. Glasser argues that the current trend toward objectivity in journalism, paradoxically, engenders its own biases.

Glasser begins by defining objectivity in journalism as an "ideology" that is "committed to the supremacy of observable and retrievable facts," wherein by ideology he means "a set of beliefs that function as the journalist's 'claim to action.'" (Compare, in this context, Lippmann's concept of a "moral code" which he says is "a scheme of conduct applied to a number of typical instances.")

According to Glasser, such an ideology, or moral code, promotes three kinds of bias. First, it is biased against the "watchdog" role of the press in favor of the status quo. In its effort to remain value neutral, it embraces the "news convention" of quoting news sources with "impeccable credentials." In practice such sources turn out to be prominent members of society—government officials, leaders, the wealthy, and so on. Since the democratic process requires the participation of ordinary citizens as much as those who are prominent, a fundamental principle of democratic society is placed in jeopardy.

The above appears to have implications for Lippmann's view that the press can record only what has been recorded for it by other institutions. The danger here seems to lie in making the press a passive recipient of official sources, which, as Glasser suggests, could undermine the "watchdog" capacity of the press. While Lippmann thinks that when "the news is uncovered for the press by a system of intelligence that is also a check upon the press," he may not take seriously enough the converse problem: that of the limited power of the press to hold in check such "systems of intelligence" once they are in operation. To the contrary, Lippmann considers the want of such institutions to be "the primary defect of popular government" to which all of its other defects can be traced.

According to Glasser, a second bias of the ideology of objectivity is its bias against independent thinking. In requiring that journalists remain impartial and value neutral, there is no longer "the need nor the opportunity to develop a critical perspective from which to assess the events, the issues, the personalities he or she is assigned to cover."

In support of the above objection, Glasser cites Rosten's study of Washington correspondents, according to which most journalists interviewed "considered themselves inadequate to cope with the bewildering complexities of our nation's policies and politics." Such a study, however, could also be used to support Lippmann's argument that journalists are not alone capable of providing the informational network necessary for promoting public opinion in a democratic society. From Lippmann's perspective, this points to the urgency of constructing well-organized informational systems from which journalists can draw the news; but, from Glasser's perspective, this would itself threaten democratic principles.

It is noteworthy, however, that Lippmann's concept of objectivity is not, per se, at odds with Glasser's emphasis on the values of creativity and imagination in journalism. Indeed, the critical reflective attitude demanded by Lippmann's sense of objectivity includes these values. It is only when the Socratic search for truth, as a method of attaining objectivity, is reserved primarily for institutions, not as a first order journalistic pursuit, that the incompatibility between creativity in journalism and objectivity arises. This incompatibility may therefore be more a matter of emphasis than an irreconcilable ideological difference. By making the "machinery of knowledge," including the Socratic method, more directly accessible to journalists, these values can be brought into line.

The third bias that Glasser attributes to the ideology of objectivity is its bias against the journalist's assumption of responsibility for what is reported. According to Glasser, since on the ideology in question "news exists 'out there'—apparently independent of the reporter—journalists can't be held responsible for it." For example, on this ideology, the journalist is not responsible for the veracity of a source's claim. Since it is a "fact" that the claim has been made, the journalist can report it without moral impunity—even if he or she knows the content of the claim to be false.

It is worth reiterating in this context that, for Lippmann, facts are not simply "out there," waiting to be discovered, since "the role of the observer is always selective and usually creative." However, even if it is supposed that journalists discover—"uncover," "expose," or "gather"—the news rather than create it, it can also be a discovery that a source's claim is false. In other words, since the falsity of a fact-claim is also a fact, the facts would be incomplete without mention of this fact. Thus, a consistent application of the ideology in question by journalists need not encourage their indifference regarding the veracity of what they report. As Lippmann points out, "if there is one subject on which editors are most responsible it is in their judgment of the reliability of the source." It is not clear, therefore, that the commitment to objectivity in journalism, even in the ideological sense examined by Glasser, will, by itself, preclude responsibility for what is reported. While the objective reporter may be ideologically unsympathetic to whether or not "the truth sometimes hurts"—and in that sense not responsible for what is reported—the question of responsibility for the veracity of what is reported is still a different matter.

Stereotypes, Public Opinion, and the Press

WALTER LIPPMANN

STEREOTYPES

Each of us lives and works on a small part of the earth's surface, moves in a small circle, and of these acquaintances knows only a few intimately. Of any public event that has wide effects we see at best only a phase and an aspect. This is as true of the eminent insiders who draft treaties, make laws, and issue orders, as it is of those who have treaties framed for them, laws promulgated to them, orders given at them. Inevitably our opinions cover a bigger space, a longer reach of time, a greater number of things, than we can directly observe. They have, therefore, to be pieced together out of what others have reported and what we can imagine.

Yet even the eyewitness does not bring back a naive picture of the scene.[1] For experience seems to show that he himself brings something to the scene which later he takes away from it, that oftener than not what he imagines to be the account of an event is really a transfiguration of it. Few facts in consciousness seem to be merely given. Most facts in consciousness seem to be partly made. A report is the joint product of the knower and known, in which the rôle of the observer is always selective and usually creative. The facts we see depend on where we are placed, and the habits of our eyes.

An unfamiliar scene is like the baby's world, "one great, blooming, buzzing confusion."[2] This is the way, says Mr. John Dewey,[3] that any new thing strikes an adult, so far as the thing is really new and strange. "Foreign languages that we do not understand always seem jibberings, babblings, in which it is impossible to fix a definite, clear-cut, individualized group of sounds. The countryman in the crowded street, the landlubber at sea, the ignoramus in sport at a contest between experts in a complicated game, are further instances. Put an inexperienced man in a factory, and at first the work seems to him a meaningless medley.

161

All strangers of another race proverbially look alike to the visiting stranger. Only gross differences of size or color are perceived by an outsider in a flock of sheep, each of which is perfectly individualized to the shepherd. A diffusive blur and an indiscriminately shifting suction characterize what we do not understand. The problem of the acquisition of meaning by things, or (stated in another way) of forming habits of simple apprehension, is thus the problem of introducing (1) *definiteness* and *distinction* and (2) *consistency* or *stability* of meaning into what is otherwise vague and wavering."

But the kind of definiteness and consistency introduced depends upon who introduces them. In a later passage[4] Dewey gives an example of how differently an experienced layman and a chemist might define the word metal. "Smoothness, hardness, glossiness, and brilliancy, heavy weight for its size . . . the serviceable properties of capacity for being hammered and pulled without breaking, of being softened by heat and hardened by cold, of retaining the shape and form given, of resistance to pressure and decay, would probably be included" in the layman's definition. But the chemist would likely as not ignore these esthetic and utilitarian qualities, and define a metal as "any chemical element that enters into combination with oxygen so as to form a base."

For the most part we do not first see, and then define, we define first and then see. In the great blooming, buzzing confusion of the outer world we pick out what our culture has already defined for us, and we tend to perceive that which we have picked out in the form stereotyped for us by our culture. Of the great men who assembled at Paris to settle the affairs of mankind, how many were there who were able to see much of the Europe about them, rather than their commitments about Europe? Could anyone have penetrated the mind of M. Clemenceau, would he have found there images of the Europe of 1919, or a great sediment of stereotyped ideas accumulated and hardened in a long and pugnacious existence? Did he see the Germans of 1919, or the German type as he had learned to see it since 1871? He saw the type, and among the reports that came to him from Germany, he took to heart those reports, and, it seems, those only, which fitted the type that was in his mind. If a junker blustered, that was an authentic German; if a labor leader confessed the guilt of the empire, he was not an authentic German.

At a Congress of Psychology in Göttingen an interesting experiment was made with a crowd of presumably trained observers.[5]

Not far from the hall in which the Congress was sitting there was a public fête with a masked ball. Suddenly the door of the hall was thrown open and a clown rushed in madly pursued by a negro, revolver in hand. They stopped in the middle of the room fighting; the clown fell, the negro leapt upon him, fired, and then both rushed out of the hall. The whole incident hardly lasted twenty seconds.

The President asked those present to write immediately a report since there was sure to be a judicial inquiry. Forty reports were sent in. Only one had less than 20% of mistakes in regard to the principal facts; fourteen had 20% to 40% of mistakes; twelve from 40% to 50%; thirteen more than 50%. Moreover in twenty-four accounts 10% of the details were pure inventions and this proportion was exceeded in ten accounts and diminished in six. Briefly a quarter of the accounts were false.

It goes without saying that the whole scene had been arranged and even photographed in advance. The ten false reports may then be relegated to the category of tales and legends; twenty-four accounts are half legendary, and six have a value approximating to exact evidence.

Thus out of forty trained observers writing a responsible account of a scene that had just happened before their eyes, more than a majority saw a scene that had not taken place. What then did they see? One would suppose it was easier to tell what had occurred, than to invent something which had not occurred. They saw their stereotype of such a brawl. All of them had in the course of their lives acquired a series of images of brawls, and these images flickered before their eyes. In one man these images displaced less than 20% of the actual scene, in thirteen men more than half. In thirty-four out of the forty observers the stereotypes preëmpted at least one-tenth of the scene. . . .

There is, of course, some connection between the scene outside and the mind through which we watch it, just as there are some long-haired men and short-haired women in radical gatherings. But to the hurried observer a slight connection is enough. If there are two bobbed heads and four beards in the audience, it will be a bobbed and bearded audience to the reporter who knows beforehand that such gatherings are composed of people with these tastes in the management of their hair. There is a connection between our vision and the facts, but it is often a strange connection. . . .

There is economy in this. For the attempt to see all things freshly and in detail, rather than as types and generalities, is exhausting, and among busy affairs practically out of the question. . . .

What matters is the character of the stereotypes, and the gullibility with which we employ them. And these in the end depend upon those inclusive patterns which constitute our philosophy of life. If in that philosophy we assume that the world is codified according to a code which we possess, we are likely to make our reports of what is going on describe a world run by our code. But if our philosophy tells us that each man is only a small part of the world, that his intelligence catches at best only phases and aspects in a coarse net of ideas, then, when we use our stereotypes, we tend to know that they are only stereotypes, to hold them lightly, to modify them gladly. We tend, also, to realize more and more clearly when our ideas started, where they started, how they came to us, why we accepted them. All useful history is antiseptic in this fashion. It enables us to know what fairy tale, what school book, what tradition, what novel, play, picture, phrase, planted one preconception in this mind, another in that mind. . . .

There is another reason, besides economy of effort, why we so often hold to our stereotypes when we might pursue a more disinterested vision. The systems of stereotypes may be the core of our personal tradition, the defenses of our position in society.

They are an ordered, more or less consistent picture of the world, to which our habits, our tastes, our capacities, our comforts and our hopes have adjusted themselves. They may not be a complete picture of the world, but they are a picture of a possible world to which we are adapted. In that world people and things have their well-known places, and do certain expected things. We feel at home there. We fit in. We are members. We know the way around. There we find the charm of the familiar, the normal, the dependable; its grooves and shapes are where we are accustomed to find them. And though we have abandoned much that might have tempted us before we creased ourselves into that mould, once we are firmly in, it fits as snugly as an old shoe.

No wonder, then, that any disturbance of the stereotypes seems like an attack upon the foundation of the universe. It is an attack upon the foundation of *our* universe, and, where big things are at stake, we do not readily admit that there is any distinction between our universe and the universe. . . .

A pattern of stereotypes is no neutral. It is not merely a way of substituting order for the great blooming, buzzing confusion of reality. It is not merely a short cut. It is all these things and something more. It is the guarantee of our self-respect; it is the projection upon the world of our own sense of our own value, our own position and our own rights. The stereotypes are, therefore, highly charged with the feelings that are attached to them. They are the fortress of our tradition, and behind its defenses we can continue to feel ourselves safe in the position we occupy. . . .

I have been speaking of stereotypes rather than ideals, because the word ideal is usually reserved for what we consider the good, the true and the beautiful. Thus it carries the hint that here is something to be copied or attained. But our repertory of fixed impressions is wider than that. It contains ideal swindlers, ideal Tammany politicians, ideal jingoes, ideal agitators, ideal enemies. Our stereotyped world is not necessarily the world we should like it to be. It is simply the kind of world we expect it to be. If events correspond there is a sense of familiarity, and we feel that we are moving with the movement of events. . . .

Anyone who has stood at the end of a railroad platform waiting for a friend, will recall what queer people he mistook for him. The shape of a hat, a slightly characteristic gait, evoked the vivid picture in his mind's eye. In sleep a tinkle may sound like the pealing of a great bell; the distant stroke of a hammer like a thunderclap. For our constellations of imagery will vibrate to a stimulus that is perhaps but vaguely similar to some aspect of them. They may, in hallucination, flood the whole consciousness. They may enter very little into perception, though I am inclined to think that such an experience is extremely rare and highly sophisticated, as when we gaze blankly at a familiar word or object, and it gradually ceases to be familiar. Certainly for the most part, the way we see things is a combination of what is there and what we expected to find. The heavens are not the same to an astronomer as to a pair of lovers; a page of Kant will start a different train of thought in a Kantian and in a radical empiricist; the Tahitian belle is a better looking person to her Tahitian suitor than to the readers of the *National Geographic Magazine*.

Expertness in any subject is, in fact, a multiplication of the number of aspects we are prepared to discover, plus the habit of discounting our expectations. Where to the ignoramus all things look alike, and life is just one thing after another, to the specialist things are highly individual. For a chauffeur, an epicure, a connoisseur, a member of the President's cabinet, or a professor's wife, there are evident distinctions and qualities, not at all evident to the casual person who discusses automobiles, wines, old masters, Republicans, and college faculties. . . .

[One's] philosophy is a more or less organized series of images for describing the unseen world. But not only for describing it. For judging it as well. And, therefore, the stereotypes are loaded with preference, suffused with affection or dislike, attached to fears, lusts, strong wishes, pride, hope. Whatever invokes the stereotype is judged with the appropriate sentiment. Except where we deliberately keep prejudice in suspense, we do not study a man and judge him to be bad. We see a bad man. We see a dewy morn, a blushing maiden, a sainted priest, a humorless Englishman, a dangerous Red, a carefree bohemian, a lazy Hindu, a wily Oriental, a dreaming Slav, a volatile Irishman, a greedy Jew, a 100% American. In the workaday world that is often the real judgment, long in advance of the evidence, and it contains within itself the conclusion which the evidence is pretty certain to confirm. Neither justice, nor mercy, nor truth; enter into such a judgment, for the judgment has preceded the evidence. Yet a people without prejudices, a people with altogether neutral vision, is so unthinkable in any civilization of which it is useful to think, that no scheme of education could be based upon that ideal. Prejudice can be detected, discounted, and refined, but so long as finite men must compress into a short schooling preparation for dealing with a vast civilization, they must carry pictures of it around with them, and have prejudices. The quality of their thinking and doing will depend on whether those prejudices are friendly, friendly to other people, to other ideas, whether they evoke love of what is felt to be positively good, rather than hatred of what is not contained in their version of the good.

Morality, good taste and good form first standardize and then emphasize certain of these underlying prejudices. As we adjust ourselves to our code, we adjust the facts we see to that code. Rationally, the facts are neutral to all our views of right and wrong. Actually, our canons determine greatly what we shall perceive and how.

For a moral code is a scheme of conduct applied to a number of typical instances. To behave as the code directs is to serve whatever purpose the code pursues. It may be God's will, or the king's, individual salvation in a good, solid, three dimensional paradise, success on earth, or the service of mankind. In any event the makers of the code fix upon certain typical situations, and then by some form of reasoning or intuition, deduce the kind of behavior which would produce the aim they acknowledge. The rules apply where they apply. . . .

At the core of every moral code there is a picture of human nature, a map of the universe, and a version of history. To human nature (of the sort conceived), in a universe (of the kind imagined), after a history (so understood), the rules of the code apply. So far as the facts of personality, of the environment and of memory are different, by so far the rules of the code are difficult to apply with success. Now every moral code has to conceive human psychology, the material world, and tradition some way or other. But in the codes that are under the influence of science, the conception is known to be an hypothesis, whereas in the codes that come unexamined from the past or bubble up from the caverns of the mind, the conception is not taken as an hypothesis demanding proof or contradiction, but as a fiction accepted without question. In the one case, man is humble about his beliefs, because he knows they are tentative and incomplete; in the other he is dogmatic, because his belief is a completed myth. The moralist who submits to the scientific discipline knows that though he does not know everything, he is in the way of knowing something; the dogmatist, using a myth, believes himself to share part of the insight of omniscience, though he lacks the criteria by which to tell truth from error. For the distinguishing mark of a myth is that truth and error, fact and fable, report and fantasy, are all on the same plane of credibility.

The myth is, then, not necessarily false. It might happen to be wholly true. It may happen to be partly true. If it has affected human conduct a long time, it is almost certain to contain much that is profoundly and importantly true. What a myth never contains is the critical power to separate its truths from its errors. For that power comes only by realizing that no human opinion, whatever its supposed origin, is too exalted for the test of evidence, that every opinion is only somebody's opinion. And if you ask why the test of evidence is preferable to any other, there is no answer unless you are willing to use the test in order to test it. . . .

NEWS, TRUTH, AND A CONCLUSION

. . . . The hypothesis, which seems to me the most fertile, is that news and truth are not the same thing, and must be clearly distinguished.[6] The function of news is to signalize an event, the function of truth is to bring to light the hidden facts, to set them into relation with each other, and make a picture of reality on which men can act. Only at those points, where social conditions take recognizable and measurable shape, do the body of truth and the body of news coincide. That is a comparatively small part of the whole field of human interest. In this sector, and only in this sector, the tests of the news are sufficiently exact to make the charges of perversion or suppression more than a partisan judgment. There is no defense, no extenuation, no excuse whatever, for stating six times that Lenin is dead, when the only information the paper possesses is a report that he is dead from a source repeatedly shown to be unreliable. The news, in that instance, is not "Lenin Dead" but "Helsingfors Says Lenin is Dead." And a newspaper can be asked to take the responsibility of not making Lenin more dead than the source of the news is reliable; if there is one subject on which editors are most responsible it is in their judgment of the reliability of the source. But when it comes to dealing, for example, with stories of what the Russian people want, no such test exists.

The absence of these exact tests accounts, I think, for the character of the profession, as no other explanation does. There is a very small body of exact knowledge, which it requires no outstanding ability or training to deal with. The rest is in the journalist's own discretion. Once he departs from the region where it is definitely recorded at the County Clerk's office that John Smith has gone into bankruptcy, all fixed standards disappear. The story of why John Smith failed, his human frailties, the analysis of the economic conditions on which he was shipwrecked, all of this can be told in a hundred different ways. There is no discipline in applied psychology, as there is a discipline in medicine, engineering, or even law, which has authority to direct the journalist's mind when he passes from the news to the vague realm of truth. There are no canons to direct his own mind, and no canons that coerce the reader's judgment or the publisher's. His version of the truth is only his version. How can he demonstrate the truth as he sees it? He cannot demonstrate it, any more than Mr. Sinclair Lewis can demonstrate that he has told the whole truth about Main Street. And the more he understands his own weakness, the more ready he is to admit that where there is no objective test, his opinion is in some vital measure constructed out of his own stereotypes, according to his own code, and by the urgency of his own interest. He knows that he is seeing the world through subjective lenses. He cannot deny that he too is, as Shelley remarked, a dome of many-colored glass which stains the white radiance of eternity.

And by this knowledge his assurance is tempered. He may have all kinds of moral courage, and sometimes has, but he lacks that sustaining conviction of a certain technic which finally freed the physical sciences from theological control. It was the gradual development of an irrefragable method that gave the physicist his intellectual freedom as against all the powers of the world. His proofs were so clear, his evidence so sharply superior to tradition, that he broke away finally from all control. But the journalist has no such support in his own conscience or in fact. The control exercised over him by the opinions of his employers and his readers, is not the control of truth by prejudice, but of one opinion by another opinion that is not demonstrably less true. Between Judge Gary's assertion that the unions will destroy American institutions, and Mr. Gomper's assertion that they are agencies of the rights of man, the choice has, in large measure, to be governed by the will to believe.

The task of deflating these controversies, and reducing them to a point where they can be reported as news, is not a task which the reporter can perform. It is possible and necessary for journalists to bring home to people the uncertain character of the truth on which their opinions are founded, and by criticism and agitation to prod social science into making more usable formulations of social facts, and to prod statesmen into establishing more visible institutions. The press, in other words, can fight for the extension of reportable truth. But as social truth is organized to-day, the press is not constituted to furnish from one edition to the next the amount of knowledge which the democratic theory of public opinion demands. This is not due to the Brass Check, as the quality of news in radical papers shows, but to the fact that the press deals with a society in which the governing forces are so imperfectly recorded. The theory that the press can itself record those forces is false. It can normally record only what has been recorded for it by the working of institutions. Everything else is argument and opinion, and fluctuates with the vicissitudes, the self-consciousness, and the courage of the human mind. . . .

If the newspapers, then, are to be charged with the duty of translating the whole public life of mankind, so that every adult can arrive at an opinion on every moot topic, they fail, they are bound to fail, in any future one can conceive they will continue to fail. It is not possible to assume that a world carried on by division of labor and distribution of authority, can be governed by universal opinions in the whole population. Unconsciously the theory sets up the single reader as theoretically omnicompetent, and puts upon the press the burden of accomplishing whatever representative government, industrial organization, and diplomacy have failed to accomplish. Acting upon everybody for thirty minutes in twenty-four hours, the press is asked to create a mystical force called Public Opinion that will take up the slack in public institutions. The press has often mistakenly pretended that it could do just that. It has at great moral cost to itself, encouraged a democracy still bound to its original premises, to expect newspapers to supply spontaneously for every organ of government, for every social problem, the machinery of information which these do not normally supply themselves. Institutions, having failed to furnish themselves with instruments of knowledge, have become a bundle of "problems," which the population as a whole, reading the press as a whole, is supposed to solve.

The press, in other words, has come to be regarded as an organ of direct democracy, charged on a much wider scale, and from day to day, with the function often attributed to the initiative, referendum, and recall. The Court of Public Opinion, open day and night, is to lay down the law for everything all the time. It is not workable. And when you consider the nature of news, it is not even thinkable. For the news, as we have seen, is precise in proportion to the precision with which the event is recorded. Unless the event is capable of being named, measured, given shape, made specific, it either fails to take on the character of news, or it is subject to the accidents and prejudices of observation.

Therefore, on the whole, the quality of the news about modern society is an index of its social organization. The better the institutions, the more all interests concerned are disentangled, the more objective criteria are introduced, the more perfectly an affair can be presented as news. At its best the press is a servant and guardian of institutions; at its worst it is a means by which a few exploit social disorganization to their own ends. In the degree to which institutions fail to function, the unscrupulous journalist can fish in troubled waters, and the conscientious one must gamble with uncertainties.

The press is no substitute for institutions. It is like the beam of a searchlight that moves restlessly about, bringing one episode and then another out of darkness into vision. Men cannot do the work of the world by this light alone. They cannot govern society by episodes, incidents, and eruptions. It is only when they work by a steady light of their own, that the press, when it is turned upon them, reveals a situation intelligible enough for a popular decision. The trouble lies deeper than the press, and so does the remedy. It lies in social organization based on a system of analysis and record, and in all the corollaries of that principle; in the abandonment of the theory of the omnicompetent citizen, in the decentralization of decision, in the coordination of decision by comparable record and analysis. If at the centers of management there is a running audit, which makes work intelligible to those who do it, and those who superintend it, issues when they arise are not the mere collisions of the blind. Then, too, the news is uncovered for the press by a system of intelligence that is also a check upon the press.

That is the radical way. For the troubles of the press, like the troubles of representative government, be it territorial or functional, like the troubles of industry, be it capitalist, coöperative, or communist, go back to a common source; to the failure of self-governing people to transcend their casual experience and their prejudice, by inventing, creating, and organizing a machinery of knowledge. It is because they are compelled to act without a reliable picture of the world, that governments, schools, newspapers and churches make such small headway against the more obvious failings of democracy, against violent prejudice, apathy, preference for the curious trivial as against the dull important, and the hunger for sideshows and three legged calves. This is the primary defect of popular government, a defect inherent in its traditions, and all its other defects can, I believe, be traced to this one.

THE APPEAL TO THE PUBLIC

. . . . Only by insisting that problems shall not come up to him until they have passed through a procedure, can the busy citizen of a modern state hope to deal with them in a form that is intelligible. For issues, as they are stated by a partisan, almost always consist of an intricate series of facts, as he has observed them, surrounded by a large fatty mass of stereotyped phrases charged with his emotion. According to the fashion of the day, he will emerge from the conference room insisting that what he wants is some soul-filling idea like Justice, Welfare, Americanism, Socialism. On such issues the citizen outside can sometimes be provoked to fear or admiration, but to judgment never. Before he can do anything with the argument, the fat has to be boiled out of it for him.

That can be done by having the representative inside carry on discussion in the presence of some one, chairman or mediator, who forces the discussion to deal with the analyses supplied by experts. This is the essential organization of any representative body dealing with distant matters. The partisan voices should be there, but the partisans should find themselves confronted with men, not personally involved, who control enough facts and have the dialectical skill to sort out what is real perception from what is stereotype, pattern and elaboration. It is the Socratic dialogue, with all of Socrates's energy for breaking through words to meanings, and something more than that, because the dialectic in modern life must be done by men who have explored the environment as well as the human mind.

There is, for example, a grave dispute in the steel industry. Each side issues a manifesto full of the highest ideals. The only public opinion that is worth respect at this stage is the opinion which insists that a conference be organized. For the side which says its cause is too just to be contaminated by conference there can be little sympathy, since there is no such cause anywhere among mortal men. Perhaps those who object to conference do not say quite that. Perhaps they say that the other side is too wicked; they cannot shake hands with traitors. All that public opinion can do then is to organize a hearing by public officials to hear the proof of wickedness. It cannot take the partisans' word for it. But suppose a conference is agreed to, and suppose there is a neutral chairman who has at his beck and call the consulting experts of the corporation, the union, and, let us say, the Department of Labor.

Judge Gary states with perfect sincerity that his men are well paid and not overworked, and then proceeds to sketch the history of Russia from the time of Peter the Great to the murder of the Czar. Mr. Foster rises, states with equal sincerity that the men are exploited, and then proceeds to outline the history of human emancipation from Jesus of Nazareth to Abraham Lincoln. At this point the chairman calls upon the intelligence men for wage tables in order to substitute for the words "well paid" and "exploited" a table showing what the different classes *are* paid. Does Judge Gary think they are all well paid? He does. Does Mr. Foster think they are all exploited? No, he thinks that groups C, M, and X are exploited. What does he mean by exploited? He means they are not paid a living wage. They are, says Judge Gary. What can a man buy on that wage, asks the chairman. Nothing, says Mr. Foster. Everything he needs, says Judge Gary. The chairman consults the budgets and price statistics of the government.[7] He rules that X can meet an average budget, but that C and M cannot. Judge Gary serves notice that he does not regard the official statistics as sound. The budgets are too high, and prices have come down. Mr. Foster also serves notice of exception. The budget is too low, prices have gone up. The chairman rules that this point is not within the jurisdiction of the conference, that the official figures stand, and that Judge Gary's experts and Mr. Fosters' should carry their appeals to the standing committee of the federated intelligence bureaus.

Nevertheless, says Judge Gary, we shall be ruined if we change these wage scales. What do you mean by ruined, asks the chairman, produce your books. I can't, they are private, says Judge Gary. What is private does not interest us, says the chairman, and, therefore, issues a statement to the public announcing that the wages of workers in groups C and M are so-and-so much below the official minimum living wage, and that Judge Gary declines to increase them for reasons that he refuses to state. After a procedure of that sort, a public opinion in the eulogistic sense of the term[8] can exist.

The value of expert mediation is not that it sets up opinion to coerce the partisans, but that it disintegrates partisanship. Judge Gary and Mr. Foster may remain as little convinced as when they started, though even they would have to talk in a different strain. But almost everyone else who was not personally entangled would save himself from being entangled. For the entangling stereotypes and slogans to which his reflexes are so ready to respond are by this kind of dialectic untangled. . . .

The effect of naming, the effect, that is, of saying that the labor groups C and M, but not X, are underpaid, instead of saying that Labor is Exploited, is incisive. Perceptions recover their identity, and the emotion they arouse is specific, since it is no longer reinforced by large and accidental connections with everything from Christmas to Moscow. The disentangled idea with a name of its own, and an emotion that has been scrutinized, is ever so much more open to correction by new data in the problem. It had been imbedded in the whole personality, had affiliations of some sort with the whole ego: a challenge would reverberate through the whole soul. After it has been thoroughly criticized, the idea is no longer *me* but *that*. It is objectified, it is at arm's length. Its fate is not bound up with my fate, but with the fate of the outer world upon which I am acting. . . .

Re-education of this kind will help to bring our public opinions into grip with the environment. That is the way the enormous censoring, stereotyping, and dramatizing apparatus can be liquidated. Where there is no difficulty in knowing what the relevant environment is, the critic, the teacher, the physician, can unravel the mind. But where the environment is as obscure to the analyst as to his pupil, no analytic technic is sufficient. Intelligence work is required. In political and industrial problems the critic as such can do something, but unless he can count upon receiving from expert reporters a valid picture of the environment, his dialectic cannot go far.

Therefore, though here, as in most other matters, "education" is the supreme remedy, the value of this education will depend upon the evolution of knowledge. And our knowledge of human institutions is still extraordinarily meager and impressionistic. The gathering of social knowledge is, on the whole, still haphazard; not, as it will have to become, the normal accompaniment of action. And yet the collection of information will not be made, one may be sure, for the sake of its ultimate use. It will be made because modern decision requires it to be made. But as it is being made, there will accumulate a body of data which political science can turn into generalization, and build up for the schools into a conceptual picture of the world. When that picture takes form, civic education can become a preparation for dealing with an unseen environment.

As a working model of the social system becomes available to the teacher, he can use it to make the pupil acutely aware of how his mind works on unfamiliar facts. Until he has such a model, the teacher cannot hope to prepare men fully for the world they will find. What he can do is to prepare them to deal with that world with a great deal more sophistication about their own minds. He can, by the use of the case method, teach the pupil the habit of examining the sources of his information. He can teach him, for example, to look in his newspaper for the place where the dispatch was filed, for the name of the correspondent, the name of the press service, the authority given for the statement, the circumstances under which the statement was secured. He can teach the pupil to ask himself whether the reporter saw what he describes, and to remember how that reporter described other events in the past. He can teach him the character of censorship, of the idea of privacy, and furnish him with knowledge of past propaganda. He can, by the proper use of history, make him aware of the stereotype, and can educate a habit of introspection about the imaginary evoked by printed words. He can, by courses in comparative history and anthropology, produce a life-long realization of the way codes impose a special pattern upon the imagination. He can teach men to catch themselves making allegories, dramatizing relations, and personifying abstractions. He can show the pupil how he identifies himself with these allegories, how long he becomes interested, and how he selects the attitude, heroic, romantic, economic which he adopts while holding a particular opinion.

The study of error is not only in the highest degree prophylactic, but it serves as a stimulating introduction to the study of truth. As our minds become more deeply aware of their own subjectivism, we find a zest in objective method that is not otherwise there. We see vividly, as normally we should not, the enormous mischief and casual cruelty of our prejudices. And the destruction of a prejudice, though painful at first, because of its connection with our self-respect, gives an immense relief and a fine pride when it is successfully done. There is a radical enlargement of the range of attention. As the current categories dissolve, a hard, simple version of the world breaks up. The scene turns vivid and full. There follows an emotional incentive to hearty appreciation of scientific method, which otherwise it is not easy to arouse, and is impossible to sustain. Prejudices are so much easier and more interesting. For if you teach the principles of science as if they had always been accepted, their chief virtue as a discipline, which is objectivity, will make them dull. But teach them at first as victories over the superstitions of the mind, and the exhilaration of the chase and of the conquest may carry the pupil over the hard transition from his own self-bound experience to the phase where his curiosity has matured, and his reason has acquired passion.

NOTES

1. E.g., cf. Edmond Locard, *L'Enquête Criminelle et les Méthodes Scientifiques*. A great deal of interesting material has been gathered in late years on the credibility of the witness, which shows, as an able reviewer of Dr. Locard's book says in *The Times* (London) Literary Supplement (August 18, 1921), that credibility varies as to classes of witnesses and classes of events, and also as to type of perception. Thus, perceptions of touch, odor, and taste have low evidential value. Our hearing is defective and arbitrary when it judges the sources and direction of sound, and in listening to the talk of other people "words which are not heard will be supplied by the witness in all good faith. He will have a theory of the purport of the conversation, and will arrange the sounds he heard to fit it." Even visual perceptions are liable to great error, as in identification, recognition, judgment of distance, estimates of numbers, for example, the size of a crowd. In the untrained observer the sense of time is highly variable. All these original weaknesses are complicated by tricks of memory, and the incessant creative quality of the imagination. Cf. also Sherrington, *The Integrative Action of the Nervous System*, pp. 318–327.

The late Professor Hugo Münsterberg wrote a popular book on this subject called *On the Witness Stand*.

2. Wm. James, *Principles of Psychology*, Vol. I, p. 488.

3. John Dewey, *How We Think*, p. 121.

4. Op. cit., p. 133.

5. A. von Gennep, *La formation des légendes*, pp. 158–159. Cited F. van Langenhove, *The Growth of a Legend*, pp. 120–122.

6. When I wrote *Liberty and the News*, I did not understand this distinction clearly enough to state it, but cf. p. 89 ff.

7. See an article on "The Cost of Living and Wage Cuts," in the *New Republic*, July 27, 1921, by Dr. Leo Wolman, for a brilliant discussion of the naïve use of such figures and "pseudo-principles." The warning is of particular importance because it comes from an economist and statistician who has himself done so much to improve the technic of industrial disputes.

8. As used by Mr. Lowell in his *Public Opinion and Popular Government*.

Objectivity and News Bias

THEODORE L. GLASSER

By objectivity I mean a particular view of journalism and the press, a frame of reference used by journalists to orient themselves in the newsroom and in the community. By objectivity I mean, to a degree, ideology; where ideology is defined as a set of beliefs that function as the journalist's "claim to action."

As a set of beliefs, objectivity appears to be rooted in a positivist view of the world, an enduring commitment to the supremacy of observable and retrievable facts. This commitment, in turn, impinges on news organizations' principal commodity—the day's news. Thus my argument, in part, is this: Today's news is indeed biased—as it must inevitably be—and this bias can be best understood by understanding the concept, the conventions, and the ethic of objectivity.

Specifically, objectivity in journalism accounts for—or at least helps us understand—three principal developments in American journalism; each of these developments contributes to the bias or ideology of news. First, objective reporting is biased against what the press typically defines as its role in a democracy—that of a Fourth Estate, the watchdog role, an adversary press. Indeed, objectivity in journalism is biased in favor of the status quo; it is inherently conservative to the extent that it encourages reporters to rely on what sociologist Alvin Gouldner so appropriately describes as the "managers of the status quo"—the prominent and the élite. Second, objective reporting is biased against independent thinking; it emasculates the intellect by treating it as a disinterested spectator. Finally, objective reporting is biased against the very idea of responsibility; the day's news is viewed as something journalists are compelled to report, not something they are responsible for creating.

This last point, I think, is most important. Despite a renewed interest in professional ethics, the discussion continues to evade questions of morality and responsibility. Of course, this doesn't mean that journalists are immoral. Rather, it means that journalists today are largely amoral. Objectivity in journalism effectively erodes the very foundation on which rests a responsible press.

By most any of the many accounts of the history of objectivity in journalism, objective reporting began more as a commercial imperative than as a standard of responsible reporting. With the emergence of a truly popular press in the mid–1800s—the penny press—a press tied neither to the political parties nor the business élite, objectivity provided a presumably disinterested view of the world.

But the penny press was only one of many social, economic, political, and technological forces that converged in the mid- and late–1800s to bring about fundamental and lasting changes in American journalism. There was the advent of the telegraph, which for the first time separated communication from transportation. There were radical changes in printing technology, including the steam-powered press and later the rotary press. There was the formation of the Associated Press, an early effort by publishers to monopolize a new technology—in this case the telegraph. There was, finally, the demise of community and the rise of society; there were now cities, "human settlements" where "strangers are likely to meet."

These are some of the many conditions that created the climate for objective reporting, a climate best understood in terms of the emergence of a new mass medium and the need for that medium to operate eff.iciently in the marketplace.

Efficiency is the key term here, for efficiency is the central meaning of objective reporting. It was efficient for the Associated Press to distribute only the "bare facts," and leave the opportunity for interpretation to individual members of the cooperative. It was efficient for newspapers not to offend readers and advertisers with partisan prose. It was efficient—perhaps expedient—for reporters to distance themselves from the sense and substance of what they reported.

To survive in the marketplace, and to enhance their status as a new and more democratic press, journalists—principally publishers, who were becoming more and more removed from the editing and writing process—began to transform efficiency into a standard of professional competence, a standard later—several decades later—described as objectivity. This transformation was aided by two important developments in the early twentieth century: first, Oliver Wendell Holmes's effort to employ a marketplace metaphor to define the meaning of the First Amendment; and second, the growing popularity of the scientific method as the proper tool with which to discover and understand an increasingly alien reality.

In a dissenting opinion in 1919, Holmes popularized "the marketplace of ideas," a metaphor introduced by John Milton several centuries earlier. Metaphor or not, publishers took it quite literally. They argued—and continue with essentially the same argument today—that their opportunity to compete and ultimately survive in the marketplace is their First Amendment right, a Constitutional privilege. The American Newspaper Publishers Association, organized in 1887, led the cause of a free press. In the name of freedom of the press, the ANPA fought the Pure Food and Drug Act of 1906 on behalf of its advertisers; it fought the Post Office Act of 1912, which compelled sworn statements of ownership and circulation and thus threatened to reveal too much to advertisers; it fought efforts to regulate child labor, which would interfere with the control and exploitation of paper boys; it fought the collective bargaining provisions of the National Recovery Act in the mid–1930s; for similar reasons, it stood opposed to the American Newspaper Guild, the reporters' union; it tried—unsuccessfully—to prevent wire services from selling news to radio stations until after publication in the nearby newspaper.

Beyond using the First Amendment to shield and protect their economic interests in the marketplace, publishers were also able to use the canons of science to justify—indeed, legitimize—the canons of objective reporting. Here publishers were comforted by Walter Lippmann's writings in the early 1920s, particularly his plea for a new scientific journalism, a new realism; a call for journalists to remain "clear and free" of their irrational, their unexamined, their unacknowledged prejudgments.

By the early 1900s objectivity had become the acceptable way of doing reporting—or at least the respectable way. It was respectable because it was reliable, and it was reliable because it was standardized. In practice, this meant a preoccupation with *how* the news was presented, whether its *form* was reliable. And this concern for reliability quickly overshadowed any concern for the validity of the realities the journalists presented.

Thus emerged the conventions of objective reporting, a set of routine procedures journalists use to objectify their news stories. These are the conventions sociologist Gaye Tuchman describes as a kind of strategy journalists use to deflect criticism, the same kind of strategy social scientists use to defend the quality of their work. For the journalist, this means interviews with sources; and it ordinarily means official sources with impeccable credentials. It means juxtaposing conflicting truth-claims, where truth-claims are reported as "fact" regardless of their validity. It means making a judgment about the news value of a truth-claim even if that judgment serves only to lend authority to what is known to be false or misleading.

As early as 1924 objectivity appeared as an ethic, an ideal subordinate only to truth itself. In his study of the *Ethics of Journalism,* Nelson Crawford devoted three full chapters to the principles of objectivity. Thirty years later, in 1954, Louis Lyons, then curator for the Nieman Fellowship program at Harvard, was describing objectivity as a "rock-bottom" imperative. Apparently unfazed by Wisconsin's Senator Joseph McCarthy, Lyons portrayed objectivity as the ultimate discipline of journalism. "It is at the bottom of all sound reporting—indispensable as the core of the writer's capacity." More recently, in 1973, the Society of Professional Journalists, Sigma Delta Chi formally enshrined the idea of objectivity when it adopted as part of its Code of Ethics a paragraph characterizing objective reporting as an attainable goal and a standard of performance toward which journalists should strive. "We honor those who achieve it," the Society proclaimed.

So well ingrained are the principles of objective reporting that the judiciary is beginning to acknowledge them. In a 1977 federal appellate decision, *Edwards v. National Audubon Society,* a case described by media attorney Floyd Abrams as a landmark decision in that it may prove to be the next evolutionary stage in the development of the public law of libel, a new and novel privilege emerged. It was the first time the courts explicitly recognized objective reporting as a standard of journalism worthy of First Amendment protection.

In what appeared to be an inconsequential story published in *The New York Times* in 1972—on page 33—five scientists were accused of being paid liars, men paid by the pesticide industry to lie about the use of DDT and its effect on bird life. True to the form of objective reporting, the accusation was fully attributed—to a fully identified official of the National Audubon Society. The scientists, of course, were given an opportunity to deny the accusation. Only one of the scientists, however, was quoted by name and he described the accusation as "almost libelous." What was newsworthy about the story, obviously, was the accusation; and with the exception of one short paragraph, the reporter more or less provided a forum for the National Audubon Society.

Three of the five scientists filed suit. While denying punitive damages, a jury awarded compensatory damages against the *Times* and one of the Society's officials. The *Times,* in turn, asked a federal District Court to overturn the verdict. The *Times* argued that the actual malice" standard had not been met; since the scientists were "public figures," they were required to show that the *Times* knowingly published a falsehood or there was, on the part of the *Times,* a reckless disregard for whether the accusation was true or false. The evidence before the court clearly indicated the latter—there was indeed a reckless disregard for whether the accusation was true or false. The reporter made virtually no effort to confirm the validity of the National Audubon Society's accusations. Also the story wasn't the kind of "hot news" (a technical term used by the courts) that required immediate dissemination; in fact ten days before the story was published the *Times* learned that two of the five scientists were not employed by the pesticide industry and thus could not have been "paid liars."

The *Times* appealed to the Second Circuit Court of Appeals, where the lower court's decision was overturned. In reversing the District Court, the Court of Appeals created a new First Amendment right, a new Constitutional defense in libel law—the privilege of "neutral reportage." "We do not believe," the Court of Appeals ruled, "that the press may be required to suppress newsworthy statements merely because it has serious doubts regarding their truth." The First Amendment, the Court said, "protects the accurate and disinterested reporting" of newsworthy accusations "regardless of the reporter's private views regarding their validity."

I mention the details of the *Edwards* case only because it illustrates so well the consequences of the ethic of objectivity. First, it illustrates a very basic tension between objectivity and responsibility. Objective reporting virtually precludes responsible reporting, if by responsible reporting we mean a willingness on the part of the reporter to be accountable for what is reported. Objectivity requires only that reporters be accountable for *how* they report, not what they report. The *Edwards* Court made this very clear: "The public interest in being fully informed," the Court said, demands that the press be afforded the freedom to report newsworthy accusations "without assuming responsibility for them."

Second, the *Edwards* case illustrates the unfortunate bias of objective reporting—a bias in favor of leaders and officials, the prominent and the élite. It is an unfortunate bias because it runs counter to the important democratic assumption that statements made by ordinary citizens are as valuable as statements made by the prominent and the élite. In a democracy, public debate depends on separating individuals from their powers and privileges in the larger society; otherwise debate itself becomes a source of domination. But *Edwards* reinforces prominence as a news value; it reinforces the use of official sources, official records, official channels. Tom Wicker underscored the bias of the *Edwards* case when he observed recently that "objective journalism almost always favors Establishment positions and exists not least to avoid offense to them."

Objectivity also has unfortunate consequences for the reporter, the individual journalist. Objective reporting has stripped reporters of their creativity and their imagination; it has robbed journalists of their passion and their perspective. Objective reporting has transformed journalism into something more technical than intellectual; it has turned the art of story-telling into the technique of report writing. And most unfortunate of all, objective reporting has denied journalists their citizenship; as disinterested observers, as impartial reporters, journalists are expected to be morally disengaged and politically inactive.

Journalists have become—to borrow James Carey's terminology—"professional communicators," a relatively passive link between sources and audiences. With neither the need nor the opportunity to develop a critical perspective from which to assess the events, the issues, and the personalities he or she is assigned to cover, the objective reporter tends to function as a translator—translating the specialized language of sources into a language intelligible to a lay audience.

In his frequently cited study of Washington correspondents—a study published nearly fifty years ago—Leo Rosten found that a "pronounced majority" of the journalists he interviewed considered themselves inadequate to cope with the bewildering complexities of our nation's policies and politics. As Rosten described it, the Washington press corps was a frustrated and exasperated group of prominent journalists more or less resigned to their role as mediators, translators. "To do the job," one reporter told Rosten, "what you know or understand isn't important. You've got to know whom to ask." Even if you don't understand what's being said, Rosten was told, you just take careful notes and write it up verbatim: "Let my readers figure it out. I'm their reporter, not their teacher."

That was fifty years ago. Today, the story is pretty much the same. Two years ago another study of Washington correspondents was published, a book by Stephen Hess called *The Washington Reporters*. For the most part, Hess found, stories coming out of Washington were little more than a "mosaic of facts and quotations from sources" who were participants in an event or who had knowledge of the event. Incredibly, Hess found that for nearly three-quarters of the stories he studied, reporters relied on no documents—only interviews. And when reporters did use documents, those documents were typically press clippings—stories they had written or stories written by their colleagues.

And so what does objectivity mean? It means that sources supply the sense and substance of the day's news. Sources provide the arguments, the rebuttals, the explanations, the criticism. Sources put forth the ideas while other sources challenge those ideas. Journalists, in their role as professional communicators, merely provide a vehicle for these exchanges.

But if objectivity means that reporters must maintain a healthy distance from the world they report, the same standard does not apply to publishers. According to the SPJ, SDX Code of Ethics, "Journalists and their employers should conduct their personal lives in a manner which protects them from conflict of interest, real or apparent." Many journalists do just that—they avoid even an appearance of a conflict of interest. But certainly not their employers.

If it would be a conflict of interest for a reporter to accept, say, an expensive piano from a source at the Steinway Piano Company, it apparently wasn't a conflict of interest when CBS purchased the Steinway Piano Company.

Publishers and broadcasters today are part of a large and growing and increasingly diversified industry. Not only are many newspapers owned by corporations that own a variety of non-media properties, but their boards of directors read like a *Who's Who* of the powerful and the élite. A recent study of the twenty-five largest newspaper companies found that the directors of these companies tend to be linked with "powerful business organizations, not with public interest groups; with management, not with labor; with well established think tanks and charities, not their grassroots counterparts."

But publishers and broadcasters contend that these connections have no bearing on how the day's news is reported—as though the ownership of a newspaper had no bearing on the newspaper's content; as though business decisions have no effect on editorial decisions; as though it wasn't economic considerations in the first place that brought about the incentives for many of the conventions of contemporary journalism.

No doubt the press has responded to many of the more serious consequences of objective reporting. But what is significant is that the response has been to amend the conventions of objectivity, not to abandon them. The press has merely refined the canons of objective reporting; it has not dislodged them.

What remains fundamentally unchanged is the journalist's naïvely empirical view of the world, a belief in the separation of facts and values, a belief in the existence of *a* reality—the reality of empirical facts. Nowhere is this belief more evident than when news is defined as something external to—and independent of—the journalist. The very vocabulary used by journalists when they talk about news underscores their belief that news is "out there," presumably waiting to be *exposed* or *uncovered* or at least *gathered*.

This is the essence of objectivity, and this is precisely why it is so very difficult for journalism to consider questions of ethics and morality. Since news exists "out there"—apparently independent of the reporter—journalists can't be held responsible for it. And since they are not responsible for the news being there, how can we expect journalists to be accountable for the consequences of merely reporting it?

What objectivity has brought about, in short, is a disregard for the consequences of newsmaking. A few years ago Walter Cronkite offered this interpretation of journalism: "I don't think it is any of our business what the moral, political, social, or economic effect of our reporting is. I say let's go with the job of reporting—and let the chips fall where they may."

Contrast that to John Dewey's advice: that "our chief moral business is to become acquainted with consequences."

I am inclined to side with Dewey. Only to the extent that journalists are held accountable for the consequences of their actions can there be said to be a responsible press. But we are not going to be able to hold journalists accountable for the consequences of their actions until they acknowledge that news is their creation, a creation for which they are fully responsible. And we are not going to have much success convincing journalists that news is created, not reported, until we can successfully challenge the conventions of objectivity.

The task, then, is to liberate journalism from the burden of objectivity by demonstrating—as convincingly as we can—that objective reporting is more of a custom than a principle, more a habit of mind than a standard of performance. And by showing that objectivity is largely a matter of efficiency—efficiency that serves, as far as I can tell, only the needs and interest of the owners of the press, not the needs and interests of talented writers and certainly not the needs and interests of the larger society.

DISCUSSION QUESTIONS

1. What does Lippmann mean by a "stereotype"?

2. According to Lippmann, even eyewitness reports typically involve stereotypes. What reasons does he provide for making this claim?

3. Lippmann states that "most facts in consciousness seem to be partly made. A report is the joint product of the knower and known, in which the role of the observer is always selective and usually creative. The facts we see depend on where we are placed, and the habits of our eyes." What do you think Lippmann means when he says that reports are "always selective"? Do you agree with him? What do you think he means when he says that reports are "usually creative"? Do you agree with him? Defend your answers.

4. Lippmann argues that there is "economy" in perceiving reality in terms of stereotypes. What does he mean by this? Do you agree with him? Defend your answers.

5. Lippmann also states that "the systems of stereotypes may be the core of our personal tradition, the defenses of our position in society." What does he mean by this? Do you agree with him? Defend your answers.

6. Lippmann argues that, while it is neither desirable nor feasible to attempt to abandon all stereotypes in favor of a completely neutral approach to experience, "what matters is the character of the stereotypes and the gullibility with which we employ them." What does he mean by this? Do you agree with him? Defend your answers.

7. As mentioned (question 3), Lippmann maintains that "a report is the joint product of the knower and the known." Yet he thinks that "objective" reports are still possible. What, then, is (are) the difference(s), in Lippmann's view, between objective and nonobjective reports?

8. What does Lippmann mean by a "moral code"? In Lippmann's view, what is the main difference between moral codes that are influenced by science and ones that are not? In your estimation, are moral codes that are influenced by science more "objective" than ones that are not? Defend your answer.

9. What does Lippmann think the chief function of the press should be in a democratic society? Do you agree with his view? Defend your answer.

10. What does Lippmann consider to be the chief obstacle that journalists confront in reporting the news? In your estimation, is he correct? Defend your answer.

11. What, according to Lippmann, can be done to make the job of journalists more manageable? In Lippmann's view, what role can expanded knowledge in the social sciences play in this regard? Do you agree with his proposal? Defend your answer.

12. Glasser contends that journalistic objectivity is an "ideology," where "ideology is defined as a set of beliefs that function as the journalist's 'claim to action.'" Discuss some of the main beliefs which, according to Glasser, comprise this ideology.

13. Glasser argues that objective news reporting is undemocratic since it is "biased in favor of the status quo." Why does he think objective news reporting favors the status quo? In your estimation, is such a bias an inevitable outcome of objective news reporting? In other words, can there be objective news reporting without such a bias? Defend your answer.

14. Glasser says that objective news reporting involves a "commitment to the supremacy of observable and retrievable facts." He also says that a "convention" of objective reporting permits journalists to make "a judgment about the news value of a truth-claim even if that judgment serves only to lend authority to what is known to be false or misleading." In your estimation, is the latter "convention" consistent with the journalistic commitment to "the supremacy of observable and retrievable facts"? Do you think journalists should ever report truth-claims they know to be false or misleading?

15. What, according to Glasser, is the significance of the *Edwards* case for the issue of objective news reporting? Do you agree with the manner in which the Court of Appeals settled this case? Defend your answer.

16. According to Glasser, objective news reporting is "biased against independent thinking." Why does he maintain this? In your view, are creativity and imagination important aspects of news reporting? If so, what roles should they play? Defend your answers.

17. According to Glasser, objective reporting is characterized by a belief in the separation of facts and values. In your estimation, is such a separation even possible? What would Lippmann say about the possibility of such a separation?

18. Glasser argues that objective news reporting is "biased against the very idea of responsibility." Why does he maintain this? Do you agree with Glasser that objective news reporting promotes such a bias? Defend your answer.

19. Against Glasser, it might be argued that the *rejection* of journalistic objectivity is biased against responsibility because it gives journalists an excuse for turning out very unobjective, inaccurate accounts. Do you agree with this latter argument? In your estimation, what view of journalistic objectivity would be most apt to promote responsible journalism? Defend your answers.

7

Multiperspectivism and the Problem of News Distortion

In the previous chapter the question of whether journalistic objectivity is possible was explored. Still, one news philosophy that provides a *further* response to the latter question is that of "multiperspectivism." In this chapter, this news philosophy and the related concepts of "news distortion," "bias" and "balance" will be examined.

In the first selection, "Multiperspectival News," Herbert Gans develops and defends a multiperspectival approach to news as a response to the problem of news distortion. According to Gans, it is not possible for journalists to provide an objective account of the news if by that is meant "a perfect and complete reproduction of external reality." Gans does not deny the possibility of grasping external reality through empirical inquiries. However, what he argues is that such knowledge is relative to the particular concepts and methods we are employing, and to the particular questions we are trying to answer. "Facts," he says, "are among other things, answers to questions about external reality." Since different people ask different questions (and make different value and reality assumptions) due to their diverse stations in life, they also perceive different facts. For example, poor people do not experience reality in the same way as do wealthy people. To the wealthy person, an unfinished meal may qualify as "garbage"; to the homeless person, who desires to know where he may obtain his next meal, the same may be perceived as tomorrow's sustenance.

Since there is no absolute standard for determining which questions are the "right" ones to ask, argues Gans, there is no absolute standard of reality; nor, therefore, is there any absolute standard of reality distortion. What, from one perspective, may be viewed as a distortion of reality, may, from a different perspective, be viewed as a fact.

Given this relativist stance concerning judgments about reality, what then is to count as fact for purposes of reporting the news? Gans' answer is to bring into the purview of news as many perspectives as (reasonably) possible. Since any one perspective is bound to be biased according to particular value and reality assumptions, the introduction of as many different perspectives as possible can serve to alleviate the problem of news distortion by providing a more "balanced" approach to the news. On this understanding, "objectivity would also attain a new meaning, for in the final reckoning, story selectors can be objective only by choosing news from several perspectives."

According to Gans, multiperspectival news would require journalists to put aside their personal values for their "prime value" which would be "perspectival diversity." Gans admits, however, that omniperspectival news is not possible. Therefore, story selectors will still need to choose among alternative perspectives. Given Gans' relativist stance, however, it is not clear how journalists may themselves remain bias-free in their selection of individual perspectives, or in their selection of standards of selection.

Gans' preference is for a "two-tiered model" of multiperspectivism according to which the current national news media would be expanded to encompass a greater number of perspectives (first tier); and according to which media catering to "specific, fairly homogeneous audiences"— specific races, religions, age groups, economic classes, interest groups, and so on—would also be expanded (second tier).

The introduction of multiperspectivism would, according to Gans, require certain changes in the manner in which stories are formated. For example, in addition to making them lengthier, "journalists would be required to organize their perspectives and, in some cases, to relate and interpret them . . . additional journalistic commentary may also be desirable, thus allowing for personal advocacy journalists in national news organizations." Similarly, the media encompassing the second tier would "devote themselves primarily to reanalyzing and reinterpreting news gathered by the central media—and wire services—for their audiences, adding their own commentary and backing these up with as much original reporting, particularly to supply bottom-up, representative, and service news, as would be financially feasible." It may be argued, however, that the introduction of these interpretive journalistic activities may themselves introduce further biases into the presentation. Moreover, since journalists' own interpretations may be taken by audiences to be authoritative, Gans' primary values of "perspectival diversity" and "greater balance" may be impaired or defeated. While Gans indicates that a multiperspectival approach to news would require journalists to cultivate "sensitivity to many perspectives, empathy with diverse sources, and above all, sufficient contact with them to breed sensitivity and empathy," it is not clear, given Gans' own stance on the relativity of reality perception, how journalists could successfully transcend their own reality and value assumptions.

In the end, Gans claims that "the fundamental justification for multiperspectival news is its potential for furthering democracy." This goal, he hopes, will be supported by bringing more groups of people into the "symbolic arena" than previously. While Gans admits that "information alone does not alter economic and political hierarchies," it can, he suggests, supply an important condition of economic and political change.

In the second selection of this chapter, "Some Reservations About Multiperspectival News," Jay Newman challenges the relativist basis of Gans' multiperspectival news philosophy. Newman argues that Gans fails to recognize an ordinary language distinction between *perspectives* and *biases*. Acording to Newman, not all perspectives are necessarily biased: a perspective is not usually considered a bias unless it is "epistemically and/or ethically unacceptable, based on false presuppositions or productive of harm or evil." Therefore, Newman argues, "in dealing with the problem of journalistic bias, we should worry much less about the question of *how many* perspectives the news media present and represent than the question of what constitutes an epistemically and morally *reasonable* perspective by which to report and interpret events." According to Newman, the failure to draw the latter distinction between rational perspectives and biased ones is to give equal standing to the moral judgments of a Socrates and an Adolph Hitler, and thus to "embrace relativism of a very radical and dangerous kind."

On the other hand, even if Newman is correct that some perspectives are morally and epistemically superior to others, it does not follow from this that journalists should attempt to limit the range of reportable perspectives to such superior ones. The reader is here reminded of John Stuart Mill's admonition (Chapter 3) against silencing an opinion even if it is false; for in this case the journalist will deprive his or her audience of the opportunity to gain "the clearer perception and livelier impression of truth, produced by its collision with error."

Nor does Newman seem to present any compelling reason to countenance the "moral and epistemic superiority" of journalists' perspectives. Newman suggests that journalists are "highly educated professionals" and that educated people may be "less biased than relatively ignorant people." Nevertheless, he does not deny that journalists may, notwithstanding their education, perceive reality through their own biased perspectives (for example, ones arising out of a white, middle-class background). Moreover, the inference from the proposition that journalists are "highly educated professionals" to the proposition that journalists are "morally and intellectually superior human beings" is not generally a sound one. However, it may well reflect the bias of at least some "educated" persons.

Newman also questions the potential of multiperspectival news to further democracy. He argues that, insofar as democratization means increasing the power of the majority, multiperspectival news is actually *un*democratic, for "while it gives power to some who have hitherto been denied it, it takes power away from 'majorities' in the process."

According to Gans, multiperspectival news is democratic because it aims at reducing "the symbolic power of now dominant sources and perspectives." However, dominant sources and perspectives are not necessarily representative of the majority. Therefore, in taking power away from them, multiperspectival news does not necessarily "take power away from 'majorities' in the process." Moreover, Newman fails to take account of the importance attached to *equalitarian* principles in democratic theory. Insofar as multiperspectival news allows every citizen an opportunity to enter the "symbolic arena," it is democratic. Since, according to Gans, multiperspectival news adds a "bottom-up view to the current top-down approach," opening up the media forum to ordinary citizens as well as those with official credentials, it is consonant with democratic principles underscoring the value of equal opportunity.

As Newman points out, however, the justification of multiperspectival news in terms of its potential for furthering democracy is independent of its justification as a solution to the problem of news distortion. Whether or not Gans' multiperspectival news philosophy is a satisfactory response to the latter problem is, indeed, no settled matter.

Multiperspectival News

HERBERT J. GANS

Discussions of news policy are customarily initiated by evaluating what is good or bad about today's news media and determining how they can be improved. But this approach often ends up with alternative print and electronic news media modeled on either a thicker and more serious *New York Times* or on the journals of opinion—and sometimes even on academic publications. Such improvements, however, are likely to drive away a significant portion of the present audience for national news. They also discourage cultural democratization, that is, making the news relevant for people not now part of the news audience. Consequently, I want to approach policy from another direction, by asking whether the news is distorted.

NEWS DISTORTION

"Distortion" has become a loosely used equivalent for "bias." In the last ten years, the news has been considered distorted because it favored one or another ideology, or was unfair to one or another set of public officials; because it was overly superficial, too concerned with personalities at the expense of issues, or overly given to dramatic action and exaggeration; because it was too preoccupied with official sources and with media events rather than with "actualities"; or because it reported too much social disorder or other bad news.

Whatever the charges (and some are justified), the assumption is that distorted news can be replaced by undistorted news; but that assumption is untenable. Even if a perfect and complete reproduction (or construction) of external reality were philosophically or logistically feasible, the mere act of reproduction would constitute a distortion of that reality. Thus, objective or absolute nondistortion is impossible.

The concept of distortion is nevertheless valid, but only as a relational one. News can be judged as distorted *in relation* to a specified standard (or ideal) of nondistortion. However, the standards themselves cannot be absolute or objective because they are inevitably based on a number of reality and value judgments: about the nature of external reality, knowledge, and truth; about the proper purposes of the news; and more often than not, about the good nation and society.[1] When the news is accused of favoring one ideology, for example, it is therefore distorted in relation to a standard of ideological balance and the ideal of a pluralist nation of coexisting ideologies. If news is judged to rely too much on official sources, the standard rests on an assumption that government is not to be trusted and, more broadly, on a theory of democracy in which ordinary people are as important as public officials. But when the news lives up to one standard, it may then be distorted in relation to a different one. . . .

Relational standards of undistorted news cannot be absolute, but they can be universal. Since they are based on values, however, they can become universal only if there is agreement on these values. Barring such agreement, all anyone can do is choose standards, argue in their behalf, and debate against those that are different. Identifying distorted news and proposing a standard for undistorted news is a political act; and while the act itself is desirable, the actor ultimately must take sides.

FACTS AND QUESTIONS

Basic philosophical concerns about the existence of external reality and about whether it can be grasped by empirical methods are not at issue here, for most critics of the news agree with journalists and most social scientists that empirical inquiry about external reality is possible. Thus, I shall not debate the possibility of determining what journalists call facts. (I will also ignore the problem that many journalistic facts are not amenable to empirical testing but are attributed opinions.)

Rather, the issue is *what* facts should become news. Even empirically determinable facts do not arise out of thin air but are fashioned out of concepts and specific empirical methods. Concepts in turn are based on reality and value judgments, and different judgments produce different concepts. But when concepts—or methods—differ, so do the resulting facts.

To put it another way: facts are, among other things, answers to questions about external reality. The population of New York City does not become a fact until someone asks how many people live in the city. Once that question is asked, in that way, the number of New Yorkers can be empirically determined; in this instance, there need be little debate about the empirical methods. Factual answers to the question of how major party candidates campaign for the presidency can also be determined empirically, although then, problems of selection and summary that always accompany the reporter's tasks begin to appear. . . .

In short, many questions can be asked about the actors and activities which now appear in, or are omitted from, the news. Consequently, news can be considered distorted for asking questions which a standard setter considers to be wrong or for using the wrong concepts to frame correct questions, or for employing the wrong methods. I want to deal with two of these issues: what constitutes the right methods and the right questions.

METHODS—AND AUDIENCES

The notion that journalists are employing the wrong methods is at the heart of most complaints, by social scientists and others, that the news is too superficial and overly addicted to dramatic action. Ostensibly, the issue is whether journalistic empirical methodology is the best way of approaching external reality; yet it cannot be separated from what questions journalists should ask because superficial facts come from superficial questions, and in order to obtain dramatic news, journalists must ask dramatic questions.

But above all, the issue concerns the audience and how it should be informed. In theory, journalists claim that their responsibility extends only to supplying information, whether or not the audience accepts it; but in practice, the product considerations exist to persuade the audience to accept it. Journalism is an empirical discipline but one which requires that its findings be presented as interestingly and in as few minutes or words as possible. . . .

THE RIGHT QUESTIONS

Whatever the discipline, distortion cannot be judged without reference to the audience. Even so, the major issue concerns what questions are to become facts—and by extension, what sets of facts should be selected, as stories, for the news. In effect, most critiques of the news accuse journalists of asking the wrong questions, and few critics have difficulty in proposing alternatives. For news policy, however, there must be agreement on what constitutes the right questions, which requires prior agreement on the relevant reality and value judgments. However, such agreement is virtually impossible to achieve, since the questions all of us consider correct, or relevant, depend on where we sit or where we stand: on our position in the national and societal hierarchies, and on the value judgments we make, partly as a result of our position in these hierarchies.

In the prototypical homogeneous society, which has never existed, everyone shares the same perspectives; but in a modern society, no one sits or stands in exactly the same place. Consequently, perspectives on reality will vary. Poor people experience America differently than do middle-income people or the rich; as a result, their attitudes toward government will also vary. Different perspectives lead to different questions and different answers, thereby requiring different facts and different news. . . .

Most important, no one can synthesize all perspectives, since some are in conflict, and in many cases, taking one perspective precludes taking others. After all, one cannot be a Marxist and a libertarian concurrently. But if a synthesis is impossible, there can be no one absolutely right or true perspective, and no single set of right questions. Individuals must choose their perspectives and, in so doing, take sides. For public agencies like the news media, which serve large numbers of people, all perspectives are relevant, and all (or virtually all) questions are right for someone. But if journalists had to consider all perspectives and answer all questions, the news would be nearly infinite in length. News and the news media can exist only if journalists restrict themselves to asking a limited number of questions at any given time. . . .

When news has focused purposes, the choice of right questions is relatively easy. If the major purpose of the news is to hasten the revolution or the return to traditional values, to publicize leaders, or to hold nation and society together, some questions are clearly wrong. But these purposes put the news at the service of specific interest groups, whose values are not necessarily public values.

Journalists operate instead with an unfocused and more public purpose: to inform the audience. So stated, however, this purpose is meaningless. Journalists cannot inform the audience about everything; but in deciding what they should include and omit, they skirt the issue of what are the right questions. . . .

Instead, I would argue that the primary purpose of the news derives from the journalists' functions as constructors of nation and society, and as managers of the symbolic arena. The most important purpose of the news, therefore, is to provide the symbolic arena, and the citizenry, with comprehensive and representative images (or constructs) of nation and society. In order to be comprehensive, the news must report nation and society in terms of all known perspectives; in order to be representative, it must enable all sectors of nation and society to place their actors and activities—and messages—in the symbolic arena. Or, as the Commission on Freedom of the Press put it in 1947, the news should include "the projection of a representative picture of the constituent groups in society."[2]

Ideally, then, the news should be omniperspectival; it should present and represent all perspectives in and on America. This ideal, however, is unachievable, for it is only another way of saying that all questions are right. It is possible to suggest, however, that the news, and the news media, be multiperspectival, presenting and representing as many perspectives as possible—and at the very least, more than today.

MULTIPERSPECTIVAL NEWS

Multiperspectival news is a label, but it also entails a conception of alternative news, which differs from today's news in five ways.

First, multiperspectival news would be *more national*. Moving beyond the current equating of the federal government with the nation, it would seek to report comprehensively about more national and nationwide agencies and institutions, including national corporations, unions, and voluntary associations, as well as organized and unorganized interest groups.

Second, multiperspectival news would add a *bottom-up* view to the current top-down approach. For example, news about federal (and corporate) policies would be accompanied by reactions not just from high officials, but from citizens in various walks of life who would be affected by these policies. If social and moral disorder news remains a news staple, the bottom-up approach would suggest that what ordinary people consider to be disorder also become newsworthy, be it petty delinquency in the suburbs or prosaic labor-management unrest in the nation's factories and offices. At the same time, multiperspectivism would include the disorder that suburban adults create for and among teenagers. Moral disorder news would cover that which a wide variety of people perceive to be amiss in society—from Marxists who see contradictions in capitalism to religious conservatives concerned with the decline in traditional morality. Although the now highly selective list of villains in the news would be enlarged, moral disorder stories would also have to report their perspectives, since these villains, too, are members of society.

Third, multiperspectival news would feature more *output* news, determining how the plans and programs of national and nationwide public and private agencies have worked out in practice for intended and unintended beneficiaries, victims, bystanders, and the general public.

Fourth, multiperspectival news would aim to be more *representative,* reporting on the activities and opinions of ordinary Americans from all population sectors and roles. (By "sectors," I mean groups according to age, income, educational level, ethnicity and religion, etc.; by "roles," I mean what people do as parents and children, employers and workers, buyers and sellers, medical and legal clients, homeowners and tenants, members of organized or unorganized interest groups, etc.) As the term implies, representative news would represent people from all walks of life in the symbolic arena: how they see America and what they deem to be its major problems, as well as what they deem to be theirs—in other words, what they consider to be important national news *about* themselves. Representative news thus means greater coverage of the diversity of opinion, from many positions in different national and societal hierarchies, and from many points on the ideological spectrum.

Fifth, multiperspectival news would place more emphasis on *service* news, providing personally relevant information for specific national sectors and roles: what people consider to be important national news *for* themselves. For example, people of different ages, incomes, and occupations who come into contact with different national agencies and institutions need national news about those agencies and institutions which touch their own lives. Changes in federal tax policy are of little relevance to people too poor to pay taxes; instead, they need news about changes in national welfare and jobs policies. Likewise, homeowners require different news than tenants about federal housing policies and administrative practices.

MULTIPERSPECTIVAL JOURNALISM

Most of the ingredients of multiperspectival news are hardly novel, but adding them to the national news, and in larger quantity than they exist at present, would require changes in the journalistic *modus operandi.* For one thing, news would have to be collected from a much larger number of more scattered and less easily accessible sources. Needless to say, the total amount of both available and suitable news would increase, which would demand a larger newshole and, as I suggest in the next section, additional national news media.

The conventional story format would also change. When several perspectives must be taken into account on any given topic, stories will naturally become longer. Moreover, journalists would be required to organize these perspectives and, in some cases, to relate and interpret them; consequently, news analyses would be necessary more often. When the news contains greater diversity of opinion from sources, additional journalistic commentary may also be desirable, thus allowing for personal and advocacy journalists in national news organizations. In the process, the news would become more ideological, with explicit ideological diversity replacing the implicit near-uniformity that now prevails.

Since sources would be recruited from all levels of society, journalists would also have to be recruited and trained to deal with them. This is not to say, for example, that only blacks could report news about and for blacks, or that producers and editors from blue-collar backgrounds would have to choose news about and for blue-collar workers. Although "insiders" might find it easier to obtain access to sources, they would also be limited in communicating to "outsiders."[3] The requisite reportorial quality is sensitivity to many perspectives, empathy with diverse sources, and above all, sufficient contact with them to breed sensitivity and empathy. In effect, beats would have to be established among different sectors of the population; and for this reason alone, multiperspectivism would have little use for today's generalists. Even so, greater heterogeneity in the personal backgrounds of journalists would probably be essential. . . .

As sources, perspectives, and therefore values multiply and diversify, journalistic objectivity becomes even more necessary than it is today. It may be epistemologically impossible, but it can exist as journalistic intent. Inasmuch as story selectors cannot include every perspective and source, their decisions to include or exclude must be free of political intent. Otherwise, they—and the news—will lose their credibility.[4] Indeed, the differences among objective journalists, news analysts, and commentators would need to be sharpened. But objectivity would also attain a new meaning, for in the final reckoning, story selectors can be objective only by choosing news from several perspectives.

Story selectors would continue to set aside personal values, for their prime value would be perspectival diversity. In the process, the journalists' enduring values would no longer play a major supporting role in story selection, although commentators could continue to apply them.

Even so, these values would not disappear; rather, they would be expressed in and by the new diversity of sources. Journalists might be adversaries less often, but they would automatically choose more adversary sources; and in the end, the amount of adversary news would increase. . . .

With more newsworthy sources and longer stories, some current selection considerations would have to be eliminated, however, and the most feasible candidate would be novelty. Were story selectors to apply multiperspectivism, they could not simultaneously supply all the latest news, even with an enlarged newshole. However, no immutable law requires that a daily television program (or newspaper) or weekly magazine emphasize the events of the day or week. Television news even now could eschew the retelling of the day's headlines, for many viewers know them already. In addition, many stories and sources deserve less topicality and immediacy than they currently receive. There is no intrinsic reason for the president to be in the news nearly every day; since the audience is not immediately affected by his actions or statements until later, these could be dispensed with and replaced by periodic but regular features which would allow for bottom-up reactions, as well as early estimates of how his words and acts might affect beneficiaries, victims, and bystanders.

Giving up novelty and the peg would be difficult for story selectors, for they are easily and quickly applied considerations. Inasmuch as a major purpose of multiperspectival news is audience exposure to many different sources, balance considerations would rise in importance. Story selectors would thus make up their story lists in part by determining which sources had not recently appeared in the news; the kind and degree of balance—which are crucial issues in making multiperspectivism operational—will be discussed in greater detail below.

MULTIPERSPECTIVAL NEWS MEDIA

. . . Reaching the millions of people in the lay audience would require an increase in the total newshole for national news, whatever the media, and there are at least two possible models. One model is centralized: it simply expands the present national news media to accommodate multiperspectivism. Each medium would supply its own brand of multiperspectival news to the present large and diverse audience, but one might guess that two-hour evening newscasts, 200-page newsmagazines, and currently non-existent popular national newspapers would be required.

The second model is decentralized: it calls for a much larger number of national news media, each designed to reach different but roughly homogeneous—and therefore smaller—audiences. There might be individual national news programs, magazines, and newspapers for adolescents, adults, and old people; for the rich, the middle class, and the poor; for suburbanites, urbanites, and rural residents; for blue-collar and white-collar workers, and professionals; for ideologically clustered audiences across the spectrum—in theory, at least, for a nearly infinite number of population sectors and roles. Each news medium would supply some uniform news, some stories on the same topics but from different perspectives, and a great deal of distinctive news relevant to each audience.

The centralized model has the benefit of exposing large audiences to a variety of perspectives; moreover, a handful of central media would provide visibility and symbolic power to these perspectives in essentially the present symbolic arena. The decentralized model would supply people with considerably more news in line with their own perspectives, but they would not be exposed to other perspectives; the symbolic arena would thus be decentralized and provincialized as well.

However, both models are probably unworkable. The centralized model requires a multiperspectival news organization, but no top editor or producer could possibly keep all perspectives in mind. The decentralized model fails on economic grounds. Independent newsgathering organizations are very expensive, and those catering to small audiences could not summon up the funds or attract the advertisers to meet these costs. While subsidies could be called for, these would need to be huge, and who would supply them?

A Two-Tier Model

A more realistic model, which combines some centralization and decentralization is conceivable, particularly since it is essentially an expansion of the currently existing array of national media. This model assumes the continued existence of the present national news media, with perhaps one or two additional network news organizations (through syndication and public television), newsmagazines, and national newspapers to come in the future, each of which would adopt a modest degree of multiperspectivism.

These central (or first-tier) media would be complemented by a second tier of pre-existing and new national media, each reporting the news to specific, fairly homogeneous audiences. Depending on audience size and interest, these could be daily, weekly, or monthly television and radio programs, as well as newspapers and magazines. Still, many would need to be subsidized . . . and even then, their news organizations would have to be small.[5] They would devote themselves primarily to reanalyzing and reinterpreting news gathered by the central media—and the wire services—for their audiences, adding their own commentary and backing these up with as much original reporting, particularly to supply bottom-up, representative, and service news, as would be financially feasible. Scattered prototypes of television and radio news programs for specific audiences are already in existence in a few large cities; the newspapers and magazines could be modeled (in makeup and staff size) on the journals of opinion, the publications of the ethnic and racial press, and the newspapers and magazines of small political parties as well as informal political groups.[6]

This model would achieve the prime aim of the news: to present and represent many more perspectives in the symbolic arena. Obviously, the two-tier model would produce somewhat less than equal representation, for the central media would be most prominent in the symbolic arena, which is why they, too, would have to become more multiperspectival.

A MODEST DEGREE OF MULTIPERSPECTIVISM

The crucial issue for the central media of my two-tier model, as well as for the national news media as they now exist, is: How multiperspectival should they become? Or, if all questions are right, which right questions should the national news media ask? Other problems aside, the issue is how to allocate a scarce resource—the national newshole—which can never be large enough to accommodate the sources and perspectives that now dominate the news as well as those called for by multiperspectivism. . . .

If the symbolic arena must be both comprehensive and representative, however, and if the arena must be so managed that journalists can accomplish their work and attract an audience, then new criteria for allocating the newshole must be developed. I do not know how this is to be done, for there are no simple formulas, and many of the judgments must, in any case, be left to the journalists. I can only make some suggestions that aim toward a modest degree of multiperspectivism.

For one thing, journalists should redefine importance considerations to give greater weight to information that is important to various sectors of the population, and less weight to nation and society as units. By that criterion, public officials—and officials of corporations, national voluntary associations, etc.—become newsworthy when their actions and statements have significant impact on one or more of the major sectors and roles into which America is divided. And stories grow in importance the larger the number of affected sectors and roles, or the more drastic the impact on a few. Impact, however, must be measured by output indicators. Social and moral disorders can be judged similarly, but they become important in two other ways: when they affect public or private policy; and when they are the actions of people who have no other means of appearing in the symbolic arena or of making their demands known to public officials.

But the essence of multiperspectivism is greater balance, which requires a higher priority to balance considerations in news judgment. In effect, journalists have to become knowledgeable about the totality, or "universe," of all possible sources and perspectives, and all sectors and roles, in America in order to represent these in the news in a balanced fashion. Currently, journalists select sources and perspectives from among those they know; instead, they must learn to choose from all those known to exist.

However, this proposal requires a complete "mapping" of all sources and perspectives in American society, by social scientists, statisticians, and journalists, which is not now, and may never be, available. In the meantime, the modest solution is to go beyond current practice by ensuring that more of the now unrepresented sources and perspectives appear in the news.

In some instances, this is relatively simple. For news about government or corporate activities, the prime additional sources, both for bottom-up and output news, are beneficiaries and victims, although identifying them requires a good deal of reporter legwork. Similarly, for the general run of political news, the universe consists of the major political parties, some minor ones, spokespersons for other groups likely to be affected by the story, and representatives of various positions on the ideological spectrum.

When the universe of sources and perspectives is very large, as for representative and service news, feasible balance criteria are harder to suggest, since journalists cannot possibly supply such news for all sectors and roles. Even so, story selectors already apply some demographic balance considerations [for example, race and sex]; they would, however, have to add other numerically and politically signifi-cant sectors and roles, which they now omit. The modest and not very difficult solution is to report more representative and service news about the now omitted people outside the middle class and professional occupations: notably the poor, blue-collar and lower white-collar Americans, the old, children and especially adolescents, racial minorities, and the people whose economic, political, and cul-tural opinions are at odds with various "mainstreams." Of course, people from these sectors and roles already appear in the news, but they are either public officials and spokespersons or deviants and oddities. If the symbolic arena is to be comprehensive and represent-ative, however, news about and for such people that treats them, their problems, and their opinions as respectfully as those of high of-ficials must be added for proper balance.

Ideally, multiperspectival balance would be achieved if the news about and for the principal sectors and roles in America were roughly equivalent to their representation in the population. For ex-ample, since close to 15 percent of the population is officially desig-nated as poor, and 20 percent earns less than the median income, balance is achieved when roughly 15 to 20 percent of the news for and about income groups deals with the poor.[7] When information about a relevant universe is readily available, journalists should use it, although I do not suggest that story selection be based on census data or that story selectors should start using slide rules. Indeed, they should not be saddled with keeping track of whether they achieve multiperspectival balance; that responsibility properly belongs to media monitors and critics. . . .

These balance considerations would, as now, be applied in conjunc-tion with others. There would be times, however, when other consid-erations might make balance impossible. If the country were involved in a major war or beset by a series of catastrophes, journalists could not supply as much representative or service news. Conversely, if the government were to launch a major anti-poverty effort, story selectors would be justified in paying more attention to the poor than their per-centage in the population might otherwise warrant. Then, too, presi-dents, other major public and corporate officials, and criminals will always be more newsworthy than their number.

Even these proposals overtax the newshole; in addition, journalists will never have sufficient time or staff to apply this kind of balance for a single story. Accordingly, multiperspectival balance can be achieved only over time—for example, over the duration of running stories and, for other news, over a year's time. In that period, journalists should be able to include some stories about all major sectors and roles, both in the news and in commentary.

As a goal, multiperspectivism resembles equality. Both are impossible to achieve completely, but each offers a target toward which to move. Just as changes in income distribution provide a feasible indicator of movement toward economic equality, so increases in the diversity of sources and perspectives in the news provide a feasible indicator of movement toward multiperspectivism.

Nevertheless, the national news media can go only so far. One of the purposes of the second tier is to continue where the central media leave off: to supply further and more detailed news for and about the perspectives of the audiences they serve. In the process, these media would also function as monitors and critics of the central media, indicating where and how, by their standards, the central media have been insufficiently multiperspectival. . . .

MULTIPERSPECTIVAL NEWS AND DEMOCRACY

The fundamental justification for multiperspectival news is its potential for furthering democracy. If the honorable cliché that democracy rests on a well-informed citizenry were accurate, no further argument would be necessary. But the cliché is not accurate, for democracies must and do function even when citizens are not well informed. The cliché reflects the Athenian conception of democracy, in which participation in government was limited to the well-informed; but today it also has a hidden agenda: the already well-informed hope that if other citizens are given the same information, they will become political supporters of the causes of the now well-informed.

Multiperspectival news is not designed to gain supporters for any specific political cause. Rather, it will enable people to obtain news relevant to their own perspectives, and therefore to their own interests and political goals, if they have any. In the process, the symbolic arena would become more democratic, for the symbolic power of now dominant sources and perspectives would be reduced.

Obviously, multiperspectivism is not apolitical, since making the symbolic arena more democratic is a political goal. Insofar as such an arena would reduce the symbolic power of now dominant sources and perspectives, it is a goal that includes some redistribution of power. The question is, how much? . . .

True, the news media redistribute symbolic power when they act as agenda setters, helping place and publicize issues in the symbolic arena, and thereby increasing the influence of supporters of these issues. Multiperspectival news would set more and different agendas, thus encouraging people to develop opinions and to act if the agenda item were relevant to their interests. In addition, the news disseminates facts, particularly about moral disorder. In the right place and at the right time, moral disorder news can create a wave of sympathy or antipathy, tipping public opinion, and power, on those issues in which public opinion counts. The conditions under which this happens, however, are partly fortuitous; and journalists cannot, by themselves, automatically tip public opinion. Even if news could deliver power, journalists only supply the news; they cannot guarantee that (or how) audiences will use it.

Multiperspectival news will not, therefore, bring about further democratization of America by itself. Democracy is a property of social structure, not symbols, requiring greater equalization of power and of people's ability to exert pressure on their government. But power cannot be equalized without economic change, for unequal economic power breeds unequal political power. Multiperspectival news could supply information about the economic and political inequities that still exist in America; but as radical journalists of every generation have learned, information alone does not alter economic and political hierarchies. . . .

[O]pposition to multiperspectival news might develop because the images of nation and society it would construct would also foster the impression that America is not a cohesive unit but an array of diverse, often conflicting groups. While I doubt that today's news media contribute significantly to social or political cohesion, multiperspectival news would, of course, contribute even less.

Whether the news media should aim to depict America as a cohesive unit or as an array of diverse groups depends on one's political values. For those who believe that cohesion and order are prime national and societal goals, multiperspectivism would be objectionable. For those who feel, as I do, that the interests of diverse groups have priority over the needs of nation and society, multiperspectival news and some decentralization of the national media are preferable. Even so, if more people obtain news relevant to their interests, and if that news helps them achieve their own goals, they may feel themselves to be part of a larger whole. In the long run, then, the country would be more cohesive in fact if not in symbol. . . .

NOTES

1. For an excellent analysis that makes this point in reviewing a number of recent bias and distortion studies, see Alden Williams, "Unbiased Study of Television News Bias," *Journal of Communication* 25 (Autumn 1975): 190–99.

2. Commission on Freedom of the Press, *A Free and Responsible Press* (Chicago: University of Chicago Press, 1947), p. 26.

3. Robert K. Merton, "Insiders and Outsiders," *American Journal of Sociology* 78 (July 1972): 9–47.

4. When too many conflicting perspectives appear in the news, objectivity can, in fact, become what Smith calls a "yardstick of reality," a perspective that is credible simply because it is detached. Anthony Smith, *The Shadow in the Cave* (Urbana: University of Illinois Press, 1974), p. 109.

5. The size and profitability of the present daytime and weekend television audience suggest that news programs for women and children could be established without subsidy. News programs for children and adolescents have, in fact, appeared from time to time, but so far none have lasted.

6. Good recent examples of publications on the Left are the weekly newspaper *In These Times* and the [former] biweekly newsmagazine *Seven Days*.

7. Jones has suggested that the amount of crime news should bear some relation to the crime rate (assuming that an accurate rate can be developed). E. Terence Jones, "The Press as Monitor," *Public Opinion Quarterly* 40 (Summer 1976): 239–43. Even if journalists continue to emphasize dramatic crimes, they can "tag" stories by reporting the rates for such crimes, thus providing some balance to the exaggerations that accompany highlighting.

Some Reservations about Multiperspectival News

JAY NEWMAN

In *Deciding What's News,* a recent study of the most influential national news media, Herbert J. Gans endorses "multiperspectivism," a news philosophy which seems to offer a partial solution to the problem of news distortion without detracting from the integrity of the journalistic enterprise.[1] He suggests "that the news, and news media, be multiperspectival, presenting and representing as many perspectives as possible—and at the very least, more than today."[2] As Gans conceives it, multiperspectival news would be more national, add a bottom-up view to the current top-down approach, feature more output news, aim to be more representative, and place more emphasis on service news.[3] "The fundamental justification for multiperspectival news is its potential for furthering democracy"; and although multiperspectival news "is not designed to gain supporters for any specific political cause," it "is not apolitical, since making the symbolic arena more democratic is a political goal."[4]

Gans realizes that in advocating a version of multiperspectivism, he is offering more than sociological analysis and developing what journalists call a "news philosophy."[5] I shall argue here that multiperspectivism is philosophically naive.

The solution to the problem of news distortion would seem to involve putting pressure on journalists to be more objective. But if Gans is right, then it is precisely in the domain where objectivity is impossible that journalistic bias does most of its damage:

> News can be judged as distorted *in relation* to a specified standard (or ideal) of nondistortion. However, the standards themselves cannot be absolute or objective because they are inevitably based on a number of reality and value judgments: about the nature of external reality, knowledge, and truth; about the proper purposes of the news; and more often than not, about the good nation and society.[6]

In the prototypical homogeneous society, which has never existed, everyone shares the same perspectives; but in a modern society, no one sits

or stands in exactly the same place. Consequently, perspectives on reality will vary. Poor people experience America differently than do
middle-income people or the rich; as a result, their attitudes toward government will also vary. Different perspectives lead to different questions
and different answers, thereby requiring different facts and different
news.[7]

Since people who come from different backgrounds and live under different circumstances have different "perspectives," different world-
views and value-systems, they view different things as important. Nothing is "objectively" important. What matters a great deal to certain
journalists or news editors may matter very little to most readers/lis-
teners/viewers. Were the problem of news bias primarily a matter of
false reports, working for objectivity would be the appropriate solution.
But if "the issue is *what* facts should become news,"[8] striving for an
unattainable objectivity is valueless. Gans proposes a way of dealing
with the kind of news distortion that results from journalists' subjective
conceptions of what matters. He suggests that national news and news
media present and represent as many perspectives as possible. News
must be made multiperspectival. The journalists' perspectives cannot
be falsified, but they can be to some extent neutralized by being jux-
taposed with different perspectives.

Since people have such very different views of what matters, many
aspects of the news can seem distorted. As Gans points out, "In the
last ten years, the news has been considered distorted because it favored
one or another ideology, or was unfair to one or another set of public
officials; because it was overly superficial, too concerned with personalities at the expense of issues, or overly given to dramatic action and
exaggeration; because it was too preoccupied with official sources and
with media events rather than with 'actualities'; or because it reported
too much social disorder or other bad news."[9]

Example: In a 1975 examination of the major news media, Patrick J.
Buchanan asks, "Can Democracy Survive the New Journalism?"[10] After
observing that, "The essence of press power lies in the authority to
select, elevate and promote one set of ideas, issues and personalities—
and to ignore others,"[11] he attacks the "New Journalism" for its anti-
military bias, Naderite grudge against big business, bias for federal social
spending, and partnership with the political and social movements of
liberalism.[12] After going on to criticize the major media's "adversary
journalism" and "negativism," he concludes that the "New Journalism"
poses a threat to American democracy.[13] In arguing that the major media
are dominated by journalists with a liberal, anti-conservative bias, Buch-

anan has spoken for a significant number of Americans who share his values and perceptions.

Gans does not share Buchanan's "conservatism" or his view that the major national media are dominated by doctrinaire anti-conservatives.[14] But the logic of Gans' multiperspectivist argument compels him to take Buchanan's grievance seriously, especially since Buchanan apparently speaks for a large number of Americans. "Ideally," Gans tell us, "multiperspectival balance would be achieved if the news about and for the principal sectors and roles in America were roughly equivalent to their representation in the population."[15] So the logic of Gans' argument compels him to hold that the national media should see to it that Buchanan's "conservative" perspective is presented and represented to the degree that it is shared by Americans. To those Americans who feel that the major news media are already too conservative, Gans can only offer the promise that multiperspectival news will try to present and represent their perspective, too.

It is one thing to envision a fair system of multiperspectival news and another to implement one. Gans quotes a member of *Time's* letters department: "Even when *Time* was conservative, most of the [critical] letters came from conservatives, and for them, no one can ever be conservative enough."[16] This statement, while misleading in one way, is instructive in another. There is no single "conservative" perspective. When Buchanan attacks the media for being dogmatically anti-conservative, many disaffected members of the audience will cheer him on; but when Buchanan starts spelling out his own views on specific issues, many people who identify themselves as "conservatives" will complain that Buchanan's brand of conservatism is not quite the same as theirs. Given the differences in their backgrounds and circumstances, Buchanan and a Baltimore stevedore will have different perceptions of many things, even though both think of themselves as "conservatives." If multiperspectivist news tries to pass off Buchanan's perspective as the rough equivalent of the stevedore's, or vice versa, it is not doing justice to either. But how inclusive can multiperspectivist news be? Every individual has a unique perspective; and in the process of grouping and classifying perspectives to make the news media more democratic, editorial bias of a dangerous kind may be operative.

Gans recognizes that omniperspectival news is impossible. So which perspectives should be included, and which should be excluded? And who should be making such judgments? If a large part of the audience is racist, should multiperspectival news include information of special interest to racists? Should editors and journalists go to great pains to present and represent the perspectives of Presbyterians, adulterers, Masons, the color-blind, astrology buffs, people who resent having to think for themselves? Should they decrease their coverage of the oppression of certain minority groups on the grounds that those groups represent a very small part of the population? And should news executives recruit as editors and journalists more Presbyterians, adulterers, et. al.? Whoever had the power to make such decisions would be able to do considerable damage with his biases.

Gans assumes that even if many perspectives cannot be presented in the news, it is better to have *more* than the national media now present. But a Roman Catholic or Jew who resents the secularism of a certain news medium may be even angrier if that medium "balances" its secularist perspective with a fundamentalist Protestant perspective. "The more, the merrier" pertains only to those invited to the party; those who have not been invited may remind us that "misery loves company": "We wouldn't feel so bad if they hadn't invited our neighbors. . . . "

Multiperspectivism is not an answer to the question of how media news can be made more objective; the advocate of multiperspectivism is not concerned with the form of news bias that is a function of insufficient objectivity but rather the form of news bias that is a result of the essential and necessary subjectivity of the journalists' "perspective." The kind of journalistic "bias" that multiperspectivism is concerned with is nothing over and above the subjective elements constituting "perspective." Multiperspectival news can be seen, then, as "multibiased" news. In such multibiased news, the various biases presented and represented do not necessarily neutralize one another. As we have seen, the combining of various biases into a package is done *by* necessarily "biased" people *for* necessarily "biased" people. The news editor's conception of what constitutes an appropriate combination of biases is likely to displease many members of the audience who do not share his values, perceptions, or "perspective." Buchanan may be pleased to see his conservative perspective presented and represented; but he will still have a grievance if he feels that his perspective has not received enough emphasis in the news editors' multiperspectival package. Indeed, he may be more critical of a system of news presentation which pretends to do justice to his perspective than one which is more obviously opposed to his perspective. It is easier to detect bias in a uniperspectival system than in a multiperspectival one. So it is not clear that presenting a package of biases will result in news which is less biased or less dangerously biased than uniperspectival news.

What sense are we to make of the multiperspectivist's claim that the national news media do not as yet present and represent enough perspectives? Every journalist has a unique perspective; journalists come from different religious backgrounds, different regional backgrounds, etc. The argument of Buchanan and many other media critics is that the major media are dominated by journalists who share certain very important values and perceptions. In a strict sense, news is already highly multiperspectival: thousands of journalists with unique perspectives are trying to inform millions of people with unique perspectives. What bothers Buchanan and a multiperspectivist like Gans is that though every journalist has a unique perspective, too many influential journalists share certain key values and perceptions. What are these key values and perceptions? For Buchanan, they are the values and perceptions of "liberalism"; for Gans, they are various professional, social, and "personal political" values and perceptions. Gans tells us, for example, that "the high value placed on civil liberties is almost an instrumental necessity, since journalistic autonomy depends on freedom of the press,"[17] and that the political values of journalists have some relation to the "upper-middle-class" status of most journalists.[18]

The judgment of journalists does reflect their educational background and professional status. But before we dismiss their judgment as the result of just one more of many possible biases, we should reflect on what is involved in being a highly educated professional. It is not clear that the news would be superior if news executives entrusted the job of informing the public to uneducated amateurs as well as educated professionals. Most people in our society believe that education is a civilizing process which helps to improve one's judgment. There is an important sense in which the educated man's "bias" is superior to the uneducated man's; some would even say that educated people tend to be *less* "biased" than relatively ignorant people. It is also widely believed that professionals are generally superior to amateurs in the practice of a craft.

A major purpose of education is to make people better human beings and better citizens. The study of philosophy, literature and history ought to give a person deeper insight into the human condition, into the nature and potential of human beings; and it ought to help him to empathize and sympathize and see things from other people's perspectives. I have not forgotten that American higher education has serious deficiencies, that many fine things have been done by those who have not benefited from higher education, and that many university graduates are highly critical of the national media. And I know that journalists share values and perceptions which are derived from sources other than higher education. Still, if journalists share many values and perceptions, perhaps it is primarily because they have been trained to be reflective, logical, fair and compassionate people and have arrived at similar conclusions as a result of carefully analyzing the relevant data. It is unfair to assume that the journalists' common perspective—to the extent that there is one—is primarily a result of the same hidden determinants that shape the perspective of a relatively unreflective, irrational person.

The term "bias" is subject to various interpretations, but when used in such contexts as "journalistic bias" and "news bias," it normally has pejorative force. In ordinary discourse, the statement, "They are biased in their reporting," carries with it the implication that those responsible for the reporting have done their job badly. "Journalistic bias" is usually associated with injustice and incompetence. It is often associated with dishonesty and selfishness. Gans offers what is, in effect, a stipulative definition of the ordinary-language locution, "journalistic bias," when he associates such bias with *perspective*. He does not point this out in his analysis, and it is not clear to what extent he is aware of it. But we are not doing justice to either ordinary language or common sense when we suggest that the very act of reporting or interpreting, necessarily based on a subjective perspective, is probably badly done and quite possibly unjust, dishonest and self-serving. To treat Mother Teresa's or Dr. Schweitzer's interpretation of the situation of the poor as being as essentially biased as the callous corporation president's interpretation is to do violence not only to ordinary language but to ideals of civilization that even the most cynical of us respect in our better moments. Similarly, to reduce pro-Nazi and anti-Nazi perspectives to the epistemologico-ethical status of pro-Nazi and anti-Nazi "biases" is to confuse ordinary speakers of English and perhaps to be too tolerant of barbarism.

"Bias" belongs to a family of concepts which includes intolerance, bigotry, discrimination, ethnocentrism, racism, prejudice, dogmatism, and close-mindedness. In analyzing the related concept of prejudice, I recently observed that when people talk about prejudice, usually they do not have all prejudgment in mind but only false and maleficent prejudgment.[19] A similar point can be made with regard to bias: in most cases, a perspective does not qualify as a bias unless it satisfies the conditions of being epistemically and/or ethically unacceptable, based on false presuppositions or productive of harm or evil. Hence, in dealing with the problem of journalistic bias, we should worry much less about the question of *how many* perspectives the news media present and represent than the question of what constitutes an epistemically and morally *reasonable* perspective by which to report and interpret events.

To reject the latter question outright as being unanswerable in principle is to embrace relativism of a very radical and dangerous kind. If such relativism is right, then the moral judgments of Socrates and Dr. Schweitzer are not superior to those of Caligula and Hitler.

Gans says that the fundamental justification for multiperspectival news is its potential for furthering democracy. His motive for advocating multiperspectivism would seem to be an admirable one; in our society, "democracy" tends to be a pro-word in much the same way as "bias" tends to have pejorative force. Now, it is important that we clearly distinguish between the pro-democracy and anti-bias motives for favoring multiperspectival news. Gans does not argue that there is a direct and necessary connection between being in favor of democracy and being opposed to news bias. There is indeed no such connection. Someone who has little or no interest in multiperspectival news' potential for furthering democracy—or even someone who is anti-democracy—can still enthusiastically promote multiperspectival news on the grounds that it offers a partial solution to the problem of news bias. Similarly, one who is deeply concerned about the need for furthering democracy may be quite willing to tolerate the most common forms of journalistic bias.

To insist that the two motives be distinguished may be to understate a key point. A critic of news bias could build an impressive case for the position that a large part of such bias exists precisely because the major news media are already *too* democratic. Far from being a manipulative elitist, the typical American newsman or news executive is someone who must consider, reconsider, and, in one sense, "respect" the values, perceptions, needs and wants of those in his audience. Even in a totalitarian system in which journalists aim primarily at satisfying a political elite, the news/propaganda media are imprudent to ignore the attitudes and concerns of the "general public." In a society like ours, where news usually must be sold, the media's attentiveness to public taste is much more important. In a capitalistic democracy, journalistic bias is largely, though not exclusively, a reflection of the bias of the "majority" of those to whom the news media speak. Of course, journalists often misjudge what the public believes; and journalists do sometimes flout public opinion. Moreover, in any complex society, there are really many "majorities," for people group together in different ways under different circumstances; everyone is at least occasionally critical of public opinion, because everyone belongs to some minorities. (Pity the poor, maligned physicians in a society dominated by patients!) Still, the national media cannot afford to alienate too many people too often. Unfortunately, the most popular judgments are not always the most perceptive or most ethical ones. On one level, democracy seems to be a matter of everyone's having a say in political decision-making; but on another level, it seems to be a matter of popular biases' taking precedence over unpopular ones. The American democratic system which has given so many freedoms to so many Americans has also tolerated and sometimes encouraged the oppression and enslavement of other Americans. In reflecting the worst as well as the best values and perceptions of the "general public," the American news media have left themselves open to many criticisms, but probably not that of being "undemocratic."

When Gans says that multiperspectival news can help to further democracy, he is thinking of its value as a means of bringing more people into the rank of decision-makers; multiperspectival news will provide "relevant" information to those who have not been able to make much use of the kind of information the media now provide. While I share Gans' view that a healthy democracy is one which involves the active participation of members of diverse groups—and respect for the rights of members of diverse groups—I worry about the importance that democratic theory attaches to what is popular. To the extent that furthering democracy is a matter of promoting popular biases, multiperspectival news is effectively undemocratic. While it gives power to some who have hitherto been denied it, it takes power away from "majorities" in the process. This form of redistributing power is quite different from the form usually associated with democratization, i.e., shifting it from a minority to a majority. It is somewhat misleading, then, to say that multiperspectival news "furthers democracy." On the other hand, the value of furthering democracy is itself something which must constantly be considered and reconsidered in the light of concrete circumstances; oppressed minorities have sometimes received more benign treatment from political elites than from the "general public."

Minorities in America have long been aware of their need for their own instruments for the transmission and interpretation of news. Countless periodicals cater to the special needs of religious, ethnic, racial, occupational and political groups. These instruments, which counter popular bias and promote their own, are responses not only to perceived bias in the national news but also to the positive need for more "relevant" information than even the most objective or most supportive national media could provide. Polish-Americans, electrical engineers, and advocates of a "single tax" policy are well aware of the natural limits to what the national media can offer in the way of information of special interest to minorities like their own; they realize that most

Americans generally have little interest in the special concerns of Polish-Americans, electrical engineers, and single-tax theorists. In our political system, minorities are permitted and sometimes even encouraged to create and make use of their own instruments for the transmission of information and ideas. Advocates of multiperspectivism should not underestimate the influence of such instruments, which efficiently perform a role that the major media could only perform poorly.

But minorities also usually believe that they deserve more consideration from the powerful national media, which is not surprising, since almost everyone believes that he deserves a greater amount of respectful attention than he now receives. For, say, Mexican-Americans, it is not enough to be able to watch television programs devoted to the "Mexican-American View of the News," since such programs are watched mainly by members of their own minority group; Mexican-Americans want other Americans to be aware of their problems, their aspirations, their contributions to American culture. And the national media speak to a national audience. Now, the national news media have often done an inadequate job of covering matters relating to Mexican-Americans, and this has, understandably enough, been resented by Mexican-Americans and those sympathetic to their various causes: To provide adequate coverage of matters relating to the many minorities and majorities in the nation, journalists and editors in the national media must constantly work at providing a reasonable "balance of interests," which is no easy task.

The multiperspectivist has lost his confidence in the ability of national journalists and editors to do their balancing work properly. Multiperspectival news is not a refined version of what we have now; it is a substitute for what we have now. But it is no coincidence that the national news has evolved in the way that it has; nor has it developed as it has primarily as a result of the decision-making of some sinister coterie of Machiavellian figures. It has developed, as we have seen, largely in response to the needs and wants of its audience. When the national media add particular perspectives to the news, or give some perspectives increased emphasis, they risk alienating those people in the audience who are uncomfortable with those perspectives. Sometimes the risk is worth taking; and sometimes it is better to alienate some people than to allow others to suffer under the status quo. But the national media cannot afford to alienate too many people too often. In any case, even those minorities (and majorities) that complain most bitterly—or most justifiably—about the bias of the national news do seem to obtain valuable information from it. To diminish whatever utility the institution now has could be to throw the baby out with the bath water.

Still, we need not be fatalistic in our acceptance of an institution which is, after all, only one of several institutions involved in the transmission of information and ideas. The national news should not be *identified* with the *public forum*. Television or radio news is one item in a package of goodies offered by a network to its audience. People with all sorts of views have access to the public forum through "talk" shows, public affairs programs, religious programs, programs directed primarily at special interest groups, editorial replies, political ads, etc. The total package offered by a television or radio network is usually multiperspectival. There is a problem of programming bias similar to the problem of news bias, and groups may feel that they do not receive adequate consideration on the program schedule as a whole; on the other hand, some people may feel that the networks already give these very same groups too much exposure. The Federal Communications Commission has put pressure on broadcasters to maintain a fair and balanced presentation of controversial issues. Such pressure need not be exerted on the printed news media. "The reason for the difference is obvious: since there is no basis on which to limit the number of publications in the United States, the extent of government regulation tolerable under the First Amendment is far narrower."[20] Anyone who is sophisticated enough to read *Time* and *Newsweek* should be able to appreciate the value of at least occasionally reading other news periodicals. Finally, it would be imprudent to underestimate the value of academic studies, books, and everyday conversation as sources of information and ideas.

My aim here has not been to present a detailed critical analysis of Gans' version of multiperspectivism. Gans treats "multiperspectival news" as a label and associates it with a variety of reforms. I find myself able to endorse most of what Gans suggests in the way of specific improvements. For example, I agree with him in objecting to the national media's tendency to equate the federal government with the nation, and I share his feeling that the national news should place more emphasis on service news.[21] Most of Gans' specific suggestions retain their appeal when they are detached from the multiperspectivist news philosophy with which he associates them; and detached they should be, for multiperspectivism is a bad news philosophy.

Gans agrees that the national news should be *national,* but he does not attach enough importance to the fact that the nation is more than a collection of groups with different perspectives. The national news media attempt to speak to Americans qua Americans, and not just to rich Americans, Polish-Americans, conservative Americans, et. al. Often they fail; often they succeed. There is nothing wrong with the assumption that some matters ought to concern all Americans; and, as a matter of fact, there are indeed some matters which *do* concern the overwhelming majority of Americans. There are even matters which concern the overwhelming majority of *human beings,* and there are a good many others which ought to. Gans tells us that he feels "that the interests of diverse groups have priority over the needs of nation and society."[22] This ambiguous statement epitomizes the confusion inherent in multiperspectivism. The nation is not just a collection of groups; it is a group. So is the human race. To be a member of these groups is to have certain rights and responsibilities. When gross injustice is committed by or against our fellow nationals or our fellow human beings, the fact is newsworthy, regardless of our biases. When the national news hides these truths behind a screen of conflicting perspectives, it has ceased to function as an instrument of civilization.

NOTES

1. Herbert J. Gans, *Deciding What's News: A Study of* CBS Evening News, NBC Nightly News, Newsweek, *and* Time (New York: Pantheon Books, 1979).
2. Ibid, p. 313.
3. Ibid, pp. 313–14.
4. Ibid, p. 332.
5. Ibid, p. 303.
6. Ibid, p. 305.
7. Ibid, p. 310.
8. Ibid, p. 306.
9. Ibid, p. 304.
10. Patrick J. Buchanan, *Conservative Votes, Liberal Victories* (New York: Quadrangle/New York Times Book Co., 1975).
11. Ibid, p. 73.
12. Ibid, pp. 75–78.
13. Ibid, pp. 84, 89.
14. Gans, op. cit., pp. 29–31, 42–52, 208–12, 312.
15. Ibid, p. 321. Cf. pp. 229–31.
16. Ibid, p. 229.
17. Ibid, p. 207.
18. Ibid, pp. 208–12.
19. In my paper, "Prejudice as Prejudgment," *Ethics* 90 (1979), 47–57, esp. 51.

20. Robert M. O'Neil, *Free Speech: Responsible Communication Under Law,* 2nd ed. (Indianapolis and New York: Bobbs-Merrill, 1972), p. 64.

21. Gans, op. cit., pp. 313–14.

22. Ibid, p. 334.

DISCUSSION QUESTIONS

1. Gans maintains that there are no objective, absolute standards of external reality. On what grounds does he maintain this? Do you agree with his position? Defend your answer.

2. According to Gans, facts arise as a result of the questions we ask. For example, he says that "the population of New York City does not become a fact until someone asks how many people live in the city." In your estimation, can facts exist prior to, and independent of, human inquiry or are they, as Gans argues, always the product of such inquiry? Defend your answer.

3. What, according to Gans, is the most important purpose of the news? Do you agree with him? Defend your answer.

4. What does Gans mean by "multiperspectival news"? Mention and briefly discuss the merit of each of the five ways Gans thinks multiperspectival news differs from today's news.

5. According to Gans, multiperspectival news would require certain changes in the ways journalists gather and organize the news. Mention and discuss the merit of some of these changes.

6. Gans sees "multiperspectival news" as a feasible response to the problem of news distortion. What does he mean by "news distortion"? Why does he think multiperspectival news helps to solve the problem of news distortion? In your estimation, does multiperspectivism adequately address this problem? Defend your answer.

7. Gans states that "objectivity may be epistemologically impossible but it can exist as journalistic intent." What does Gans mean by this statement? In your estimation, has Gans satisfactorily addressed the issue of journalistic objectivity? Defend your answer.

8. According to Newman, not all human perspectives are necessarily biased. What does Newman mean by a "biased" perspective? In your estimation, are all human perspectives necessarily biased? Are some perpectives less biased than others? Defend your answers.

9. Gans discusses three different conceivable models of multiperspectival news media: a "centralized" model, a "decentralized" model, and a "two-tier" model. Describe briefly the main features of each of these models. Which of these models does Gans favor? Why? In your estimation, are any of these models desirable? Defend your answer.

10. Gans admits that omniperspectival news (that is, news that represents *all* American perspectives) is not possible. Instead, he proposes the more modest

goal of greater (perspectival) "balance." What does Gans mean by "balance" in this context? What suggestions does he make toward this end? Do you agree with these suggestions? Defend your answer.

11. In your estimation, does the national news *already* provide a sufficiently "balanced" portrayal of the news? Defend your answer.

12. Newman contends that the national news is just one item in a network's package of programs wherein "the total package offered by a television or radio network is usually multiperspectival." In your estimation, are such network *packages* already sufficiently "balanced." Defend your answer.

13. Gans states that "the fundamental justification for multiperspectival news is its potential for furthering democracy." Why does Gans think that multiperspectival news has a potential for furthering democracy?

14. What criticisms does Newman make of Gans' attempt to link multiperspectival news to democracy? Do you agree with Newman's criticisms? Defend your answer.

15. Gans contends that "the interests of diverse groups have priority over the needs of nation and society." What criticism does Newman make of this contention? Do you agree with Newman's criticism? Defend your answer.

8

Logical Foundations
of News Reporting

While the question of objectivity in journalism remains a philosophically controversial matter, studies in logic and the social sciences have suggested at least one path. In consonance with Walter Lippmann's plea (Chapter 7) for the development of cognitive machinery for the "detecting, discounting and refining" of prejudices, these studies might be seen as providing specific standards or guidelines for objective news gathering and reporting as well as certain standards or guidelines against which readers and viewers may objectively assess and comprehend (print and nonprint) news presentations. In this chapter, some of these criteria will be discussed.

In the first selection, "Understanding Errors and Biases that Can Affect Journalists," S. Holly Stocking and Paget H. Gross point to the failure of journalism and journalism education to draw upon recent research by cognitive psychologists concerning the kinds of errors and biases that can affect the processing of information. According to Stocking and Gross, although more research aimed explicitly at the way *journalists* mentally process information in reporting and gathering the news is seriously needed, there are a number of specific errors and biases that "have been found in a variety of professions across a variety of tasks"; which suggests to them that "they probably show up in journalists' work as well."

Although Stocking and Gross draw primarily from cognitive psychology in their examination of various errors and biases, several of the errors and biases they consider are also studied in the branch of philosophy known as logic. Moreover, since the latter discipline is directly concerned with providing standards for assessing the adequacy of *reasoning,* it may prove helpful to keep in mind certain of its fundamental concepts.

Reasoning itself can be understood as a process of *making infer-ences*. That is, when people reason, they come to conclusions on the basis of evidence. Even eyewitnesses make inferences in reporting what they claim to perceive. For example, on the basis of certain vi-sual evidence a person may claim to have witnessed two armed men robbing a store. However, what actually may have appeared to the eyewitness was two running figures waving objects. That these figures were men (as opposed to women in men's clothing), that the objects in their hands were really guns (as opposed to water pistols), and that they had stolen something out of a store, are all inferences from the immediately given, but not themselves immediately given. Since there are many factors that can affect the quality of such infer-ences—including prejudices, prior expectations, values, poor eye-sight, visual conditions, emotional stress, etc.—Stocking and Gross caution journalists against committing "the eyewitness fallacy," the fallacy of overestimating the reliability of eyewitness reports as com-pared with other sources of information.

In logic, inferences are distinguished into two kinds: *deductive* and *inductive* variants. An inductive inference is one in which the conclusion can be inferred with some degree of probability—but never with absolute necessity—from the evidence given in support of it. Accordingly an inductive fallacy occurs when a conclusion is defended on evidence that does not support its probability. For example, a journalist who surveyed mostly residents residing near the projected construction site of a pro-posed airport would not have a good probability estimate that most of the residents in the county are opposed to the building of the airport. In such a case, the reporter would have employed a "biased sample." On the other hand, a sample that included a significant number of people from diverse sectors of the county—including ones not near the pro-posed construction site—would provide a more adequate probability index.

In contrast to an inductive inference, a *deductive* inference is one whose conclusion *must* be true (it is not merely rendered probable) given that the evidence is true. Accordingly, one commits a deductive fallacy when one mistakenly thinks that a conclusion necessarily follows from the evidence at hand. For example, a journalist would commit a deductive fallacy if he tried to deduce that "People who are not prom-iscuous don't risk getting AIDS" from the (true) evidence that "People who are promiscuous risk getting AIDS." Since there are other risk factors besides promiscuity, the conclusion in question would not nec-essarily follow. On the other hand, the deductive inference from "People who are promiscuous risk getting AIDS" to "People who don't risk getting AIDS are not promiscuous" is a perfectly valid one.

Since some deductive fallacies are quite common among the general population it is reasonable to think that journalists may have some problems with making deductive inferences. Unfortunately, however, while many of the inferences Stocking and Gross discuss are inductive ones, they do not also consider any deductive ones. More interdisciplinary research, which includes the study of logic (both inductive and deductive kinds) as well as cognitive psychology, would therefore appear to be indicated.

In the second selection of this chapter, "Devices of News Slanting in The Print Media," Howard Kahane explores some of the ways in which newspaper and magazine editors may (consciously or not) build their own prejudices into their stories. In contrast to Stocking and Gross, Kahane is not here chiefly concerned with correcting the cognitive processes of journalists; rather his primary concern appears to be that of providing *readers* with an understanding of various devices used by journalists to slant the news in order that they can avoid being misled by these devices.

Two caveats to Kahane's discussion seem to be in order. First, it should not be read as an exhaustive account of all devices of news slanting that journalists can employ. For example, one common one that is not addressed in this selection is *cardstacking*. In the latter a journalist creates a distorted picture of reality by selectively mentioning details of an issue or event. For example, an editor who is anti-gay might include the fact that a given child molester is a homosexual, whereas on other occasions the sexual preference of heterosexual child molesters is omitted. Thereby, it is made to appear that gays are more frequent child molesters than are heterosexuals. This in turn can reinforce a popular prejudice in the reader unless, of course, he or she is aware that the cards have been stacked against gays.

Second, Kahane's discussion of the "emotive meaning" of words (that is, the positive or negative "emotive charges" that some words possess) should not be taken to imply that journalists cannot use emotively active words constructively. For example, the reader may recall the following statement by John Dewey (as cited by Berny Morson in Chapter 1): "Artists have always been the real purveyors of news, for it is not the outward happening itself which is new, but the kindling by it of emotion, perception and appreciation." Indeed, if journalists are to "kindle emotion" in readers, then they may need to employ words that impart emotion. For example, in order to "kindle" the emotion, perception and appreciation of the casualties of war, the journalist may need to employ highly negatively emotionally charged language (for example, "mutilated," "dismembered," "the stench of rotting flesh"). Nevertheless, to say that emotive meaning can be used constructively is not to deny Kahane's important point that it can also have objectionable uses, as when it is used to distort or conceal important facts.

In the final selection of this chapter, "Organizational Biases of Network News Reporting," Edward Jay Epstein explores "the rules and logic that shape network news." According to Epstein, much of the bias in news reporting does not stem from personal biases of individual reporters working within news organizations, but rather from the news organizations themselves. While newspapers and magazines also have their "organizational biases," Epstein suggests that television news "provides perhaps the clearest case of the process by which reality is systematically reconstructed by news organizations." According to Epstein, the forces behind such systematic reality restructuring include constraints of time, audience, advertisers and local affiliates. For example, the inability of many viewers to grasp complex issues, coupled with the demand by advertisers that viewers' interest be maintained, make inevitable an oversimplified presentation of reality.

What implications does Epstein's view have for the problem of objectivity in the network news? According to Epstein, "Dealing with such distortions involves the same problem as dealing with systematic distortions in a map. No map presents a perfect picture of reality. However, if one understands that such areas as Australia and Greenland are reduced in size, it is feasible to use a map to understand the geography of the world." But, as Epstein himself acknowledges, the network news, unlike the map, does not provide any key that allows the viewer to adjust for systematic distortions.

Epstein suggests that "if news media clearly and honestly stated the constraints and limits under which they operate, the adjustment would be far easier." But such a suggestion, it might be rejoined, would be self-defeating for the network, since the assertion or implication that the news contains distortions would be likely to turn the viewer off, a result that would not suit the advertisers who keep the network news on the air.

Perhaps it is bias of the institutional sort that presents the most serious practical challenge. As Stocking and Gross suggest, the problem of errors and biases in journalists' processing of information is "a problem we may be able to do something about" through the training of journalists. However, the restructuring of the network news' internal logic in order to repair systematic institutional distortions may require more sweeping changes.

Finally, Epstein's assumption that the network news is systematically distorted might itself be challenged. It might be argued that the charge of systematic distortion assumes that there is, in the first place, some "objective" reality that the networks are remiss in reporting. Since any news report will inevitably be a product of some set of subjective factors, it must be shown that those that currently shape network news are somehow more objectionable than other possible subjective sets. For example, the ability of the current news format to hold viewers' attention and understanding may be superior to other perhaps more complex reality constructions that undermine the latter goals. Therefore, to refer to the current format as systematically distorted or as institutionally biased may be to overlook the virtues of the current news perspective as well as the relative status of reality perspectives. However, for those who do not accept this relativism or who have more confidence in the ability of the viewing public to see beyond simplistic news forms and content, such a response to Epstein may not be satisfactory.

Understanding Errors and Biases That Can Affect Journalists

S. HOLLY STOCKING AND PAGET H. GROSS

In the last fifteen years, psychology has witnessed an explosion of knowledge about how human beings process information. Much of this new knowledge concerns limitations and biases in perception, memory, and reasoning.

Research on eyewitness testimony has highlighted the distortions in perception and memory that can plague observers, particularly observers under stress at the moment of observation or recollection. Similarly, studies on the way people make inferences have shown us that people often favor anecdotal information over more reliable base rate statistical information. Even when instructed to be "objective," they often seek and select data according to preexisting expectations or theories.

Other research has documented the difficulties people have evaluating risk. Still more research has shown that people easily ignore sampling biases, fail to understand regression effects, often believe they "knew something all along" even if they didn't, tend to attribute the causes of people's behavior to dispositional rather than to situational factors, and often imagine association between events where none exists. Significantly, many of the errors and biases to which people fall prey only get worse under time constraints.

For journalists who pledge allegiance to objectivity and/or fairness as they observe and interpret people and events, such knowledge is potentially of great relevance. Yet only a small percentage of what we know appears to have found its way into journalism classrooms, most of it in upper-level or graduate courses that consider how audiences, as distinct from journalists, process information.

Moreover, hardly any of this knowledge seems to have found its way into courses and textbooks that train students to write, edit, and report the news. Even those texts that do devote space to documented distortions in interviewing and observation (cf. Rivers & Harrington, 1988) have either ignored more recent findings on cognitive error and bias or drawn upon but a small portion of this research.

Given the growing demands on journalists to report and interpret the activities of an increasingly complex society and the demonstrated importance of the news media for setting public and private agendas, this is a shame. It is also a problem we may be able to do something about.

In the pages that follow, we will outline some of the more important errors and biases in thinking that psychologists have documented in recent years. We have little formal knowledge about the existence and operation of such biases in journalists (as we have noted, and lamented, in Stocking & Gross, 1988). However, we do know they have been found in a variety of professions and across a variety of tasks (cf. Loftus, 1979; Sims, Gioia, & Associates, 1986; and Rogoff & Lave, 1984), leading us to think they probably show up in journalists' work as well. We hope that journalism educators, when alerted to these common errors and biases, will be motivated to learn more about them and seek ways, in classrooms and textbooks, to bring them to the attention of their students.

THE EYEWITNESS FALLACY

As everyone knows, "seeing is believing." When someone says, "I saw it with my own eyes," people listen, believe, and remember.

Indeed, psychologists who have studied the impact of eyewitness testimony in jury trials have found that jurors, when reaching a verdict, give much more weight to eyewitness testimony than they do to other kinds of evidence (Loftus, 1979).

Not surprisingly, journalists seem to understand intuitively the power of eyewitness accounts. Thus, as van Dijk (in press) has pointed out, editors so value first-hand reports that they "may even send a special envoy to places where already dozens of other reporters are present" (p. 78).

The problem is that eyewitness accounts, while more convincing than hearsay accounts, are not always reliable. Research on eyewitness testimony (c.f., Loftus, 1979) is very clear about this fact: Observations can vary and err as a function of a variety of factors such as prejudice, temporary expectations, the types of details being observed, and stress. It is very easy, in other words, for one's observations (and one's memories about observations) to be distorted or flat-out wrong.

In one of the most well-known demonstrations of the fallibility of observations, reported in Loftus (1979), Hastorf and Cantrill (1954) examined people's perceptions of a football game between Dartmouth and Princeton. The game, one of the dirtiest and roughest played by either team, was filmed and shown to students on each campus. Students were instructed to note any rule infractions they saw and to rate them as either "flagrant" or "mild."

In spite of instructions to be completely objective in their observations, students at the two schools perceived the infractions very differently. More precisely, students at Princeton saw the Dartmouth players make 9.8 infractions, more than twice the number of infractions they saw their own team make (4.2). Moreover, they saw the Dartmouth players make more than twice as many infractions as Dartmouth students saw their team make. Princeton students tended to rate the violations by their own team as mild and those committed by the Dartmouth team as flagrant. Dartmouth students were more evenhanded when they saw the film, seeing about the same number of infractions for both teams (4.3 by Dartmouth and 4.4 by Princeton), but they also tended to see the violations of the opposing team as more flagrant than violations by their own team. Obviously, people don't always see what others see; even when instructed to be objective, they often see what they want to see.

It is perhaps an obvious point that one's personal prejudices can unconsciously affect the accuracy of one's observations; personal prejudice is usually what journalism educators mean when they warn about "bias" in the news. However, research on eyewitness testimony (Loftus, 1979) suggests that other factors besides personal prejudice can lead to unreliable eyewitness reports, among them: temporary expectations, expectations from past experience, and stress.

Eyewitness accounts can also be unreliable when the event has been witnessed infrequently and for a short period of time, when violence has been involved, when a long time has elapsed between witnessing the event and reporting it, or when the witness is under stress at the time of recollection. Researchers have also found that information introduced after an event has taken place can alter the memory of it; thus, if a reporter witnesses a concert and then reads a competitor's article on the concert, the reporter may alter his own memory of the event to conform to information contained in his competitor's account.

The point in all this (and much more, contained in Loftus, 1979) is simple: People, journalists included, may put more weight on eyewitness accounts than they do on other kinds of evidence. Unless journalists are aware of the ways that eyewitness accounts can be biased and erroneous, they, like juries, may fallaciously assume that such accounts offer more truth than they do. Such assumptions could, in turn, influence reporters to "count on" such accounts and prematurely limit their reporting efforts.

UNDERUTILIZATION OF STATISTICS

Related to people's tendency to weight eyewitness accounts more than other types of evidence is a tendency for people to favor anecdotal or case history information over base rate statistical information (information about the percentage of cases in the population).

This tendency to underutilize more reliable base rate information, to focus on specific individuals and make less use of information about the population from which individuals come, has been vividly demonstrated in a study by Hamill, Wilson, and Nisbett (1980). In this study, subjects read a magazine article about a Puerto Rican woman who had a number of unmanageable children by a succession of common-law husbands. When this anecdotal case was presented along with base rate statistics indicating that 90 percent of welfare recipients "are off the welfare rolls by the end of four years," subjects regarded the case history as more informative than the more reliable base rate statistics. Put another way, the statistical facts had less impact on people's views about the laziness and hopelessness of welfare recipients than did the single vivid case.

Just why people favor anecdotal information over base rate information is unclear. It may be because the information contained in anecdotes is usually more vivid (Nisbett & Borgida, 1975; Nisbett & Ross, 1980), or it may be that the information in anecdotes seems more relevant (Tversky & Kahneman, 1978). But regardless of the precise reason, what the Hamill et al. study and related research suggests for journalists, who routinely use anecdotes to "personalize" the news, is a need to handle anecdotal information with considerable caution.

Some sources are masters of the anecdote. Intentionally or unintentionally, they may present anecdotal data that do not square with more abstract statistical information. If reporters fall victim to the tendency to favor vivid anecdotal information over pallid but reliable statistics, they, and their audiences in turn, may be misled.

CONFIRMATION BIAS

Intellectually, most of us probably realize that preconceived ideas shape how we view, interpret, and remember information. But what we may not realize is the extent to which such notions bias us.

In recent years, psychologists have conducted research revealing that preconceived ideas can be very powerful indeed in shaping what we see, understand, and remember. In fact, so powerful are their effects that it is hard to imagine they do not affect the work of journalists and journalists-in-training.

The tendency for people to seek, select, and recall data according to preexisting expectations or theories is called the "confirmation bias." To understand its pervasiveness, it is important to understand how it works.

Two processes seem important here. First, when people seek information with respect to one theory, they are unlikely to seek information with respect to another theory simultaneously. People, in short, test theories one at a time, or sequentially. So, for example, the person who is testing a theory about the negative impact of feminism on women's lives is unlikely to test theories about its positive impact as well. Similarly, the individual testing the theory that there is a "crime wave" against the elderly (Fishman, 1980) is unlikely to test the opposite theory that there are no crimes against the elderly.

Secondly, as people seek information with which to test their theories, they show a dramatic tendency to use a theory-confirming strategy. For example, a reporter who has theorized that there is a crime wave against the elderly may unconsciously seek out sources that confirm this theory—the potential and actual elderly victims in a bad part of town, the head of a crime prevention program for the elderly, etc. Further, the reporter may ask questions of these sources—about increases in reported crimes, efforts to reduce crimes, and the like—that confirm the theory, without asking probing questions that might disconfirm the hypothesis (Snyder & Swann, 1979).

Not only may expectations influence the sources to which reporters turn and the types of questions a reporter may ask, but they also may influence journalists' evaluation and selection of data. One prevasive bias in perceivers' decisions about what information is most relevant or credible is the tendency to regard information that is consistent with one's a priori theories as the worthiest pieces of information (Darley & Gross, 1984; Hayden & Mischel, 1976; Snyder & Gangestad, 1981). Thus, when one is testing a theory about the nature, causes, or outcome of an event, the information that will be selected as most useful is information that is consistent with and confirming of one's theory.

Information that runs counter to one's theories is discounted a number of ways. For one thing, disconfirming evidence may be regarded as transient or situationally induced. For example, a political figure who is thought to be honest and forthright and who is then caught in lies about events may be regarded as momentarily confused, or without recall, or perhaps induced to perform dishonestly by misguided advisers or the pressure of office (Ross, Lepper & Hubbard, 1975). Even if journalists themselves do not interpret actions in this way, they may regard such interpretations by others as highly credible and so give them prominent play.

Secondly, disconfirming evidence may be regarded as arising from poor or shoddy sources. Thus, one may be particularly critical of the methodology of the disconfirming study, and, in fact, so critical that the study may be discarded as entirely unreliable. Reporters may similarly discard sources (persons or resources for data) that are disconfirming of their theories by virtue of their judged unreliability.

Fishman (1980), in his account of how a series of events in New York City came to be linked together as a "crime wave," noted that once a crime wave was established in journalists' minds it took on a life of its own, guiding reporters' perceptions of hitherto unconnected crimes and city police officers' as well. "A week and a half after the coverage started, the police wire was steadily supplying the press with fresh incidents almost every day." Even when a reporter examined police crime statistics and discovered that crimes against the elderly had actually decreased (*not* increased) compared to the previous year, the crime wave theme remained in place. As Fishman tells it, "The reporter was puzzled and eventually decided to ignore the police figures. He felt they were unreliable and incomplete, and anyway he had to do the story as originally planned because the whole issue was too big to pass up or play down" (p. 5).

If people, including journalists, are unaware of the extent to which they seek to confirm their expectations and theories, it may be in part because the processes that allow this to happen operate below the level of consciousness. Reporters may honestly believe they are objectively considering all sides to an issue, while in practice they are processing information in a way that confirms what they expect or believe.

MISPERCEPTIONS OF RISK

Every day, on the news, from their friends, in the movies, people hear about risk—the risk of diseases, natural disasters, technological mishaps, nuclear war, auto emissions, passive smoke. And, based on what they hear, people perceive some risks as greater than others. But are they right?

Psychologists have done a great deal of research on people's perceptions of risk in recent years, and their findings include the following:

- Anything that makes a hazard appear very memorable or imaginable, such as a recent disaster, vivid film, or media coverage, can influence one's perception of risk; thus, someone who has just seen the movie "Jaws" may overestimate the probability of being attacked by sharks on their vacation to the ocean, and someone who has just seen "The Towering Inferno" may overestimate the probability of being killed in a high-rise fire.
- People overestimate the risk of death from dramatic or sensational causes, such as homicide, accidents, cancer, and natural disasters, and underestimate the risk of death from the undramatic causes such as diabetes, emphysema, and asthma, causes which kill one at a time and are common in nonfatal form.
- When people lack strong opinions about hazard, they are highly susceptible to the way risk information is presented; thus, the way information is framed (whether, for example, one says "*only about one percent* of the nation's five million chemical processing units handle hazardous waste materials that could result in runaway reactions," or "*as many as 50,000* of the nation's five million chemical processing units handles hazardous waste materials . . .") can have a major effect on perceptions.

In short, researchers have found that people have a great deal of difficulty accurately perceiving risk (Slovic, 1986).

Not surprisingly, some of these same difficulties have revealed themselves in news media coverage of risk (c.f., Combs & Slovic, 1979). Thus, it appears that journalists, like lay perceivers, process risk information poorly.

"Reporters obviously need to be educated in the importance and subtleties of risk stories," psychologist Paul Slovic has written in an article detailing some of the difficulties inherent in informing and educating the public about risk (Slovic, 1986). In obvious agreement, a number of psychologists, mass communication researchers, and other groups have produced materials and events, including articles, pamphlets, films, and workshops, to help reporters understand and clarify risk issues (c.f., Fischoff, 1985a, 1985b; Risk Reporting Project, 1986; Institute for Health Policy Analysis, 1984).

Since the news media are a dominant source of information about risk, it seems incumbent upon journalism educators to alert students to the ways in which they may err (and be influenced by the intentional and unintentional errors and biases of sources) as they process information about risk. It also seems incumbent upon us to alert them to some of the ways they can minimize such errors and biases.

SAMPLE ERRORS AND BIASES

Although journalism educators have recognized for some time the need for journalists to pay attention to biases in formal poll data (c.f., Wilhoit & Weaver, 1980), they have given relatively little attention to the need for journalists to attend to sampling biases in other realms, though they probably should. Researchers have found, for example, that people can and often do ignore biases in existing samples of information (Fiske & Taylor, 1984).

In one of the few textbook examples of this shortcoming in journalism, Tankard (1976) points to how journalists covered the Watergate hearings during the 1970s. One reporter, using letters reportedly sent to Senator Ervin's committee, concluded that televised hearings were appreciated by audiences, while another reporter, judging from call-ins to television stations, concluded just the opposite (pp. 51–52). Apparently, neither reporter stopped to consider the inherent biases in the samples they drew upon in reaching their conclusions.

MISUNDERSTANDING OF REGRESSION

People have a poor understanding of regression, the fact that extreme events will, on the average, be less extreme when observed again. As a result, they often use extreme events to predict future extreme events (Jennings, Amabile, & Ross, 1982). In journalism, regression effects are sometimes appreciated, as when a literary critic raves about a first book but at the same time urges readers to wait for the next book because previous experience suggests that second novels often are not as good as first ones. However, other times they may not be appreciated, as when reporters herald the first very positive results of a study on a new drug. The study may show positive results, even great results, but it is only one study, and chance alone may have accounted for the findings.

HINDSIGHT BIAS

Psychologists have found that once people learn the outcome of an event, they tend to exaggerate their ability to have foreseen it. Thus, in one experiment, students were asked to predict the likelihood of various possible outcomes of President Nixon's forthcoming trips to Moscow and Peking. When, in the wake of Nixon's journey, the students were unexpectedly asked to recall their initial predictions, they remembered them as very close to what they now knew had happened (Fischoff & Beyth, 1975). This tendency to overestimate what could have been foreseen is known as the "hindsight bias" or the "I-knew-it-all-along" phenomenon, and it seems to have been operating in much of the post hoc moralizing about journalistic coverage of the shuttle disaster (I knew or would have known, so others should have too); it may also have been operating when Sen. William Proxmire bestowed "Golden Fleece" awards on research that documented or explored the "obvious," though many journalists didn't recognize the fact.

ILLUSORY CORRELATION

Sometimes, psychologists have found, people greatly overestimate the frequency with which two characteristics or events are related, or they even impose a relationship where none exists (c.f., Crocker, 1981; Jennings, Amabile, & Ross, 1982). This phenomenon, known as illusory correlation, has been demonstrated in a number of circumstances, but particularly when two things happen to be associated in meaning. Thus, if journalists commonly associate "longhairs" with demonstrations (that is, they expect to see people with long hair at demonstrations), they may overestimate the frequency with which long-haired people attend such events. Likewise, if reporters associate university-based artists with state grants for the arts, they may overestimate the frequency with which such artists (as distinct from community-based artists) have been awarded such grants.

Some of the research on illusory correlation (c.f., Chapman & Chapman, 1982) appears to suggest that expectations can also lead people to impose illusory causal (as distinct from simple correlational) relationships between characteristics or events. Consider the journalist who notices that an abnormally high number of children living near a chemical spill have been born with birth defects. In the reporter's mind, chemical accidents often cause human health problems; if there is an increase in birth defects following a chemical accident, it would appear that the increase must be due to the accident. In the face of such strong prior expectations, it may never even occur to the reporter that a simple increase in the birth rate may have caused the unusually high number of defects.

FUNDAMENTAL ATTRIBUTION ERROR

In journalism texts and journalism classrooms, we do considerable talking about journalists' role as "interpreters" of behavior and events; we tell students not only to report behavior and events but also to explain the reasons behind behavior and events. But for many of us, that is as far as our training takes us. We provide no real understanding of what goes into making causal inferences and the biases and errors that can, and often do, occur. As a result, we send out students who, in their role as interpreters, are likely to commit a number of cognitive errors. Some of these errors are documented in attribution theory research, which concerns how people make causal inferences about their own and others' behavior.

Research on one such error, the ubiquitous "fundamental attribution error," suggests that one is more likely to attribute another person's behavior to his or her own dispositional qualities than to situational factors (Jones & Harris, 1967). Thus, reporters discovering a case of scientific fraud at their local university are more likely to explore the theory that the person was a "bad apple" than to explore the theory that the "barrel itself was rotten." There are documented exceptions to the fundamental attribution error, of course, but the tendency needs to be recognized.

CONCLUSION

There are numerous other documented biases and errors in people's thinking (see Fiske & Taylor, 1984). But our point, we hope, has been made: In most skills courses and most journalism texts, we put great stock in observable facts without adequately emphasizing some of the ways observations can vary and err. We warn our students to be wary of their own biases, but we appear to do very little to demonstrate how easily biases and prior expectations can affect their selection of data.

We encourage students to "personalize" the news but fail to warn them adequately of the dangers, often unwittingly reinforcing the cognitive tendency to favor case histories or anecdotal information over important base rate information. In the same vein, we encourage coverage of activities that pose social or environmental risks, yet say little or nothing about the errors people commonly make when assessing risk. In these and many other small ways, we may be unknowingly failing our students and our profession.

The need—to learn more about such errors and biases, and to bring what we know and learn into the educational setting—is great. Admittedly, it may not be easy. Most of us have all we can do in a term to teach students the traditional fundamentals of interviewing, observation, and mining documents. To bring this knowledge into the classroom successfully will require us to develop exercises that will provide opportunities for learning about cognitive distortions without sacrificing the basics.

Teachers' manuals for undergraduate texts in social psychology often contain exercises for demonstrating such errors and biases; some of these might be modified for use in writing, reporting, and editing classes, but others will have to be developed from scratch. We must also work to integrate this and related knowledge into traditional journalism textbooks. Some materials produced by cognitive social psychologists are accessible enough to use as readings for undergraduate journalism majors (c.f., Loftus, 1979; Stanovich, 1986), but most are not. It is imperative that those capable of translating psychological research be involved in producing and testing classroom-appropriate materials.

Whether journalists and journalists-in-training will be receptive to efforts to meet this need is another matter; another cognitive tendency that psychologists have documented is the "overconfidence phenomenon," or the tendency for people to overestimate the accuracy of their judgments (Fischoff, Slovic & Lichtenstein, 1977). Also uncertain is whether journalists, even if receptive, will be able to inhibit these errors and biases, particularly under time constraints, which have been found to exaggerate such problems (Kruglanski & Freund, 1983).

Still, there is evidence that, at least under some circumstances, people can inhibit some of these biases. Simply telling people to be unbiased won't lessen people's tendency to maintain a theory in the face of disconfirming evidence. However, some research suggests that telling people to consider carefully how they are evaluating evidence and to watch their biases as they go through the process of interpreting data does help (Lord, Lepper, & Thompson, 1980). Asking people to explain why the theory might be wrong has also worked in some experiments (Anderson, 1982).

By doing nothing, we can be almost certain that journalists, to the extent that they do make these mistakes, will be condemned to repeat them.

REFERENCES

Anderson, C.A. (1982). Inoculation and counter-explanation: Debiasing techniques in the perseverance of social theories. *Social Cognition, 1,* 126–139.

Chapman. L.J., & Chapman, J.P. (1982). Test results are what you think they are. In D. Kahneman, P. Slovic, & A. Tversky (Eds.), *Judgment under Uncertainty: Heuristics and Biases.* N.Y.: Cambridge University Press, 239–248.

Combs, B. & Slovic, P. (1979). Newspaper coverage of causes of death. *Journalism Quarterly, 56,* 837–843.

Crocker, J. (1981). Judgment of covariation by social perceivers. *Psychological Bulletin, 90,* 272–292.

Darley, J.M. & Gross, P.H. (1983). A hypothesis-confirming bias in labeling effects," *Journal of Personality and Social Psychology, 44,* 20–33.

Fischoff, B. (1985a). Environmental reporting: What to ask the experts. *The Journalist,* Winter, 11–15.

Fischoff, B. (1985b). Cognitive and institutional barriers to 'informed consent.' In M. Gibson (Ed.), *Risk, Consent, and Air,* Totowa, N.J.: Rowman & Allenheld.

Fischoff, B. & Beyth, R. (1975). 'I knew it would happen': Remembered probabilities of once future things. *Organizational Behavior and Human Performance, 13:* 1–16.

Fischoff, B., Slovic, P. & Lichtenstein, S. (1977). Knowing with certainty: The appropriateness of extreme confidence. *Journal of Experimental Psychology: Human Perception and Performance, 3,* 552–564.

Fishman, M. (1980). *Manufacturing the News.* Austin, Tex.: University of Texas Press.

Fiske, S.T. & Taylor, S.E. (1984). *Social Cognition.* Reading, Mass.: Addison-Wesley Publishing Company.

Hamill, R., Wilson, T.D., & Nisbett, R.E. (1980). Insensitivity to sample bias: Generalizing from atypical cases. *Journal of Personality and Social Psychology, 39,* 578–589.

Hastorf, A. & Cantrill, H. (1954). They saw a game: A case study. *Journal of Abnormal and Social Psychology, 49,* 129–134.

Hayden, T. & Mischel, W. (1976). Maintaining trait consistency in the resolution of behavioral inconsistency: The wolf in sheep's clothing? *Journal of Personality and Social Psychology, 44,* 109–132.

Institute for Health Policy Analysis. (1985). *Health Risk Reporting; Roundtable Workshop on the Media and Reporting of Risks to Health.* Washington, D.C.: Georgetown University Medical Center Institute for Health Policy Analysis.

Jennings, D.L., Amabile, T.M. & Ross, L. (1982). Informed covariation assessment: Data-based vs. theory-based judgments. In D. Kahneman, P. Slovic, and A. Tversky (Eds.), *Judgment under Uncertainty: Heuristics and Biases.* N.Y.: Cambridge University Press.

Jones, E.E. & Harris, V.A. (1967). The attribution of attitudes. *Journal of Experimental Social Psychology, 3,* 1–24.

Kruglanski, A.W. & Freund, T. (1983). The freezing and unfreezing of lay inferences: Effects on impressional primacy, ethnic stereotyping and numerical anchoring. *Journal of Experimental Social Psychology, 19,* 448–468.

Loftus, E.F. (1979). *Eyewitness Testimony.* Cambridge, Mass.: Harvard University Press.

Lord, C.G., Lepper, M.R. & Thompson, W.C. (1980, September). Inhibiting biased assimilation in the consideration of new evidence on social policy issues. Paper presented at the meeting of the American Psychological Association, Montreal, Canada. (Cited in Fiske and Taylor, 1984)

Myers, D.G. (1983). *Social Psychology.* New York: McGraw-Hill Book Company.

Nisbett, R.E. & Borgida, E. (1975). Attribution and the psychology of prediction. *Journal of Personality and Social Psychology, 32,* 932–943.

Nisbett, R.E. & Ross, L. (1980). *Human Inference: Strategies and Shortcomings of Social Judgment.* Englewood Cliffs, N.J.: Prentice-Hall.

Risk Reporting Project. (1986). Piscataway, N.J. University of Medicine and Dentistry of New Jersey–Rutgers Medical School.

Rivers, W.L. & Harrington, S.L. (1988). *Finding Facts: Research Writing Across the Curriculum* (Second Edition). Englewood Cliffs, N.J.: Prentice Hall.

Rogoff, B. & Lave, J. (1984). *Everyday Cognition: Its Development in Social Context.* Cambridge, Mass.: Harvard University Press.

Ross, L., Lepper, M.R. & Hubbard, M. (1975). Perseverance in self-perception and social perception: Biased attribution processes in the debriefing paradigm. *Journal of Personality and Social Psychology, 32,* 880–892.

Sims, H., and Gioia, D.A. & Associates. (1986). *The Thinking Organization.* San Francisco: Jossey-Bass.

Slovic, P. (1986). Informing and Educating the Public about Risk. *Risk Analysis, 6, 4,* 403–415.

Snyder, M. & Gangestad, S. (1981). Hypothesis-testing processes. In J.H. Harvey, W. Ickes, & R.I. Kidd (Eds.), *New Directions in Attribution Research: Vol. 3.* Hillsdale, N.J.: Erlbaum.

Snyder, M. & Swann, W.B. Jr. (1978). Hypothesis-testing processes in social interaction. *Journal of Personality and Social Psychology, 36,* 1202–1212.

Stanovich, K.E. (1986). *How to Think Straight About Psychology.* Glenwood, Ill.: Scott Foresman.

Stocking, S. H. & Gross, P.H. (1988). How Journalists Think: A Proposal for the Study of Communicatory Behavior. Paper presented to Theory and Methodology Division, Association for Education in Journalism and Mass Communication annual meeting Portland, OR.

Tankard, J.W. (1976). Reporting and the scientific method. In M. McCombs, D.L. Shaw, & I. Grey, *Handbook of Reporting Methods.* Boston Houghton Mifflin Company.

Tversky, A. & Kahneman, D. (1978). Causal schemata in judgments under uncertainty. In M. Fishbein (Ed.), *Progress in Social Psychology* Hillsdale, N.J.: Erlbaum.

van Dijk, T.A. (in press). *News as Discourse* New York: Erlbaum.

Wilhoit, G.C. & Weaver, D.H. (1980). *Newsroom Guide to Polls & Surveys.* Washington, D.C. American Newspaper Publishers Association.

Devices of News Slanting in the Print Media

HOWARD KAHANE

The key to understanding any institution, from the PTA to the U.S. Department of Energy to NBC to the Soviet Politbureau, is that they are run by human beings who have the same sorts of defects and virtues as the rest of us. We should remember that the people who gather the news often have *biases* or *prejudices* that distort their finished product.

In the first place, remember that a given class tends to see itself more kindly than others might. We should expect that the rich will be more understanding of the problems of the rich than of ordinary folk. And it is the rich, obviously, who own or control most of the media. From which it follows, by some valid deductive rule or other, that those who own or control the media will be more understanding of the problems of the rich than of ordinary folk. (Remember, however, that it is we ordinary folk who buy the newspapers and watch the television ads, a fact that acts as a counterforce.)

Second, the media have been managed primarily by men, who have done most of the reporting, too. The result is sex discrimination not only in hiring (recall the *Reader's Digest* and *New York Times* sex discrimination suits) but also in the way news is slanted. But times are changing. These days we rarely encounter loaded language of the kind illustrated by this *New York Daily News* headline (29 May 1974):

> ## 2 CAREER GIRLS ARE MURDERED
> *Librarian strangled on E. Side;*
> *Time, Inc. Girl Shot in W'chester*

By the way, imagine reading the analogous headline in your local newspaper.

> ## 2 CAREER BOYS ARE MURDERED
> *Librarian strangled on E. Side;*
> *Time, Inc. Boy Shot in W'chester*

But the most deep-seated media prejudice, as it has been in America as a whole, is race prejudice. Busing, for instance, became a big issue in the United States only when courts started ordering white students to be bused. The busing of blacks to inferior segregated schools received little notice prior to 1954—editors and reporters, like most white Americans, hardly gave a second thought to the education of blacks.[1] . . .

Now let's look at the devices used to slant stories (primarily in newspapers and magazines).

STORIES CAN BE PLAYED UP OR DOWN

Within limits, you can bury a story, if you don't like it, or give it page one space if you do. The *Canton* (Ohio) *Repository* may have set some sort of record on this in its 28 July 1974 issue. Under the front-page headline "Wowee. . . . What a Weekend," the *Repository* devoted most of its front page to an account of the first National Football League exhibition game of the season, plus a description of ceremonies surrounding the induction of four new members into Canton's Football Hall of Fame. Relegated to a bottom corner of page one was the decision of the House Judiciary Committee to recommend impeachment of President Nixon, a key event in one of the biggest ongoing news stories in American history.

A *New York Daily News* headline during the 1976 primary campaigns had it this way, in large type: "REAGAN BEATS FORD IN NEB.," below which they tell us in much smaller type: "But President Wins in W. Va." Had they been for Ford, they could have reversed that quite easily. . . .

MISLEADING OR UNFAIR HEADLINES CAN BE USED

Many more people read the headline on a story than read the story itself. So even if a story is accurate, a misleading headline distorts the news for many readers. Here are a few examples:

New York Daily News:
> *Secret Bar Study Pounds Five Judges*

New York Times headline (same general story):
> *Bar Report Clears 3 on State Bench*
> *of Accusations Leveled in Magazine*

Hartford Times (21 May 1972):
> *North Viets Repelled in Attack*

Hartford Courant (same day, same general story):
S. *Vietnam Repulsed in Push Toward Beleaguered An Loc*

Boston Globe (same day, same general story):
Battle See-Saws at An Loc

Hartford Times (18 September 1970):
$500 Million U.S. Aid to Israel

But below, in the AP story, we learned that:

> *President Nixon* reportedly *was preparing today to promise Israel Premier Golda Meir . . .* officials say no final decision on exactly what the package will contain has been made.

The Washington Post (7 March 1979, headline for story on page D7):
Recession Only Inflation Cure, Economist Says

Same newspaper (same date, headline for story on page D10):
NAM Asserts Inflation Only Cure for Recession

(This item is from the *Columbia Journalism Review's* regular back-page feature, *"The Lower Case,"* May/June 1979, which also contained this headline from the *New York Post:* "Bishop defrocks gay priest.")

INFORMATION CAN BE BURIED WELL INTO A STORY

In playing a story one way or another, the headline obviously is most important (next to its location), since it is read by many who never read further. But the first few paragraphs are more important than what follows, for the same reason—readership drops off after that point.

For instance, a television debate between three Connecticut candidates for the U.S. Senate was played quite differently by the *Hartford Courant* and the *New York Times* (28 October 1970). The *Courant* started their story with three paragraphs on Senator Thomas J. Dodd's performance, while the *Times* went five paragraphs before mentioning any participant other than Lowell P. Weiker, Jr.

NONNEWS FEATURES CAN BE SLANTED

Editorials, of course, are expected to be slanted, except that it is called editorializing and is not contrary to the rules of objective reporting (as are most of the devices discussed so far). Similar remarks apply to the custom of selecting political columnists and cartoonists who espouse the "right" point of view.

But any nonnews feature of a newspaper or magazine can be, and often is, used to intrude political bias. Even photos are so used—papers run more and better photos of candidates they support than they do of their opponents.

During the Watergate period, with the Nixon presidency collapsing, the *Boston Globe,* anti-Nixon all the way, ran an *extremely* unflattering photo of Nixon on a story headlined, "Nixon felt besieged by bureaucrats." Under the photo we read (the quote is from the Nixon tapes):

> Fire, demote him or send him to the Guam regional office. There's a way. Get him the hell out.—President Nixon (AP photo from files).

Few will notice that small print (AP photo from files); most readers must have believed the photo was of Nixon saying the very words quoted, instead of, as a matter of fact, having been taken at another time during a political address. . . .

FOLLOW-UP STORIES CAN BE OMITTED

When the Office of Economic Opportunity (OEO) was established to help the poor, it was played up as big news, showing that America does indeed provide opportunity for all. But when the Nixon administration effectively throttled OEO, this news was buried in small print on back pages.

Similarly, the Attica prison uprising and massacre (notice that emotive word) were big news, including a promise by Attica Commissioner Oswald to implement prisoners' demands for twenty-eight improvements, which Oswald agreed were "reasonable and desirable." But later reports that none of the twenty-eight improvements were made received hardly any play at all.

The media covered Richard Nixon's political campaigns from 1946 through 1972. Stacked away in their files, their "morgues," were mountains of items on Nixon campaign rhetoric and performance, showing that Nixon's performance bore little relation to his campaign promises. Worse, it showed Nixon's attacks on his opponents *always* consisted primarily of *false dilemma, straw man,* and *ad hominen* arguments. Yet it was rare for a news outlet to follow through on the news and point out this great disparity between his words and subsequent actions or between his portrayal of opponents' positions and their actual positions.

Follow-up stories rarely make headlines, primarily for two reasons. The first is that they are relatively difficult to obtain. It takes much less time and effort to report a prison uprising than to investigate day-to-day prison conditions. The second is that the public (and media) conception of "news" is what is *new,* and therefore different. Follow-up is reporting on "old news," which isn't really news. But isn't it news if, say, a president of the United States fails to keep his word, or a bill passed by Congress fails to get implemented? . . .

EMOTIVE LANGUAGE CAN BE USED

If the purpose of a sentence is to inform, or to state a fact, some of its words must refer to things, events, or properties. Some of its words thus must have what is commonly called *cognitive meaning.* The sentences made up of them also may be said to have cognitive meaning—provided, of course, that they conform to grammatical rules.

But words also may have *emotive meaning*—that is, they also may have positive or negative overtones. The emotive charges of some words are obvious. Think of the terms "nigger," "wop," "kike," "queer," and "fag." Or think of four-letter sex words, which even in this permissive age rarely appear in textbooks.

The emotively charged words just listed have negative emotive meanings. But lots of words have positive emotive overtones. Examples are "freedom," "love," "democracy," "springtime," and "peace." On the other hand, many words have either neutral or mixed emotive meanings. "Pencil," "run," and "river" tend to be neutral words. "Socialism," "politician," and "whiskey" tend to have mixed emotive meanings. . . .

Con artists take advantage of the emotive side of language in two very important ways: First, they use emotive meaning to mask cognitive meaning—to whip up emotions so that *reason* gets overlooked; and second, they use emotively neutral terms, or euphemisms (less offensive terms used in place of more offensive ones), to dull the force of what they say and thus make acceptable what otherwise might not be.

Until very recently, *New York Daily News* editorials were famous for their use of emotively charged expressions. A relatively mild *Sunday News* editorial (8 September 1974) on a campaign reform bill started with the title "A Snare and a Delusion" (compare that with the emotively less charged "An Unsatisfactory Bill," or even "A Misguided Bill"). It then referred to the bill's "*ogreish* feature" and the idea of "*saddling* the taxpayers with the cost of campaigns" (compare: "assessing the taxpayers . . . "), finding the saddling "*obnoxious*" (not just "ill advised" or "wrong"). Some other emotively charged expressions it used were "well-disciplined *band of zealots*," "*grab control*," "*ridiculous*," and "increase the clout." . . . The *Vancouver Sun* (15 July 1975) headlined its story about American and Soviet spacemen "Astronauts *Chase* Cosmonauts Into Space" (italics added). This had a much better ring than the more accurate "American Astronauts *Follow* Soviet Cosmonauts Into Space." A *National Enquirer* article (September 7, 1982), headlined "A *Juicy* Way to *Waste* Your Tax Dollars," started out: "*Fruitcakes* at the National Science Foundation . . . " (italics added). Now if, say, *U.S.A. Today* had started one of their articles: "Fruitcakes at the *National Enquirer.* . . . "

IGNORANCE CAN BE CLOAKED IN A FALSE
AURA OF AUTHORITY

Way back in the 1920s and 1930s, *Time* magazine developed a "you are *there*" style of news reporting, which became an essential part of the "*Time*style" that all newsmagazines have copied at one time or another. In their 2 November 1970 issue, *Time* ran a story whose main point was to emphasize how much of our air effort in Vietnam had been turned over to the South Vietnamese. *Time* reported that:

> "The target today is a suspected enemy location near the gully behind that clump of trees," says the American Forward Air Controller (FAC) from a tiny spotter plane just above the treetops some 30 miles northwest of Saigon.

Obviously, if *Time* reporters are so knowledgeable that they can quote word for word the remark of a FAC man in action, they surely must have been correct about the main point of their article—which happened to be quite controversial. . . .

The same issue of *Time* contained an article on Charles Reich's book. *The Greening of America,* which started out:

> Sociology has spawned more games than Parker Brothers. But all the *divertissements* rest upon a single process—the breakup of phenomena into categories. It has been so ever since Auguste Comte invented the

"science" and divided human progress into three stages, theological, meta-physical and positive.

Forgetting the question whether any one person invented sociology, does the *Time* writer really understand the complex philosophy of Comte to which he so blithely refers?

Whatever the answer may be in that particular case, it seems true that experts in various fields frequently find errors when *Time* and *Newsweek* report on their own areas of knowledge. This fact casts serious doubt on the general competence of newsmagazine writers who talk so flippantly of technical matters. Here is a particularly revealing flub, which occurred in *Time's* 14 April 1967 review of the autobiography of the philosopher Bertrand Russell. Wrote the *Time* reviewer:[2]

> [Russell's] historic collaboration with Alfred North Whitchead . . . that resulted, after ten year's labor, in the publication of *Principia Mathematica*, named after Newton's great work, *which in many respects it superseded.*

The writer didn't mention in which respects Russell's work superseded Newton's *Principia,* since there aren't any. Newton's *Principia* formed the foundation of mechanics, a topic on which Russell's *Principia* has nothing to say.

Few foreign correspondents know the language or customs of the countries to which they are sent. (The same is true to a lesser extent of our diplomats.) The result is that correspondents tend to stay in big cities, in particular capital cities, where they're fed handouts by government agents and others who speak English. You can't interrogate people whose language you don't understand. The results of this cultural incompetence of reporters is well known in the case of Vietnam, but the same thing happens in most foreign countries. . . .

NOTES

1. Virtually all reporters, editorial employees, and owners of the major news outlets in the United States at that time were white. The vast majority still are.

2. Pointed out by a *knowledgeable* layman, C. W. Griffin, Denville, New Jersey.

Organizational Biases of Network News Reporting

EDWARD JAY EPSTEIN

. . . There is a legitimate concern with bias in news reporting. Unfortunately, critical audiences tend to assume that the bias they detect is the personal bias of the reporter whom they see on television or whose by-line is at the top of the article. This reduces the issue to one of personal fairness (or ignorance), and the remedy most often suggested is to replace or educate the newsman. This focus on personal bias tends to distract attention from the far more important issue of organizational bias. Indeed, if the organization is "tilted" in its preferences in one direction, news will tend to be distorted regardless of the fairness—or unfairness—of the individual newsman. Just as a roulette wheel mounted on a tilted table tends to favor some numbers over other numbers no matter how fair the croupier might be, a news organization that is tilted in a certain direction because of the way it is structured will also tend to favor certain types of stories over others. When confronted with such a biased wheel, it would obviously be unprofitable to attempt to explain its outcomes by studying the biases of the croupier. To understand the criteria by which the media decide what is news, it is necessary first to describe the interests and values of the news organizations.

PROCESSING NETWORK NEWS

Television news provides perhaps the clearest case of the process by which reality is systematically reconstructed by news organizations. To begin with, network news organizations have, unlike some newspapers and magazines, absolute control over their product. Av Westin, vice-president of ABC News, described the process of control candidly in a memorandum (Epstein 1975, p. 200):

> The senior producers decide if the story has been adequately covered and they also estimate how long the report should run. In most cases, cor-

244

respondents deliberately overwrite their scripts giving the producers at home the option of editing it down: selecting which portions of the interviews are to be used and which are to be discarded. . . . In some cases, the senior producer "salvages" a report by assigning the correspondent to redo his narration or by sending a cameraman to refilm a sequence.

Under such a regime, a correspondent has little opportunity to insert in a news story personal values that run counter to the network's objectives. Nor does the description in the Westin memorandum quoted above apply only to ABC. During the year I spent observing NBC's and CBS's news operations, I saw even more rigorous controls maintained on news stories—including constant review by network executives.

In controlling the news product, the network organizations attempt to satisfy certain basic requirements that will allow them to continue as viable businesses. They must maintain a national audience for their advertisers, a need which, in turn, requires that the news programs be accepted by the affiliated (but independently owned) stations around the country. They must satisfy the ground rules laid down by the Federal Communications Commission (FCC), which licenses and monitors television stations. They also must maintain credibility as news media. And they must conform to budgetary and time restrictions to maintain profitability.

The Pressure of Time

Out of these basic requisites flow the rules and logic that shape network news. The most obvious constraint is time. The networks allocate only thirty minutes each night for their network news programs. From this time budget, approximately seven minutes must be deducted for commercials and non-news items. This leaves only twenty-three minutes for the presentation of between five to eight filmed news stories and the narration of other news events. Confronted with this reality, the producers of network news programs have no choice but to limit most of the news stories to a duration of two to four minutes. This enforced brevity leaves little room for presenting complex explanations or multifaceted arguments. In practical terms, two to four minutes is not sufficient for providing the historical context or detailed geographic situations of most events. To make news stories understandable to a national audience in this brief slice of time, producers find that they have to be reported almost entirely in the present/future tense. The focus is on what is happening, not why it is happening or what the root causes are. This time requisite ineluctably leads to a picture of society as unstable. If great events happen without cause or historic context, then it appears—at least, to constant viewers of network news—that any institution is capable of foundering, collapsing, or being overthrown without evident cause.

The Audience and the Advertiser

A second requisite that shapes television news is audience maintenance. It is assumed by network executives that if the stories on a news program are unclear, confusing, or visually uninteresting, a portion of the audience will switch the channel to another network. Such a loss of audience would not only lessen the advertising revenues from the news program, it would—even more important—lessen the revenues from all the network programs that follow, since the news program is regarded as a "lead-in" for the network's evening of entertainment programs. Network executives therefore insist that news stories have both visual interest and visual clarity. In attempting to satisfy this requisite, news producers have come up with a common formula for audience maintenance.

The first assumption made by news executives and producers is that viewers' interest is most likely to be maintained through easily recognizable and palpable images; conversely, it is most likely to be distracted by unfamiliar or confusing images. This has special force in the case of dinnertime news when, according to studies, the audience has fewer years of formal education than the population at large— and when a large proportion of the viewers are children. In practice, therefore, cameramen, correspondents, and editors are instructed to seek and select pictures that have an almost universal meaning. Stories thus tend to fit into a limited repertory of images, which explains why so often shabbily dressed children stand for poverty, why fire— symbolically—stands for destruction, and so forth. Since television is regarded as a medium for the "transmission of experience" rather than for "information," complex issues are represented in terms of human experience; inflation, for example, is pictured as a man unable to afford dinner in a restaurant. The repertory, of course, changes. But at any given time, images—especially emotional ones, which are presumed to have the broadest possible recognition—are used to illustrate news events.

A second assumption in this logic of audience maintenance is that scenes of potential conflict are more interesting to the audience than scenes of placidity. Virtually all executives and producers share this view. Network news thus seeks situations in which there is a high potential for violence but a low potential for audience confusion. News events showing a violent confrontation between two easily recognizable sides in conflict—for example, blacks versus whites, uniformed police versus demonstrators, or military versus civilians—are preferable to those in which the issues are less easily identifiable. Even when the conflict involves confusing elements, however, it usually can be reconstructed in the form of a two-sided conflict. Network news therefore tends to present the news in terms of highly dramatic conflicts between clearly defined sides.

A third, closely related, assumption is that the viewers' span of attention—which is presumed to be limited—is prolonged by action or by subjects in motion, and is sharply reduced by static subjects such as "talking heads." As has been previously discussed, the high value placed on action footage by executives leads to a three-step distillation of news happenings by correspondents, cameramen, and editors, all of whom seek the moment of highest action. Through this process, the action in a news event, which in fact may account for only a fraction of the time, is concentrated and becomes the central feature of the happening. This helps to explain why news on television tends willy-nilly to focus on activity.

A fourth assumption made by news producers is that stories are more likely to hold viewers' attention if they are cast in the form of the fictive story, with a discernible beginning, middle, and end. One NBC vice-president suggested to news producers that all stories should have rising action, a climax, then a falling action, and a seeming resolution. According to analyses done by NBC's audience research experts (see Epstein 1973, p. 263), this form would "lock" the audience into the news story. Since the film is generally reedited by the producers, it is relatively simple to cast most happenings in this fictive form. The net effect, however, is that reality is reconstructed into a series of events that never actually happened in the form in which the audience witnesses them. Events do not necessarily begin, build, and resolve themselves in terms of the visual data that are available to a television news team. Yet all the behind-the-scenes oscillations, twists, and contingencies of reality are neatly ironed out.

Networks and the Local Stations

Another basic requisite flows from the demand of affiliated stations that network news be differentiated from their own local news programs. It must appear to be national news. The problem is, of course, that all news is local in the sense that it occurs in some locality. Network producers resolve this tension by combining a series of local reports into a single national story. For example, the opening of a new subway line in Washington, D.C., may be considered a local story; it can be converted, however, into a national story by commissioning and fusing stories about subways in two or three other cities and then subsuming them all under a nationwide theme such as "Can the Cities Survive?" This process of nationalizing the news yields a constant agenda of national crises in place of local happenings.

Finally, governmental regulation of television imposes another basic requisite on producers: they must appear to be fair on controversial issues by presenting opposing views. This requisite is satisfied by soliciting views from spokesmen of two opposing sides in a dispute—and then editing these conflicting views into a "dialogue." To avoid obvious disparities, the producers usually seek the most articulate spokesman for each side. Not only does this treatment tend to reduce complicated issues to a mere debate, point/counterpoint style, but it also gives presumptive legitimacy to both sides.

MEDIA RESTRICTIONS AND REALITY

Organizational requisites cannot by any means explain all the outputs of television news. The personal quirks of producers, editors, and reporters contribute to news programs. There are also indisputable fashions and trends that change the level of consciousness of news reporting. The organizational requisites do explain, however, many of the built-in tilts that influence television news.

Print media have a different set of organizational requisites. Most afternoon newspapers, for example, face the problem of delivery: the news must be reported, written, printed, and delivered to newsstands spread over a metropolitan area before commuters have returned home from their jobs. They also must find news that has occurred after the deadlines of the morning newspapers. This severe restriction on time, coupled with union regulations that restrict periods in which the paper can be printed, have led the afternoon newspapers to focus their coverage on sports, horse racing, and stock markets. Morning newspapers, news magazines, and monthly magazines face different sets of organizational problems.

One question finally must be asked: Given these constraints, do the media present a picture of reality upon which rational men may make decisions? In spending over a year watching the three television networks collect, analyze, and present data in the form of news stories, I concluded that these pictures of reality were systematically distorted by organizational requirements. Dealing with such distortions involves the same problem as dealing with systematic distortions in a map. No map presents a perfect picture of reality. However, if one understands that such areas as Australia and Greenland are reduced in size, it is feasible to use a map to understand the geography of the world. Similarly, news itself requires some adjustments to compensate for systematic distortions.

If news media clearly and honestly stated the constraints and limits under which they operate, the adjustment would be far easier to make. Unfortunately, they tend to hide rather than to explain these constraints. News magazines, for example, print a false publishing date on each issue (usually a week after publication). This deception makes it difficult for the reader to ascertain the point when news had to be cut off because of the deadline. The value of news to the public would be greatly enhanced if news organizations revealed, rather than obscured, the methods by which they select and process reality.

REFERENCES

1. Epstein, Edward Jay. 1975. *Between Fact and Fiction.* New York: Vintage Press.
2. ———, Edward Jay. 1973. *News from Nowhere.* New York: Random House.

DISCUSSION QUESTIONS

1. What is "the eyewitness fallacy"? What, according to Stocking and Gross, is its significance for reporters?

2. According to Stocking and Gross, people tend to favor anecdotal information over statistics. Why do you think people might prefer anecdotes to statistics? What implications might this have for news reporting? In your estimation, should reporters always favor statistics over anecdotes in news reports? Defend your answers.

3. Consider the following case. A reporter investigating the hypothesis that

pornographic literature is causally linked to sex crimes notices that many of the sex offenders she interviewed read pornographic literature. Would this reporter be justified in concluding, on the basis of the latter interviews, that there is, indeed, a causal link between pornography and sex crimes? Defend your answer.

4. What is the "fundamental attribution error"? Give some examples of how journalists might fall into this error.

5. Consider the following case. A journalist who is doing a story on prison conditions in the United States visits several prisons across the nation that have had long-standing reputations for their "hellish" environments. On the basis of these visits, which also included extensive interviews with inmates, the journalist writes a story describing the unsatisfactory conditions prevailing in U.S. prisons today. Has this journalist committed any errors in compiling her story? Defend your answer.

6. What is "regression"? Give some examples of how regression errors might occur in news reporting.

7. What is the "hindsight bias"? What significance does it have for journalists?

8. Discuss some factors that can distort one's perception of risk. What, in your estimation, are some possible ways in which reporters, in reporting information about risks, can guard against misrepresenting those risks?

9. According to Kahane, three principle sources of media prejudice are class, sex, and race. Briefly describe or provide examples of some ways in which each of these prejudices can shape the news in terms of *what* gets reported or *how* it gets reported.

10. What is the difference between "cognitive meaning" and "emotive meaning"? Give some examples of words that have primarily cognitive meaning. Give some examples of words that have strong *negative* emotive meaning. Give some examples of words that have strong *positive* emotive meaning.

11. In your judgment, does "objective" news reporting require that reporters use only words that have primarily cognitive meaning? Are reporters at least sometimes justified in using strong emotive language? Defend your answers.

12. Kahane suggests that news reporters sometimes "cloak" their ignorance of facts behind a "false aura of authority." What does he mean? In your estimation, is there anything a reporter can do to avoid this pitfall?

13. What, according to Kahane, are some reasons why follow-up stories do not usually make headlines? In your estimation, should editors give greater weight to follow-up stories than they presently give to them? Defend your answer.

14. Look through newspapers or magazines to locate examples of at least three different devices of news slanting that have been discussed by Kahane. Bring these examples to class and be prepared to discuss them.

15. What does Epstein mean by an "institutional bias"? Why, according to Epstein, is much of the bias in television news of the latter sort?

16. In your estimation, do time constraints lead to reality distortions in television news? Defend your answer.

17. What role do advertisers play in shaping network news? Are there limits to the extent to which a network ought to allow itself to be influenced by advertisers? For instance, what, in your estimation, is the ethical responsibility of a network in cases in which airing a story would conflict with the interests of the advertiser?

18. Discuss the four assumptions which, according to Epstein, news executives and producers make about audience maintenance. Are each of these assumptions justified? Do you agree with Epstein that these assumptions lead to reality distortions in television news? Defend your answers.

19. Epstein says that "all news is local in the sense that it occurs in some locality." If this is true, then what is the difference between local news and national news? Is this a real distinction or just another way in which reality is distorted, as Epstein suggests? Defend your answers.

20. Epstein maintains that governmental pressures on the networks to be fair on controversial issues leads them to "reduce complicated issues to a mere debate, point/counterpoint style," which "gives presumptive legitimacy to both sides." What, in your estimation, is the merit of such a format? Is it, as Epstein suggests, a further reality distortion within network news? Defend your answers.

21. Discuss the merit of Epstein's suggestion that network news distortions might be handled in a manner similar to that of systematic distortions in a map.

22. In general, do you agree with Epstein that network news presents a distorted view of reality? Defend your answer.

23. If you were able to revise the current structure of network news, what aspects, if any, would you change? Defend your answer.

9

Philosophy and Journalistic Education

It has sometimes been said that a firm grounding in the liberal arts is an important, if not *the* most important, requisite of preparation for a career in journalism. However, the role(s) played by philosophy itself in such a liberal journalistic education has remained largely uninvestigated. More specifically, it may be asked, what contributions can the study of philosophy—including traditional areas such as ethics, logic, and epistemology (the theory of knowledge)—make to journalistic education? In this final chapter, the latter question will be considered.

One response to this query is to say that the study of philosophy is a constructive activity for journalists and prospective journalists because it bears upon the cultivation of skills and understanding that can be useful in practice. In the first selection, "Applying Philosophy to Journalism," Anthony Serafini takes such a route in trying to justify the inclusion of philosophy in journalistic education.

According to Serafini, philosophy and journalism bear certain resemblances, which make the study of philosophy complementary to that of journalism. First, he argues, both fields function as "interpreters, so to speak, of the work of other people in other fields" without having a subject matter of their own. Second, like philosophy, journalists also deal with "fundamentals," the journalist probing and interrogating in persistent pursuit of the truth much as does the philosopher.

In addition, Serafini argues that journalists should have more training in philosophy rather than other disciplines such as economics and history because philosophy is, in its essence, concerned with the cultivation of critical reasoning skills, which are also, presumably, important requisites of journalistic competence. In particular, journalists could benefit from coursework in logic, which directly teaches reasoning skills such as those involved in making sound (deductive as well as inductive) inferences and in avoiding logical fallacies. In this regard, it is noteworthy that Stocking and Gross (Chapter 8) have defended a similar point—coming to the same conclusion, however, from their studies in cognitive psychology rather than philosophy.

Serafini discusses the potential contributions of several different philosophy courses to journalistic education, including philosophy of language, ethics, and epistemology. For example, he contends that the study of epistemology could make a useful contribution to journalistic education, since "very similar questions [to those raised by epistemologists] can be raised as to the nature, definition of, and epistemic criteria of knowledge in the super-charged, critical situations that journalists often must deal with . . . " For instance, once exposed to the philosophical problem of attaining absolute certainty, even in sense observations, a journalist might be less apt to commit what Stocking and Gross have called the "Eyewitness Fallacy," the fallacy of overestimating the reliability of eyewitness testimony as in news reporting (Chapter 8).

Will coursework in philosophy do for prospective journalists what Serafini hopes it will do? It might plausibly be argued that the value of a philosophy course for journalistic education would depend upon the nature of the philosophy course in question. For example, logic courses that concentrate on practical reasoning might be more beneficial than those with a less practical emphasis. Epistemology courses that spend most of their time on such problems as finding the necessary and sufficient conditions of knowledge, or on theories about whether any statements can ever be "incorrigible," may be instructive insofar as they exemplify the methods of careful analytical thinking, but much of the relevance of their contents to journalism (where such relevance exists) may be lost within an elaborate labyrinth of theories. If so, then perhaps courses in philosophy may prove to be more useful for these purposes if their contents are more carefully tailored to the problems that actually confront journalists. Thus, an epistemology course that explored the connections between various theories of knowledge and journalistic concerns such as journalistic objectivity would, according to this view, be more useful than one that simply, or even for the most part, stuck to the latter abstract theories.

In the second selection, "What Can Philosophy Do For a Journalist?," Franklin Donnell examines and criticizes some of Serafini's contentions about the value of philosophy in journalistic education. For example, he maintains that Serafini's attempt to build an analogy between philosophy and journalism ignores relevant differences between the two fields. According to Donnell, the subject matter of journalism is broader than that of philosophy, including within its scope even very specific events and anything that might interest some audience. Moreover, the sense in which journalists probe for "fundamental" issues is different than the philosophical sense since journalists are concerned with getting at specific events, their causes and explanations, rather than at "general features of being and value that occupy philosophers."

One major contention of Donnell is that the study of philosophy is too large and demanding a task for a journalist to fulfill successfully without making a full-time professional commitment to the study of philosophy. According to Donnell, a practicing journalist who is confronted with a difficult philosophical problem has two options: (1) "buy a point of view" in light of whatever training and reading he or she has done, or (2) consult a professionally trained philosopher. Donnell opts for the second option on the grounds that it is the most efficacious path to the truth.

However, it might be argued that Donnell is treating the above options as mutually exclusive when in fact they are not. Embarking upon one's own philosophical studies does not necessarily exclude an occasional conference with a professional philosopher.

Moreover, Donnell likens a philosophical problem in journalism to "any complex medical, legal, or engineering problem" in which an expert is consulted for advice. However, there are few philosophers today who would consider themselves to be "expert advice givers." Most philosophers who deal in applied issues (medical ethicists, business ethicists, and so on) may offer clarification of the relevant issues, but they would not normally offer "solutions." For example, a medical ethicist may attempt to clarify the morally relevant issues and concepts surrounding the question of whether or not a particular comatose patient should be withdrawn from life support. However, the ultimate decision would then rest with others—for instance, the physician and family or the court. If so, then philosophically trained journalists would still benefit from their own philosophical lights even if, on some occasions, they thought it useful to seek further philosophical clarification from a professional philosopher.

It might also be argued that Donnell is exaggerating the task of making enlightened philosophical judgments. While the levels of complexity at which philosophical problems can be considered may be boundless, there may nevertheless be levels of complexity that suffice for practical purposes, and are within the reach of philosophically enlightened journalists.

Donnell does agrees that there are cogent reasons for making at least some elementary training in philosophy part of journalistic education. Nonetheless, Serafini's contentions that "philosophy has a rather special place in journalistic education," and that it should be given greater weight than other studies such as economics and history, are still further matters.

Against Serafini, some would argue that the greatest weight in journalistic education should be given to courses that teach technical skills such as, for instance, news reporting, editing, headline writing, newspaper makeup, and copyreading. Such a view would therefore attach little or no significance to liberal arts studies, including philosophy, as preparatory for journalistic practice.

However, one criticism of the view in question is that it promotes conformity and loss of independent thinking. For example, John C. Merrill has stated that "perhaps to far too great a degree journalism education does tend to turn journalism students into robots who can walk 'sure-footedly' into the world of Establishment journalism. It does discourage 'unprofessional' practices and techniques, creativity and individuality, by instilling in all the students the 'proper ways' of journalism."[1]

If Merrill's above-cited concern is taken seriously, then perhaps there is a further reason for including the study of philosophy in the education of journalists (although not necessarily to the exclusion of journalism coursework or as a priority above other liberal arts). The study of philosophy does, indeed, have a propensity for stimulating independent thinking.

NOTE

1. John C. Merrill, *The Imperative of Freedom: A Philosophy of Journalistic Autonomy* (New York: Hastings House Publishers, 1974), p. 142.

Applying Philosophy to Journalism

ANTHONY SERAFINI

In 1951—the thirteenth year of the Nieman Fellowship program for professional journalists at Harvard—Professor Edward Walsh of the Department of Journalism at Fordham University surveyed the Fellows of that year for their views on education for journalists. The results were striking. Many of the finest journalists of the day had grave reservations about the value of any sort of extended formal education in journalism. And of those that did support such education, the majority appeared to believe that, at the very least, the education of a journalist ought to consist of heavy doses of liberal arts courses. Lou Lyons himself, the esteemed Curator of the Nieman program spoke as follows: "In general, I am for providing the maximum chance for studies of a general nature, history, literature, philosophy, economics, sociology, etc., and a minimum of time on techniques of journalism. . . . My impression is that journalism programs are tending toward a greater concern for educational background and a lesser time for techniques and that this is, in most instances, good."[1]

Dana Adams Schmidt of the *New York Times* responded by urging that " . . . the best preparation for journalism is a four-year liberal arts course followed by a postgraduate year at a school of journalism such as the one at Columbia . . . I do not believe in four years, or even two years of undergraduate journalism courses. Journalism is not a body of knowledge like law or medicine; it is primarily a technique. And one year should be plenty of time to master the technique in so far as it can be mastered at school."[2]

Hoke M. Norris of the *Winston-Salem Journal* echos similar sentiments when he urges that, "I do think the liberal arts education is the best preparation for journalism."[3]

Schmidt's opinion is perhaps a bit more extreme than most, but his sense of the nature of journalism education still exists. Even today, the controversial Accrediting Council for the Association for Education in Journalism and Mass Communications embodies these skeptical philosophies in its stated requirement that no school of journalism or mass communications should devote more than one-quarter of its course work to "technical" training in e.g., news reporting, editing, advertising and so forth. Failure to follow these guidelines has in recent history, precipitated the flap at the Boston University program: they lost their accreditation and the controversy over this dramatic turn of fate is still sending shock waves through journalism schools throughout the nation.

Procedural and legal questions aside, the Boston University crisis does raise once again the doubts and fears of the Nieman Fellows of thirty-six years ago. If, indeed, journalism is not a body of knowledge, but a technique, then serious questions arise as to what, exactly, journalists should know. In the rest of this paper I wish to analyze the role of philosophy in journalism education. I believe an argument can be made that philosophy has rather a special place in journalistic education.

Why? On the conceptual level, there are certain structural similarities between journalism and philosophy. In a sense, both are "meta" disciplines. While the above critics argue that journalism has no "content" of its own, is this not, in a way, also true of philosophy? Perhaps we all recall our freshman philosophy courses, where we were told that philosophy is "parasitic" on other disciplines—that philosophy takes as its subject matter, *other* fields of knowledge. Ergo, one has philosophy of religion, philosophy of science, philosophy of education, etc.

Is not this much also true of journalism? The "subject matter" of the journalists' activity is precisely that which forms the content and subject matter of other fields of knowledge, much as is the case with philosophy. There are, e.g., science journalists, whose job is to write crisp accurate prose about science—interpreting its results to the world of nonscientists at large. But science—that which the science journalist writes of—is not part of any mythic body of knowledge called "journalism." *Mutatis mutandis,* the same is true of the political journalist, whose livelihood is parasitic upon the subject-content of politics and political goings-on in the real world. Thus there is a natural, ontological fellowship between journalists and philosophers.

Put differently, the journalist's activity is also a "meta" activity (though not in precisely the same sense that philosophy is): it, too, takes as its subject matter, the ideas and concepts of *other* fields. True, there is a difference in that philosophy's job is not (or not merely) to act as a conduit for information, but to clarify fundamental assumptions (Does God exist? Is matter real?) about other disciplines.

Even so, daring to press the analogy further, it could be argued that journalism too, in its own way, deals with "fundamentals." The journalist's way of dealing with 'fundamental assumptions' consists in the probing, interviewing (yes, even intimidating) of politicians, scientists, tyrants and butchers in dogged pursuit of the truth (Who *really* ordered such-and-such a raid, or arms deal, or political ouster: who *really* runs U.S. foreign affairs?)

Thus it seems, that since both fields are interpreters, so to speak, of the work of other people in other fields, it is logical to assume that the sort of understanding and concerns a philosopher must have may well be similar to the sort of understanding and skills a journalist should have.

But there are other reasons why, in my judgement, a journalist should have more training in philosophy rather than, say in economics or history (without denying the importance of the latter). If philosophy has a practical *raison d'etre* it is, arguably, critical, reasoned thought, the avoidance of logical fallacies and the construction of sound arguments as well as the drawing of sound inferences and the making of solid inductive leaps. Few, I think, would dispute the general principle—the role and importance of logic in everyday life. Thus it is important that journalists have sound training in logic, in order to avoid errors in reasoning that could destroy the credibility of a presidency or—in the worst case scenario—the world.[4]

According to most historical critics, as well as virtually all contemporary practitioners, the job of journalism is merely to 'state facts,' to convey information from one arena to another—from, e.g., the most private corridors of governmental bureaucracy, to the most public street-corners of every village and town—without the intrusion of any journalists' personal biases, whims, caprices or prejudices. This, of course, is the much-discussed problem of "objectivity" in journalism.

Yet, when I had the opportunity of teaching journalistic ethics for the first time at the University of Massachusetts' journalism department in 1982, I was staggered by how unaware most academic journalists were of the vast literature on "objectivity" written by philosophers. In all the literature I covered, in preparation for the course, there occurred not a single mention, for example, of Israel Scheffler's classic *Science and Subjectivity*.

By contrast, the reams of *journalist*-authored literature on the topic leaned toward the naive and simplistic. Most articles leaned toward an apparently tempting as well as confessional/self-therapeutic conclusion that journalistic "objectivity" is impossible anyway, so why pretend to it? A natural conclusion of course, especially since it tends to exonerate journalists from responsibility when grossly *un*objective pieces find their way to print.

In fact, had journalists been aware of the vast amount of work already done on objectivity (where the journalistic version of the problem is merely a special case), they might have realized that the tempting above-mentioned conclusion is still very much up in the air from a philosopher's perspective.

My purpose in this paper is not to argue for or against such conclusions: they may, in the long run, even be correct. The point however is that this is an instance of reflecting about philosophical matters in ignorance of the literature (a special case of the *general* problem of lack of communication between academic displines).

What most journalists do not appreciate, regarding this vexing question of "objectivity," is that (a) the problem is not peculiar to journalism and (b) a vast literature on it exists and stretches back for centuries. How profitable could a journalist's investigations of the concept of objectivity (as applied to journalism), be, if he or she has to constantly reinvent the wheel?

What I found were journalists exploring a lot of dead ends, propounding arguments that philosophers had dismissed years earlier, and so forth. I also found that some few journalists had done some really original work. But the point, again, is that the entire investigation is riddled with inefficiency. If philosophers have already done considerable spade work on objectivity, why should journalists not take advantage of it?

More specifically still, most journalists appeared not to have heard of, say, the Heisenberg Uncertainty Principle, with its rather obvious possible implications for the observer as intruder or interferer with the observational process.[5] Is the Uncertainty Principle a merely theoretical concern at the level of day-to-day life, important only at the sub-atomic level? Or does it have a macroscopic counterpart which "infects" the macroscopic observations of the journalists, making it impossible for the journalist to report on a phenomenon without, in some way, also becoming part of it (Can one "merely" broadcast a hostage crisis without *ipso facto* becoming part of it?).

Then too, there are epistemological problems critically important for, but not unique to journalism. Philosophers have long concerned themselves with such classic epistemological questions as the nature, definition and limits of human knowledge. Yet it is difficult to imagine any human activity where this problem is more acute or of greater immediate urgency than journalism. The importance of the issues for journalism can be seen merely by surveying some classic epistemological problems and seeing how they apply to journalism.

One example of such an epistemological problem, is the alleged "incorrigibility" of physical object assertions. Can we ever be absolutely certain that any given assertion about the physical universe is true? Austin, e.g., in *Sense and Sensibilia* argues that incorrigibility is an unattainable chimera, while philosophers like Norman Malcolm argue that incorrigibility is possible with respect to physical object assertions.

Naturally, the examples philosophers typically pick to discuss epistemic problems lack a certain urgency. Austin talks about the concept of evidence where claims are made about the presence or absence of pigs,[6] while Malcolm discusses inkwells on desks in front of him.[7] This, of course, is sound enough, as such philosophers are concerned to establish general truths about knowledge, and examples picked from anything but "ordinary" situations could distract readers from the analysis.

Yet very similar questions can be raised as to the nature, definition of, and epistemic criteria of knowledge in the super-charged, critical situations that journalists often must deal with—and how much the more important is it to establish epistemic criteria in such situations. Knowing the alleged fragility of even the most ordinary claims to knowledge, it is just conceivable that journalists would pause a bit when confronted with informants swearing with "absolute certainty" that such-and-such happened or so-and-so killed someone. As philosophy professor and journalism professor Odell and Merrill, respectively, suggest, "when one claims, as journalists must constantly do, that some event took place in the past, on the grounds that certain witnesses are willing to attest to it, one's claim is nowhere nearly so well grounded."[8]

In the *Thaetetus,* the question is raised as to what, precisely, are the conditions under which a person can be said to KNOW that a proposition, p, is true. As Chisholm recasts this scheme[9] S can be said to know that p is true if and only if: p is true, S believes p, and S has "adequate evidence" that p is true. I would note that this too has applications to journalistic practice. Under what circumstances does a certain degree of evidence count as "adequate evidence" in journalism? And will this differ among the different media? Arguably, the evidential standards of newspaper journalism have to be lower than magazine journalism. For example: In a daily paper, the reporter has 24 hours to check on his facts, while in a magazine story he or she may have several months thereby allowing for more time for fact-checking. Epistemic criteria for issues remain uncharted territory: again, the importance of philosophy in journalistic training—as a vehicle for epistemic consciousness-raising at the very least—is immeasurable.

On still another front, one can note that the main tool of journalism is, after all, *language*. Would not journalism be better prepared to carry out its tasks if they had *some* inkling of how the variety of theoretical views in that branch of philosophy known as the philosophy of language could affect the day-to-day practice of journalism? To pick just one possibility: during my teaching at the University of Massachusetts, I noted that a favorite topic of discussion among academic journalists (usually, by the way, retired newspapermen) was the relative importance of "hard" journalism vs. "soft" journalism—the importance of hard news vis-à-vis comic strips, crossword puzzles, advice columns and so forth. Most journalists again fall into the initially tempting view that, "of course" hard journalism is "more important" than soft.

But it has to be noted that this view depends on the parallel, yet far more fundamental question of the nature and purpose of language *per se*. As any student of philosophy knows, the early positivists tended to view the "fact-stating" function of language as having far greater value than emotive and other uses of language. Indeed they viewed it as being virtually the only legitimate use of language. And this ancient prejudice is the mirror and philosophical underpinning for the "hard" journalism bias. In later years, of course, many positivists softened their views. This occurred in the later Wittgenstein. He softened his view and treated such "second-class" uses of language as joke-telling, story-telling, exclamations, etc. as equally valid members of the tree of language uses.

A deeper appreciation of the very nature and function of language itself would, virtually inevitably, assist the journalist in thinking more carefully and deeply about the relative importance of "hard" news (analogue to 'fact-stating' use of language) vis-à-vis "soft" news (analogue to emotive, illocutionary,[10] satirical, etc., functions of language).

Finally, of course, there are many vexing problems in journalistic ethics. Since this is, in a way, the most obvious application of philosophy to journalism and journalistic practice, I leave it for last. But despite the rather obvious importance of journalistic ethics, given such scandals as the Myron Farber and Janet Cooke[11] cases in recent years, the situation is even worse than it is with the problem of "objectivity." At least a literature on the latter, by philosophers, existed, though journalism is not tapping it. But philosophers aren't even *writing* all that much about issues in journalistic ethics.[12]

It is surprising how neglected this field is by philosophers and how philosophizing in a vacuum—theorizing without being informed by history—has gone on by journalists. Outside of censorship, and occasional pieces on the ethics of advertising, there are still relatively few traditional problems in journalistic ethics that academic philosophers discuss. There is little on junketing, propaganda and the news, 1st vs. 6th Amendment conflicts, etc.

Partly for that reason, partly because of a general lack of communication between the fields, other ethical issues in journalism are tackled by journalists in seat-of-the-pants fashion. Journalists struggle and flounder helplessly in the logico/linguistic/epistemic tangles of a free press vs. a fair trial, reporter conflicts of interest, responsibilities to sources, etc.

Unaware of and thus unable to draw nourishment from such doctrines as act and rule utilitarianism, Nozickian ultraminimal states, deontological ethics, prescriptivism, Rawlsian decision procedures for ethics, etc., academic journalists continue to drown and die in the intellectual debris of their own creation.

And, predictably, a retreat into the safety of some kind of primitive relativism ("each reporter has to work out this issue for himself") is almost a foregone conclusion.

What is to be done? I am arguing that philosophy should join hands with academic journalism, partly because the two fields are cousins anyway (because of the structural similarities and affinities between the disciplines that I outlined earlier). At the very least, it would provide for variety, efficiency and diversity in departments of journalism and consequently, in the thought processes of the graduates of such schools.

Education, therefore, may hold the key to correcting journalism's epistemological deficiencies. Just as medical schools now hire philosophers full-time to handle, say, medical ethics as well as medical epistemology, journalism schools could do likewise. As a further development along these lines, new models of journalism education are possible. One conceivable model might require that those interested in careers in journalism take a normal, four-year liberal arts program, with at least a minor in philosophy, possibly followed by four years as a working journalist. After that, and where feasible, their respective newspapers, magazines or stations could send them on a year's "sabbatical" to return, Nieman-style, to a major university to sit in on philosophy courses of their choosing. They could also meet periodically in seminars with distinguished visiting philosophers and journalists to exchange ideas.

NOTES

1. *Robert A. Hutchins, A Free and Responsible Press* (Chicago: University of Chicago Press, 1947), p. 11.

2. Ibid., pp. 13–14.

3. Ibid, p. 14.

4. See for example, Howard Kahane, *Logic and Contemporary Rhetoric* (Belmont, CA: Wadsworth Publishing Co., 1980). Strictly a logic text, this work nonetheless has far more examples of fallacious reasoning taken from the various news media, than from any other source.

5. Teachers of philosophy are, of course, used to bright physics students handing in papers "vindicating" free will on the basis of this famous principle. Even so, the principle is not without some philosophical import. See, for example, Millic Capek's *The Philosophical Import of Contemporary Physics* (New York: Van Nostrand Company, 1961), especially, pp. 238–40 & 289–94.

6. J. L. Austin, *Sense and Sensibilia* (New York: Oxford University Press, 1962), p. 110, and generally all of Chapter IX.

7. Norman Malcolm *Knowledge and Certainty* (Englewood Cliffs, NJ: Prentice-Hall, 1963) the essay "Direct Perception" ("The Verification Arguments," in the same volume is also relevant).

8. John C. Merrill and Jack S. Odell, *Philosophy and Journalism* (White Plains, NY: Longman Publishing Co., 1983), p. 55.

9. Roderick Chisholm, *Theory of Knowledge* (Englewood Cliffs, NJ: Prentice-Hall, 1970), p. 6.

10. For a more detailed discussion of this theme, see my article, "Achievements, Illocutions and the Concept of Teaching," in *Educational Theory* (spring 1976).

11. In April of 1981, Janet Cooke of the *Washington Post* received a Pulitzer Prize for a poignant account of an 8-year-old heroin addict named "Jimmie". Days later it was discovered that the story was a total fabrication. Miss Cooke returned the prize and resigned in disgrace.

12. I recently issued a call to philosophers for papers for an anthology on ethics that I'm under contract to put together: so far, none of the papers I've received has been in the area of communications ethics.

What Can Philosophy Do for a Journalist?

FRANKLIN DONNELL

In "Applying Philosophy to Journalism,"[1] Professor Serafini argues that the study of philosophy should have an important place in the academic training of journalists, perhaps as a required minor program in college, and even as the theme of sabbatical years later in life, when the journalist will sit in on philosophy courses at major universities.

Now I can think of two reasons for a person in a certain vocation to go out and learn something. One reason is that learning it could either help to avoid some ill or to increase some good that is liable to come to people in that vocation, as when it is said that every physician ought to learn about liability law or study principles of sound investing. The other kind of reason, however, and the usual one, for saying that a person in a certain vocation ought to study something is simply that doing so makes one better at that vocation. I will assume that Professor Serafini's view is that students of journalism ought to study philosophy because doing so will make them better journalists.

Hard journalism is like a technique or craft, both in that it is the producing of something and in that there are standards for doing it well or badly. Let us say that hard journalism is the technique of using beliefs about what one has read or heard or observed to produce a media presentation, where such a presentation always contains (or implies: as in photo journalism) statements about what has gone on in the world and often contains statements interpreting this news, i.e., explanations of why it has gone on and reasons why it is likely to have certain effects. Among the marks of a successful journalistic presentation must be that its statements are true and relevant to the topic, that the sentences by which they are made are clear and readable and organized in a consecutive way that is easy to follow, that the explanations and predictions are both insightful and shown to be reasonable to believe, i.e., supported in ways that conform to accepted principles of logic, and that the whole thing keeps the reader's attention. If crafting presentations like this is central to being a good journalist, then we may understand Professor Serafini's thesis to be that studying philosophy helps a journalist to do just *that*.

Why should we think that studying philosophy makes a better journalist? Early in his paper, Professor Serafini points out similarities between journalism and philosophy. Recasting what he says to explicitly support the point that studying philosophy makes a better journalist might generate the following argument:

> Studying philosophy makes one better at philosophy.
> Philosophy is similar to journalism.
>   So it is likely that studying philosophy makes one better at journalism.

This is an analogical argument, hence one that will be strengthened by citing relevant ways in which philosophy and journalism are similar and weakened by citing relevant ways in which they are different. Professor Serafini seems to strengthen the argument by suggesting that journalism and philosophy are similar in having no special subject matters of their own, but in being concerned instead with kinds of events that are the subject matters of various fields of study, such as economics or sociology. He also says that philosophy and journalism are similar in that they both deal with "fundamentals."

The analogy is weakened, I suggest, by the consideration that the subject matter of journalism is much broader than that of philosophy, in that (a) it extends to anything that might be of interest to some audience and (b) it includes historical events in all their specificity, whereas most philosophy is investigation of very general features of the world, such as the nature of time, or truth, or right and wrong.

As for Professor Serafini's second point of resemblance, philosophy is indeed about "fundamentals," and journalists may probe "fundamentals" as well. But the cash value of "fundamentals" in the two cases seems very different. A journalist's fundamental truths are likely to concern specific events and empirical hypotheses that explain the subject of her reportage—get to the root of the matter—and relate it to other events—disclose the broader picture. They are rarely about those general features of being and value that preoccupy philosophers. Here again is a difference between journalism and philosophy that weakens the argument.

A further objection to the argument lies in the consideration—a counter-analogy—that there are activities, such as storytelling or the graphic art of illustration, that resemble journalism in treating of events that are of interest to special studies while having no subject matter peculiar to themselves, but which are not activities likely to be improved by the study of philosophy.

Other reasons Professor Serafini gives for his contention are clearly appropriate in light of the marks of good journalism mentioned above. Thus, being good at journalism involves being able to write with clarity and precision, and this is an ability that is likely to be enhanced by the reading and writing of philosophy. Moreover, both in explaining what has gone on and in drawing conclusions about the future, the journalist must proceed, if the presentation is to be reasonable, according to principles of deductive and inductive logic, hence according to principles one learns in studying a branch of philosophy, namely, logic.

To these reasons why a journalist should study philosophy, I would add two more.

First, references to the history and problems of philosophy may crop up in materials that the journalist is working on, and ideas from philosophy may also figure in a journalist's interpretation of the news. So studying philosophy makes one a better journalist simply by leaving one better equipped to deal with philosophic ideas in assignments that may come one's way.

Secondly, and in a different vein, any good introductory study of philosophy should acquaint a student with the diversity of plausible, yet incompatible, points of view that have been advanced and defended in philosophy. And from this sense of the difficulty of philosophic issues should arise a healthy caution about accepting the declarations about the nature of reality, morality, and the good community that journalists, and the people they write about, sometimes make with great conviction. Rights issues provide abundant illustration. Claims about the rights of fetuses on the one hand and rights of those that bear them on the other, about rights to property vs. rights to be provided for, about rights to speak freely vs. rights to be protected from disruptive social forces unleashed by words—all of these claims can and have been argued for, and argued for plausibly. Philosophy is very hard: witness the complex ideas Professor Serafini mentions in talking about being informed about ethics, "act and rule utilitarianism, Nozickian ultraminimal states, deontological ethics, prescriptivism, Rawlsian decision procedures for ethics." Each of these ideas is surrounded by a vast literature of argument and counterargument produced by highly trained intellects. Philosophy is very hard. There are plausible arguments for and against almost any philosophic thesis, and the glib or impassioned answer almost certainly disregards the plausibility of contrary views. In Hume's view, good philosophy, which for him was grounded in a scepticism tempered by common sense, serves to "diminish their fond opinion of themselves, and their prejudice against antagonists"[2] in those who might otherwise be swept away by ideas. If writing only what is true is a mark of a good journalist, then the caution about embracing slogans of philosophy that studying the subject should bring ought to help to make one a good journalist.

Some other reasons why a journalist should study philosophy that are suggested by Professor Serafini's paper seem to sit poorly with the idea that philosophy is a very hard subject. I say 'suggested' because in the passages I have in mind Professor Serafini is simply discussing how useful formal study of philosophy must be to a journalist who has to take a stand on certain philosophic issues. I am going to interpret these passages as arguments to the point that studying philosophy is likely to make one a better journalist and then expatiate on why I find this idea problematic.

Thus Professor Serafini writes as if there are problems of metaphysics and epistemology about which a journalist might well want to be concerned. Approaching the matter with my questions in mind, it might be said that this concern—speaking now just of epistemology and the nature of adequate evidence—is appropriate, because a mark of good journalism is that it says only what is true. But if a story contains only truths, it is very likely that the journalist intended to write only what is true. And if she intends to write only what is true, then she intends to write only what she knows to be true. And if she thinks she knows something to be true, that will be because she thinks she has adequate evidence for it. Yet the problems of what counts as adequate evidence for a claim to knowledge and whether such claims are really justifiable at all are enduring problems of epistemology. Hence plying the craft of journalism well seems to presuppose an understanding of epistemology.

Moreover, being a good journalist involves not only making well-crafted packages of information, but also refusing to present information in ways that are unfair to persons written about or persons supplying information. But questions about what makes behavior immoral, and how to justify answers to this question are enduring problems of moral philosophy. Hence plying the craft of journalism well seems to presuppose an understanding of moral philosophy.

There is, however, an obvious difference between these principles about the nature of adequate evidence and moral wrongness and the logical rules that are so clearly of importance to good journalism. The difference is that the ideas about the nature of knowledge and moral wrongness are enduringly controversial: they are ongoing subjects of philosophical investigation. What one learns in elementary logic is at least as settled a part of learning as what one learns in first year geology, or first year Constitutional History, or first year accounting. If such knowledge is needed to make a better journalist, then the student of journalism can simply dig in and learn it. But whether or not it is possible to be objective (vs. subjective) in describing the world, or what puts us in a position to have knowledge about the world, or what can settle it that a certain behavior is morally wrong are questions whose answers cannot be looked up in textbooks. Few philosophers working in English and American traditions would be ready to say that their answers can be known at all.

Obviously, there are textbooks in philosophy, and they provide information. But the information they provide is mostly about different points of view on philosophic issues and some of the argumentation that has been given in support of them. And in the actual pursuit of philosophy the argumentation can achieve great complexity, pulling in an array of issues that may have seemed far removed from the original topic. Argumentation on the subjectivity of moral judgments devolves 'naturally' into argumentation on issues from philosophy of language, philosophy of psychology, epistemology, and metaphysics, which is just to say that this, and most, philosophic issues are immensely complex, and that an informed judgment on a philosophic thesis is likely to require a considered understanding of a vast web of issues of which it is a part.

Now to the point. Professor Serafini may be read as saying that an adequate view of such matters as the possibility of objectivity, the nature of adequate evidence, and the nature of moral wrong are necessary, or at least desirable, for being a good journalist, and that studying philosophy as an undergraduate should put one far enough on the road to having such an adequate view as to make it all worthwhile. My criticism of this is that achieving an adequate view of these big issues in philosophy can be little less than a full-time job, a professional commitment to philosophy, hence not something one can hope to achieve if one has a full-time commitment to another vocation, be it science, law, business, or journalism. Certainly that minor in philosophy—a mere peek at the subject, relatively speaking—will not get one far towards a grasp of the issues in their real complexity.

What, then, is a journalist, or any professional person to do when in the course of professional life moral or epistemological issues arise that one wants to take a stand on? Professor Serafini's view appears to be that the professional person must tackle them himself. Hence an undergraduate training in philosophy, one that can avoid reinventings of the wheel, is desirable. But I have suggested that a genuinely informed judgment on a philosophic issue is very hard to come by, requiring acquaintance with and reflection upon a very large net of philosophic theses and the argumentation for and against them, such that a person is not likely to be in a position to make such a judgment unless she gives a lot of her life and energy to philosophical investigations. So the options for a practicing journalist puzzled by a moral or epistemological issue and unready to drop the matter seem to be (a) simply to buy a point of view that seems right in view of whatever academic training in philosophy one has had and whatever extra reading one has done, realizing that there is a great deal more out there that is relevant but unknown to one; (b) behave as one would with any complex medical, legal, or engineering problem, and go to a respected professional in the field, in this case a respected professional philosopher, hoping to receive a judgment that reflects extensive study of the issue in its complexity, together with some arguments in favor of the judgment that the professional person thinks are especially weighty. If it is important to write only what is true, I submit that (b) is the path of choice.

NOTES

1. Anthony Serafini, "Applying Philosophy to Journalism," in *Applied Philosophy* 3 no. 4 (1987): 45–49.
2. David Hume, *An Enquiry Concerning Human Understanding*. Sect. XII, Part III.

DISCUSSION QUESTIONS

1. What similarities does Serafini claim exist between journalism and philosophy? What criticisms does Donnell make of Serafini's comparison between these two fields?
2. In your own estimation, in what ways, if any, are philosophy and journalism alike? In what ways, if any, are they different? How, if at all, do any such similarities or dissimilarities bear upon the question of the value of philosophy in journalistic education? Defend your answers.
3. What, according to Serafini, are some reasons why students of journalism should study epistemology (the theory of knowledge)? Do you agree with him? Defend your answer.
4. What, according to Serafini, are some reasons why students of journalism should study logic? Do you agree with him? Defend your answer.
5. Serafini argues that journalists should have more training in philosophy

than other liberal arts disciplines. Why does he believe this? Do you agree with him? Defend your answer.

6. What reasons, beyond those cited by Serafini, does Donnell suggest might be given for including at least some introductory courses in philosophy in journalistic education? Do you accept these reasons? Defend your answer.

7. According to Serafini, one "conceivable" model of journalistic education is one in which the student enrolls in a four-year undergraduate liberal arts program with at least a minor in philosophy, "possibly followed by four years as a working journalist," and then, perhaps, a one-year return "to a major university to sit in on philosophy courses of their choosing." What problems, if any, do you see with such a proposal? What, if any, are its positive features? Do you think that such a proposal is, on balance, a good idea? Defend your answers.

8. Donnell claims that practicing journalists who seek answers to philosophical problems would be better off consulting a professionally trained philosopher rather than attempting to use their own philosophical training to solve these problems. Why does Donnell believe this? Do you agree with him? Defend your answer.

9. In your estimation, what is the value, if any, of including the study of philosophical issues in journalism, such as those covered in this volume, in journalistic education? Do you think a course on philosophical issues in journalism (or one that includes such issues) should be a *required* course, as distinct from an elective course? Defend your answers.

10. If you were to develop your own journalism curriculum, what courses would you include and in what measure? That is, how much weight would you attach to technical courses in journalism as opposed to liberal arts courses? What specific technical courses, if any, would you require? What specific liberal arts courses, if any, would you require? What courses would you treat as electives? Defend your answers.

SELECTED BIBLIOGRAPHY

Aristotle, *Nichomachian Ethics*. Trans. W. D. Ross. In *The Basic Works of Aristotle*. Ed. Richard McKeon. New York: Random House, Inc., 1941.

Austin, J. L. *How to Do Things with Words*. 2 ed. Cambridge, MA: Harvard University Press, 1975.

Barry, Vincent E., and Joel Rudinow. *Invitation to Critical Thinking*. 2 ed. Forth Worth: Holt, Rinehart and Winston, Inc., 1990.

Bayles, Michael D. *Professional Ethics*. Belmont, CA: Wadsworth Publishing Co., Inc., 1989.

Bentham, Jeremy. *Utilitarianism*. In Samuel Gorovitz, ed., *Mill: Utilitarianism, Text and Critical Essays*. New York: The Bobbs-Merrill Co., Inc., 1971.

Berger, Fred R. "The Right of Free Expression." *The International Journal of Applied Philosophy* 3, no. 2 (Fall 1986), 1–10.

Braden, Maria. "Stamping Out Automatons." *The Quill* 74 (May 1986), 26–28.

Brandt, Richard B. *Ethical Theory*. Englewood Cliffs, NJ: Prentice-Hall, Inc., 1959.

Callahan, Joan C., ed., *Ethical Issues in Professional Life*. New York: Oxford University Press, 1988.

Clifford, W. K. "The Ethics of Belief." In Leslie Stephen and Sir Frederick Pollock, *The Ethics of Belief and Other Essays*. London: Oxford University Press, 1947.

Cohen, Elliot D. *Making Value Judgements: Principles of Sound Reasoning*. Melbourne, FL: Robert E. Krieger Publishing Co., 1985.

———. *Philosophers at Work: An Introduction to the Issues and Practical Uses of Philosophy*. New York: Holt, Rinehart and Winston, 1989.

Cranberg, Lawrence. "Plea for Recognition of Scientific Character of Journalism." *The Journalism Educator* 43, no. 4 (Winter 1989), 46–49.

Day, Louis A. *Ethics in Media Communications: Cases and Controversies*. Belmont, CA: Wadsworth Publishing Company, 1991.

Dewey, John. *The Public and Its Problems*. New York: Henry Holt and Co., 1929.

Dorfman, Ron. "The Puzzle of Objectivity: The Objective Posture." *Et Cetera: A Review of General Semantics* 44 (Fall 1987), 312–15.

Edel, Abraham. *Interpreting Education*. Buffalo, NY: Prometheus Books, 1989.

Elliott, Deni. "On Deceiving One's Source." *International Journal of Applied Philosophy* 6, no. 1 (Summer 1991), 1–9.

————, ed. *Responsible Journalism*. Beverly Hills, CA: Sage Publications, Inc., 1986.

Elliston, Frederick A. "Whistleblowing: The Reporter's Role." *International Journal of Applied Philosophy* 3, no. 2 (Fall 1986), 25–36.

Elliston, Frederick A., et al. *Whistleblowing Research: Methodological and Moral Issues*. New York: Praeger Publishers, 1985.

Engel, S. Morris. *With Good Reason: An Introduction to Informal Fallacies*. 4 ed. New York: St. Martin's Press, 1990.

Epstein, E. J. *News from Nowhere*. New York: Random House, 1974.

Feinberg, Joel. *Social Philosophy*. Englewood, NJ: Prentice-Hall, Inc., 1973.

Flores, Albert, ed. *Professional Ideals*. Belmont, CA: Wadsworth Publishing Co., Inc., 1989.

Frankena, William K. *Ethics*. 2 ed. Englewood Cliffs, NJ: Prentice-Hall, Inc., 1973.

Giere, Ronald N. *Understanding Scientific Reasoning*. New York: Holt, Rinehart and Winston, 1979.

Gifford, N. L. *When in Rome: An Introduction to Relativism and Knowledge*. Albany, NY: State University of New York Press, 1983.

Goldman, Alan H. *The Moral Foundations of Professional Ethics*. Totowa, NJ: Rowman & Littlefield, 1980.

Gould, James A. "Political Free Speech Ought to Be an Absolute." *Applied Philosophy* 1, no. 1 (Spring 1982), 65–70.

Grcic, Joseph. "Freedom of Speech and Access to Mass Media." *The International Journal of Applied Philosophy* 4, no. 1 (Spring 1988), 51–58.

Hirst, R. J., ed. *Perception and the External World*. New York: Macmillan, 1965.

Hutchins, Robert A. *A Free and Responsible Press: A General Report on Mass Communication: Newspapers, Radio, Motion Pictures, Magazines, and Books*. Chicago: The University of Chicago Press, 1947.

Kultgen, John. *Ethics and Professionalism*. Philadelphia: University of Pennsylvania Press, 1988.

Ladd, John, ed. *Ethical Relativism*. Belmont, CA: Wadsworth Publishing Co., 1973.

Martin, June C. "The Case of the Lost Ethic: Making Moral Decisions." *The Journalism Educator* 43, no. 1 (Spring 1988), 11–14.

Martin, Mike W. *Everyday Morality: An Introduction to Applied Ethics*. Belmont, CA: Wadsworth Publishing Co., 1989.

Merrill, John C. "Is Ethical Journalism Simply Objective Reporting?" *Journalism Quarterly* 62 (Summer 1985), 391–93.

————. *The Imperative of Freedom: A Philosophy of Journalistic Autonomy*. New York: Hastings House Publishers, 1974.

Moore, W. Edgar, Hugh McCann, and Janet McCann. *Creative and Critical Thinking*. Boston: Houghton Mifflin Company, 1985.

Murphy, Sharon, and James E. Murphy. "A New Look at the New Journalism." *The Quill* 72 (April 1984), 19–21.

Newman, Jay. *The Journalist in Plato's Cave*. Rutherford, NJ: Fairleigh Dickinson University Press, 1989.

Patterson, Philip, and Lee Wilkins. *Media Ethics: Issues and Cases*. Dubuque, IA: Wm. C. Brown Publishers, 1991.

Plato. *The Republic*. Trans. Francis MacDonald Cornford. New York: Oxford University Press, 1945.

Pullen, Rick D. "Newspaper Codes of Ethics: Unenforceable and Impractical." *International Journal of Applied Philosophy* 3, no. 2 (Fall 1986), 11–16.

Quine, W. V., and J. S. Ullian. *The Web of Belief*. 2 ed. New York: Random House, 1978.

Rawls, John. *A Theory of Justice*. Cambridge, Mass.: Harvard University Press, 1971.

Ross, W. D. *The Right and the Good*. London: Oxford University Press, 1930.

Rowley, William E. "Three Dimensional Objectivity." *The Quill* 72 (March 1984), 17–21.

Russell, Bertrand. *The Problems of Philosophy*. London: Oxford University Press, 1972.

Sartre, Jean-Paul. *Existentialism and Human Emotion*. New York: Philosophical Library, 1985.

Serafini, Anthony, ed. *Ethics and Social Concern*. New York: Paragon House Publishers, 1989.

Smith, Ted J. "Journalism and the Socrates Syndrome." *The Quill* 76 (April 1988), 14–20.

Wasserstrom, Richard A. *Morality and the Law*. Belmont CA: Wadsworth Publishing Co., Inc., 1971.